THE PETALS

THE PETALS

JOGEN KHAN

KALPAZ

The Petals

ISBN: 978-81-7835-779-9

Published in 2009 in India by
Kalpaz Publications
C-30, Satyawati Nagar,
Delhi-110052
E-mail: kalpaz@hotmail.com
Phone : 9212729499

Printed at : Singhal Print Media, Delhi

Contents

Preface

The Petals is the collection of nine short stories based on real life experiences of men, women and children as envisaged by the author. Man's inter-action with each other to survive in the best possible way, under the Divine authority, is always in jeopardy. Human foibles, short-comings, animosity, deprivation, and denial of both divine and civil rights are the meanest characteristics possess by man against each other. Extreme of one of it destroys one if it is not sensibly substituted in doing something good.

A family is ruined if one looses his/her balance in life. Too much stress on emotional traits of an individual ignoring the welfare of the rest of the family could cause danger to ones' life. A youth living unrighteous, unprincipled and lecherous life will escalate into his doom, yet a small child rising to the occasion in spite of leading an impoverished life could bring prosperity, if the luck favors him in his enterprise. An ignorant domestic help, cursed by all around him for his low stature in society could turn up to be a sagacious wise man, lending his support to the others in difficulties.

As no one should judge a book by its cover only, so no one should come to the conclusion of something mischievous or sinful just looking at the profile of a person. One has to go deep into the matter. The mysterious soul has to be taken into account while judging a person and his character.

The adage, every dark cloud has a silver lining, is proved appropriate in the case of a jilted lover. The pain inflicted by an avaricious and unscrupulous dame does not mean the end of the road but there is always someone who would lend the precious support in the need of a frustrated man and would be a part of his destiny.

Above everything else on earth, widely occupied by human beings, there is the realm of the celestial existence, the residents of Arch Angels and other celestial beings. God, the Supreme head of all the creatures below is living a layer above the firmament. He commands and rules over everything down below, animate and inanimate objects alike in the Universe. The devil and its cronies hover around the fringes of the Universe can only create trouble and challenge the power of the Supreme God-head, but never successful to capture the hearts of the human being with its evil design. The entire lot is defeated thoroughly with the master stroke administered by the Divine one.

About the Stories

The subject matter of all the stories portrayed in the book entitled 'The Petals' are based on true life-stories one could encounter in man's action and inter-action with each other while living in this mortal world. These new experiences blended with sweet and bitter knowledge of life are the keynotes of these stories. In the race of achieving excellence one is always is the winner. He has the honor of triumphant entry into the realm of glory, the rest are the losers, so follow the disgraceful existence. But in the eye of the Supreme Being all are equal, both the losers and winner are His children.

Two stories elaborated here are, firstly 'The Heavenly Asylum' titled by the author was related to four of us by one of the members of Calcutta Special Police while on duty during a crucial soccer league match played on Mohan Bagan field by the two arch rivals, East Bengal and Mohan Bagan, way back in mid seventy of the last century. We took the field three hours before the scheduled start of the game. It poured for half an hour incessantly, drenched us from head to foot. The story of a ruined family was told to us by one of the officers in a different form to bring relief to our wet and dry conditions. The protagonists Mr. Jha and his spouse Asha are concocted personality, not related to any living or dead characters. Imagination and speculation were used elaborately while writing the story.

Secondly 'The Providential decree', was a fictitious story which I heard while studying at Barisha High School in the primary section. The substitute teacher to occupy the non-teaching period told us several stories on varied subjects. I have elaborated the bare outlines of a similar story he so passionately acquainted us with his imaginative quality of a story teller.

Hanif in the story titled 'The Waiter' is an example of a true person of substance whom one could rarely come across in life. He is an ordinary person not considered to be included in page 3 of any newspaper of the country. The wise and sagacity blended with emotion and love for humanity of an ordinary waiter of an insignificant restaurant in Calcutta is projected in the story.

The little Hassan was standing under a mango grove and was staring at the ripe succulent fruits hanging from the branches of 'Fazli' mango tree. He stands there every day while the mighty Kenchanjonga Express passes through the mango grove after crossing the Malda Railway Station in West Bengal. The author encountered the absorbing scene during one of his innumerable journeys he took to Darjeeling in connection with music, traveling in the express train.

The two stories 'The Malai Mandir Bus Stop' and 'The Bond' based on the lives of two different personalities of the weaker section of so called society, suffering from serious ailments, yet have influencing effect on the ordinary passers by. The mere presence of these characters in the midst of people with diverse nature, possessing different ideologies and varied opinions of life is the crux of the stories. They impersonate the creator of mankind, who descends on earth seldom to guide people to live righteous life. The author encountered the fascinating scenes during his daily walks at 7' 45 am in two spots — the crossing of Rao Tularam and Outer Ring Road in the corner of West End Colony, where a leprosy afflicted beggar was begging to sustain life. He was seen with another man offering him a packet everyday at a particular time of the day. Suddenly one day the man disappears and the beggar began to get cured. Who was He? While seeking the answer to the question the onlookers also began to change from skeptical persons to men and women of honour and simplicity. The second one is the story of a frail hilly girl boarding a bus at a particular time of the day. At first the sundry passengers hated her but soon she became the cynosure of all eyes. The mere affliction of leukemia changed the minds of all inquisitive onlookers. Here also the hateful minds transformed into loving ones.

'The Destiny' is based on the scene witnessed in front of a house every morning in the posh West End Colony where an aged driver was mopping the car of a wealthy person residing in the house. When a Nepali girls of 14 years old carried two milk containers to fetch milk from the nearby Mother Dairy booth. The young boy of the house wanted to settle down in the U.K. the land of hope and glory but failed to do so due to entanglement in a mysterious wedding ceremony, where a girl was involved. The jilted young man lost all hope of marriage and began to hate sweeter sex entirely. An insignificant, obscure and caring girl brought back the faith in him eventually.

Acknowledgements

I owe a great deal to my beloved granddaughter Madhurima, who has inspired me to go ahead with my writings in sundry ways, Ramen and Sangeeta, her parents.

Mrs. N. Williams, Mrs. Sikha, (the respected teachers), Mr. M. Banerjee, Arpita Dasgupta, Pinki Gomes, Shourabh Atri, Shshank Nautiyal, Parakh Oswal (My students), Brother Dinesh of Delhi Brotherhood Society and a few selected friends for recognizing my .001 percent talent. Above all I thank God for his ubiquitous presence in all my activities.

1

The Heavenly Asylum

Mr. Jha longed for a house of his own where peace would reign supreme forever. After hard work and dedicated services rendered to the commercial establishment where he was employed for several years, he got one. In fact he built one palatial building in the heart of the city after his marriage with a girl from an army family that became a landmark of the area.

"This man has a taste" remarked his distant neighbour.

"He must have accumulated unaccountable wealth in fraudulent means." Said his next-door neighbour.

"I'm sure he must have inherited a huge property from his ancestor somewhere and spent the amount here to live a happy life." Commented the third.

All these people spoke among themselves because Mr. Jha did not interact with his neighbour so intently as it was expected of him to do. He was a simpleton, homely by nature and was devoid of any social characteristic.

It was in one of those propitious evening he married Asha, the beloved daughter of Colonel Sethi, the retired Infantry commander of the fifth battalion of the Army. Mr. Jha knew Asha even before their marriage. They met in several parties at the garrison headquarters of the army and the intimacy grew from the courteous wishes to a lifelong bond. It was neither a matchmaker's vociferous, useless introduction nor an arranged marriage but a perfect understanding of the duo after a long discussion of the intricacies of life and the responsibility entailed thereafter of bringing up the offshoots in the traditional way in the healthy atmosphere of a perfect dwelling place. The sacrament of marriage would bind them together in harmony, love and care for each other.

After a couple of meetings between the parents of the couple, the day was fixed for the great event.

" Asha, if you do not mind 1 would like to call you by your first name." Mr. Jha believed in speaking his mind openly.

"You're at liberty to call me by my first name." She gave the direct reply to his proposal. "I hope you will like my company?" he shot a simple query.

"It is obvious," she replied as a matter of fact.

This was the first intimate conversation they had before marriage over the phone.

The wedding ceremony was lavishly and elaborately performed. The relatives, friends and the well wishers of both the families blessed the couple profusely. They wished them the best of everything that they could think of and the world could offer them.

"May their home be an ideal one."

" May all the blessings of God bestow upon them."

"May they prosper in health, wealth and wisdom."

"May they be blessed with lovely children."

There was no exchange of dowry and animosity between the two families, only the goodwill, best wishes and blessings of the elders were solicited.

The disposition of God is always contrary to human expectations. But in the case of this particular family it was not so. Within a year Mrs Jha had given birth to a bony boy. They named him Rahul, a sophisticated common name widely used in the affluent society.

"He is the apple of our eyes." People heard Mr. Jha saying to his friends in sundry times. "My child will be famous and add laurels to the family's growing popularity." Asha told her friends at the club, in the social gatherings in the house and outside parties.

Rahul was born on the day when Mr. Jha got the letter from the Chairman of his company elevating him to the post of Assistant Manager of the business establishment. The couple rejoiced at the bounty of Providence and the occasion was celebrated with a party where all the elites of the city and the friends were invited. Their happiness knew no bounds. The relatives and friends reaffirmed their previous benedictions and wished the family a happy life.

Within three years of their marriage Mini, a pretty girl was born and Mr. Jha got another promotion. He became a full-fledged manager. Again the relatives, friends and neighbours gathered around them to make merry. The only talk among them was how their prediction had come true. Asha also kept her busy in setting up their house and to make it an ideal one.

The new house they built in the posh locality of the city was named, "Heavenly Asylum". Asha was its sole architect. She herself designed the house, chose the colour and decorated it to her own taste and to her heart's content. The children grew up well under her care and she groomed them to the norms and pattern of the affluent society she belonged to. The mother showered Rahul with excessive love and her father pampered Mini.

Minor altercations were common affairs between husband and wife like any other home, but the dispute was always settled between them amicably. On an occasion such as this the children profited most since one of the parents would try to cover up the matter by bringing a gift of his choice or taking the family out for a sumptuous treat. Usually Mr. Jha was the looser.

The people living in the close proximity of their house envied their life. They felt jealous of their happiness. Mr. Taneja lived two buildings away from the Heavenly Asylum. He was a brute by nature. He mellowed down as he came within the vicinity of the Jhas. Mrs. Taneja heard commenting,

"Why can't we live like the Jha's?" There's seems to be no trouble, no misunderstanding, no quarrel and no lack of cohesion among the inmates of the H.A. Perfect harmony prevailed in the whole atmosphere and it influenced the other people who came in contact with the Jha's.

The years passed by. The vicissitudes of life affected a and sundry people in their respective domain, but the Jha's were hardly changed. The family grew from strength to strength in wealth and power. They prospered beyond measure.

"I want a cycle to ride to school" Rahul asked his father one day. It was a bombshell to Asha. She never expected her son to ride to school on a bicycle like the ordinary boys. "Why, what's the trouble?" she asked him in annoyance.

"Nothing, Mom. All my friends ride cycle and show off. I just stand there and watch their movements." Rahul said innocently.

"Why we have such swanky cars, not one but two. Is it not enough for you?" She expressed her disgruntled state over the issue.

"Perhaps he has taken a fancy to the newly found adventure. It is the natural trait in all growing up boys." Mr. Jha tried to bring an amicable and judicious solution to the problem.

Mini caught the thread and asked for a gorgeous Sari to adorn to her best friend's birthday party.

" This is no longer a fashionable dress to be worn by a girl of your age. Only the grown up girls wear them during marriage parties." Asha did not quite like the inordinate demand of her daughter.

She turned to Papa for a solution. Mr Jha was forever ready to lend his helping hand to his beloved daughter. He took the middle path and said,

"Mini, Mama is right. You've to listen to her. The saris of your size are difficult to come by in the market. They are sold in Benaras. When I go there next I will get one of the best."

Whether she was convinced or not was a debatable question, but for the time being there was a truce between the mother and daughter. Mr. Jha obviously kept his promise and got her a beautiful Sari during his next outing to Mumbai.

After ten years of their marriage, the Jhas gained a lot both mentally and physically. The children went to study in two prestigious schools in the city. The family now possessed three cars, one happened to be a Mercedes and additional sprawling bungalow with an exquisite garden in nearby hill station, a steady handsome income. What more could a family want!

Most of her spare moment Mrs. Jha used to be in social and charitable works. She was quite pretty to look at and her amiable nature drew her co-workers towards her. Her presence in every activity of the social organization acted as an elixir. A little sweet smile on her face transformed many depressed and dejected souls to a life of meaningful living. In addition to these she maintained poise and gait in her manner and walk.

Similarly Mr. Jha was handsome too. He was hardworking and a man of wisdom. It was not only his upbringing and public school education that earned him the coveted job, but he had also the shrewdness and understanding of the minds and intention of the people who had elevated him in this exalted position.

The couple was made for each other.

God created man in his own image and bestowed upon him all that he could - strength, vigour, character, wisdom, etc., but God created woman out of necessity. After the Creation of man, the Lord God felt, " It is not good that the man should be alone, I will make a help mate for him." And the supreme being caused a deep sleep to fall upon Adam (the first man), and he slept" and took one of his ribs from above his heart, and made her a woman, and brought her to man. Subsequently, the man called her woman because she was taken off from the man. For centuries she was considered a weakling and under dog, although a 'lib' had been granted to her universally in the recent past.

The tranquil atmosphere in which the Jhas were living was shattered all on a sudden one afternoon with the delivery of a letter, stamped "Her Majesty's Governmen". Ajay, an old flame of Mrs. Jha had written to her from London to resume their old acquaintance. Both Ajay Sharma and Asha studied together in St. Xavier's College, Mumbai. Like a flash of lightning it reminded Mrs. Jha of her salad days. She was disturbed mentally and agitated physically.

Strange is the passion of human beings. It wears him off if he does not control it. Man is the worst victim of his uncontrollable passion. In the fit of passion he forgets joy, happiness, discretionary power, concentration of mind and peace. His mind is subject to sorrow, suffering, disillusionment and depression. Passion is a sense object.

" When man muses on sense object, attachment to them arises, from attachment arises desires, from desire anger comes forth. From anger comes delusion, from delusion loss of memory, from loss of memory destruction of discrimination. From destruction of discrimination he perishes". Gita ch. II verses 62 and 63.

Mr Jha noticed a change in his wife's attitude.

"Darling is there anything amiss?" asked Mr. Jha one evening as he sauntered through the parlour where his wife was brooding on the letter.

" Have I left anything undone, or, have I done something to annoy you?"

Mrs. Jha smiled a forced smile but did not say anything.

"Of late I have been noticing that you do not find interest in our household activities." Continued Mr. Jha in a low voice. It was his mother who taught him never to hurt anybody's feelings. He remembered his mother and applied the same principle here. The result was inevitable. She burst out into an ear splitting wailing as a last resort to cover up her weakness.

"Why are you crying Mummy? Have we done anything to bring sorrow to your happy life?" Rajat asked her while he heard the cry.

Mini too was upset at the incident when she came to know about it.

"I know the reason why you are so unhappy." Mr. Jha said coolly.

"Nothing to worry about. Let your friend be mine also." He added.

Such a statement from Mr. Jha came to her as a bolt from the blue. Her tears disappeared like the last raindrop evaporates from the earth's crust due to heat. She was rejuvenated

Life began again at the heavenly Asylum. Mrs. Jha went on doing her daily chores but refrained from doing too much of outside work. Her gratefulness to her husband knew no bounds. She became a loving mother again to her children. The neighbours heaved deep sigh of relief. The gloom, frustration and fear of loss disappeared completely from the house. Henceforth, the entire atmosphere of the Heavenly asylum was transformed into one of jollity, frolicking and gaiety. Parties were held frequently to celebrate the social, family and national occasions for the neighbours, friends and relatives. It was heard of Mr. Jha to say at the end of each social gathering,

"Darling I wish to bring you out into the limelight of the social fabric where everyone takes notice of your entire personality, attractiveness and integrity. Wasn't this party a grand success?"

"Yes. It was fabulous. I am very happy." She acknowledged greeting with a simple reply coyly.

Rahul and Mini took the opportunity of mother's good mood and forced her to spend more money on their favourite stuff like electronic gadgets, junk foods and fashionable clothes.

"Mummy will you please attend to my school's play on next Saturday? I'm the hero of the play. All the parents of my friends participating in the play will be attending." Rahul asked his mother expecting a favorable reply.

" Of course my son. It is my great privilege to attend the concert. I will make you a new dress for the occasion. It will dazzle the eyes of all your friends and their relatives. I will do anything to help my son to carve a niche among his friends."

"What about me?" Mini butted into the intimate conversation between mother and son. "Nothing. You are not taking part in the play. You suck your thumb." Rahul said just to annoy her.

"Don't worry. I've not forgotten you. You get the surprise on the appropriate day." Mrs. Jha consoled her daughter in the apt manner like a mother.

All of a sudden the inmates of the house were aroused one morning with the sharp sound of the doorbell. A servant opened the door. Within a few moments they heard a loud knock on their bedroom door. After a great deal of reluctance Mrs. Jha opened the door. A telegram had arrived from London. She tore opened the envelope and read the content which read,

"Reaching I.G.I. Airport on Saturday Morning, Ajay."

The news had a mixed reaction on Mrs. Jha. She was in a fix and did not know what to do. She handed the telegram nonchalantly to Mr. Jha. By now he had woken up. He took the telegram and read it. He had only one expression on his face, a beaming smile.

" I must go to the Airport myself to fetch Ajay"; he quipped instinctively to ease her tension and worry.

On Friday evening, Mrs Jha looked very worried. She took quite a long time to dress up, an indifferent attitude towards everything overcame her once more. At dinner she talked very little and sparingly.

" Mummy will you be coming to my concert tomorrow?" Rahul asked in excitement. Mrs. Jha was startled at the sudden reminder of her promise to attend the programme in school on Saturday

"I will try." A small answer from her did not assure Rahul of the belief he had of his mother's presence at the concert.

Mini caught up the thread and asked her mother a simple familiar question dominated in any day to day household conversation,

"Are we not going to the shopping Mall on Saturday afternoon?"

To this Mrs. Jha had no reply. She kept quite and looked the other way. Realizing the unpleasant situation Mr. Jha intervened and said,

" You have to understand that your Mummy will be very busy to tomorrow and will be unavailable to accompany both of you to your promised engagements. Instead I will go with you to the Shopping Mall in the afternoon and to school to attend the concert in the evening." The children were rather surprised at the sudden change in their mother's attitude towards them. She even looked at them indifferently. Only once she looked into the eyes of her husband.

Mr. Jha passed the night peacefully. In fact on that night he snored the loudest. Turned sides on the bed only once and had a couple of pleasant dreams, all related to his office work. Mrs. Jha spent the night in agony. Her thought centered around one topic only whether she should continue in the same way with Ajay as she did in the days of yore.

She got up several times during night. She even swallowed several sleeping pills, but to no avail. The much sought after sleep deluded her.

Woman, 'frailty is thy other name.' The creator has endowed her with all the beauty of Nature. The red rose is ingrained on her cheeks. The precious emerald is spread in her hairs, the sweet song of the Nightingale is in her voice, the sheet of gold is pasted on her skin, two green sapphires are embedded in her eyes and a slender touch of reeds is revealed in her feature. But alas she has an infernal heart. Most crooked, devious and deceitful. It is a gift from the devil. The eternal grandeur of the Himalayan snows are mixed with the fierce force of the tropical storm. The soothing effect of the dawn and the sunset has got entangled in the mid-day scorching sun.

The alarm clock rang at three sharp in the morning. Mr. Jha woke up promptly, completed his morning ablution at great speed, dressed himself up as neatly as possible and went down to the garage to the car to keep ready for the journey. In the mean time Mrs. Jha also got herself ready to go out. She looked extraordinarily brighter and more cheerful this morning. After having a hearty breakfast in silence they set out in their Mercedes for the Airport. During the half an hour drive to the Airport Mr. Jha tried to speak sporadically in monosyllables to break the monotony of the tedious drive but received no answer from his wife. Once only she said, 'Fine' when he enquired about her health and the reason for keeping silence.

" Rahul seems to be growing up fast. All his clothes are shrinking. He needs a few pairs of good outfits."

" Mini is looking pretty nowadays. She has become stylish too. I like her latest hair style."

"How are your days? The American NGO is spending dollars in real earnest to eradicate the contagious diseases in the city. I'm sure you are involved in the project."

" The Sensex is rising in an astronomical rate. The country is bound to raise both economical and industrial lives of the people."

All the above questions went unanswered. She sat like a dummy in the car never looked at him for an instant. Mr. Jha thought the silence was golden so withdrew from the battlefield.

But he was not a person who had been cut out to remain silent for long. He cracked a couple of old familiar jokes in between to enlighten her spirit. He even hummed a few disharmonic false to tunes from the old Hindi film songs. She was as dumb as the Sphinx. But nothing could deter Mr. Jha.

He went on and on with his usual pranks. But she became more silent.

The B.A. plane landed in time. Ajay was easily identifiable in the midst of the embarking passengers. He was tall, fair complexioned and handsome. He had an imposing personality. He wore a light blue coloured suit, which bore the mark of Saville Row of the shopping complex in London. Pair of dark glasses made his look more attractive. He walked slowly in dignified manner; every step he took was well measured.

As he walked through the tarmac to the security enclosure and afterwards crossed the custom checkpoint in the airport, Mrs. Jha's heart began to palpitate in nervousness. It was very difficult to discern at that point of time whether it was in agony or ecstasy, perhaps the later. It was simply the joy of meeting an old friend, a joy, full of reminiscences. It had no impact on Mr. Jha. He was unconcerned and unperturbed.

"Hallo, darling, " Ajay greeted her in a familiar, affectionate and friendly tone. "Hallo." She made the simple and short reply. But the tone was full of mirth and excitement.

Mr. Jha took the trouble of collecting his suitcase from the exit gate and carrying it to the car in a trolley. All through this Mrs. Jha was deeply engaged in conversation with Ajay. A peal of laughter from them sometimes even surpassed the din of the Airport. While walking, unconsciously their hands locked in, the arms embraced each other and often Ajay even pulled her towards him. They were in deep conversation, forgetting the world around them.

Mr. Jha always rose to the occasion when it was demanded of him. That was the secret of his success. In this case also he rose steadily to that inevitable position where the demand was for presumptuous guts and unpretentious sacrifice. Mr. Jha did not wait for ceremony but introduced himself to Ajay and welcomed him heartily to the city. They all climbed together in the front seat of the car. Mr. Jha sat at the wheel, his wife next to him and Ajay at the other end. She was squeezed in between them. Both Mrs. Jha and Ajay were tightlipped and excepting the occasional remarks by Mr. Jha, the drive to the house was quiet. Mr. Jha asked Ajay about the English weather, Big Ben, Mrs Thatcher and her economic policy, the Cricket at Lord's and the latest fashion sweeping the country ——--Levis, Wrangler, or Hara.

" I'm sure you have a long holiday". Mr. Jha asked Ajay.

" Not exactly. Just two weeks." Drawled Ajay.

"Where can I drop you?" Asked Mr. Jha as soon as they reached the heart of the city.

"Oh, at the Taj." Ajay replied indifferently being very prudish.

"Why not spend the day with us?" Mrs. Jha dropped the invitation without asking her husband. It was the first time that she had spoken after entering the car at the Airport. "Yes, why not? It's a splendid idea. Mr. Jha reiterated further, "It's an excellent idea indeed."

The children were at the door to receive them. So Ajay had a Royal welcome. They went off to school after greeting Ajay. A shed of disgruntle feelings was discernible on their faces. Mini looked rather annoyed at the sight of a stranger too close to her mother.

"I don't like that man." She confided her unhappiness to Rahul on the way to school. "Don't worry he's not going to stay in our house. He has booked a room in a hotel." Rahul tried to pacify her in the natural way a brother ought to be doing.

Mini did not spend the day well in the school. She felt as if a void was created between her mother and her. She rushed home after school as usual, hoping to meet her mother and ask her about the man. Unfortunately her desire remained unfulfilled. Her mother had gone out already. Mrs. Jha did not come back home till the time she went to bed.

Ajay spent the day at the Heavenly Asylum in the company of both the Jhas. It was spent with lots of fun and frolic. Mrs. Jha seemed to have a new lease of life.

A spate of new visions had dawned before her. Many old, common and intimate friends came to meet them at the Taj Hotel. The next few days were rather heavily booked for them. Asha spent her days with her friends at the Taj Hotel ignoring her real responsibility at home. The children initially assumed their mother was heavily engaged in her social works. Perhaps the coming of her friend had intensified her work, but soon they realized their mother was engaged in some other ways. It spelt disaster.

Mr. Jha was tied up very much with the office work that week so he too stayed out of the house almost all days. The MNC office Directors had come to visit all the branches of the company in India. Being one of the regional directors he had to show them around. He had innumerable luncheon meets with the clients and endless meetings with the board of directors to sort out the future course of the company. He came back to the Heavenly Asylum in the late evenings, but was forced to spend the time alone, or occasionally with the children, since they too were busy with their studies. Mrs Jha was practically out of the house every evening. She came back home often after mid-night and some nights she did not come home at all. On a day such as this the children felt miserable. They missed their mother a lot.

"What has happened to Mom? She does not come home these days. Has she gone to see Nunny?" Rahul asked his father one day.

"No she is here. She must be very busy with her work." Mr. Jha told a lie to cover up his wife's folly.

" I miss mummy." Mini just uttered her frustration in a nutshell

"Don't cry baby your mother will be with you within a couple of days". He uttered another lie to console her children.

Towards the end of the fortnight of Ajay's stay in India Mrs. Jha put on a look of aloofness. She never cared for the children as much as she used to do previously. There was no show of love and care on her part towards the children. She even stopped talking to them.

The children also distanced them from her company. A strange situation prevailed in the Heavenly Asylum. Mr. Jha bore it patiently.

Two days before Ajay's departure for England Mr. Jha was surprised to find his wife standing at the door in the evening as if to welcome him after a long voyage.

"Hallo, Darling." Mr. Jha greeted his wife with a luscious and spontaneous smile. "Hallo, dear." Mrs. Jha replied in a subdued tone.

"So nice to see you at home." Mr. Jha said. " Aren't you going out?" He added with a genial smile.

"I'm awfully busy today, dear. Staying back home only to see you." After a few seconds silence she continued,

"I'm in a terrible dilemma." She said without looking at him.

" Don't hesitate to spell it out." Replied Mr. Jha. " I'm always at your service."

She hesitated for a few seconds. But observing cordial demeanor of her husband she opened her mouth and blurted out to him,

" Do you know darling, Ajay wants me to go to London with him." She said without a stutter.

Mr. Jha was dumb-founded. He was speechless for a few seconds, but recovered as the meaning of the words sunk in. Surprisingly he was a changed man in the very next moment. In a situation such as this any man with an ordinary heart would have given vent to his inner feeling of in discretionary animal instinct but not Mr. Jha. He was made of sterner stuff. He controlled his emotion and gave the felling as if nothing had happened. " Of course darling, a little change of place will do you a world of good. Moreover, I have to go on to foreign tours myself to see our overseas offices in the East. Most probably after the tour I'll be taking over the management of all the Indian concerns of the company. I'll be off this weekend."

"Is Mummy going to leave us?" The worried children asked their father as soon they got the wind of her departure.

"No, She is not going to leave us. She will stay away from us for a while." Mr. Jha tried to be more positive and informative about the subject,

"Children you have to be self-reliant. Your Mom will pay a short visit to her relatives in London." He continued to convince them. It was a stark lie, but there was no other way he could find to pacify the children. They were too sensitive.

" She did not come to my school programme and now she will be absent on my birthday." Lamented Rahul at the situation prevalent now of which he was a participant. "Now no one would sit beside me while doing the home work. I will feel lonely without her." Mini expressed her deep sorrow at the sad news of her mother's idiosyncrasy.

The very first thing Mr. Jha did the next morning was to call a distant Aunt of his to come and stay in the house with the children for a short while. Being a widow and a septuagenarian, she often obliged people whom she knew well. After a lot of hesitation and expressions of surprise she agreed to come over. Quite a number of eyebrows were raised among the people in the elite society in the neighborhood, but Mr. Jha put on a bright smile on his face against ensuing odds. Since then and till her departure he kept himself busy with the office work.

Within three days of her announcement she bade Good-bye to all and left the house without a ceremony. The children were given the impression that she had gone to visit her aunt in the U.K.

Mr. Jha too was to catch a plane for the Far East and Australia en route to Europe with in another five days. He made all arrangements for his aunt and the children's stay at home as comfortable as possible. Everybody watched him on the day of his departure. There was no sign of unhappiness or complaint. A genuine smile was visible on his face.

After three weeks of successful trip abroad and a promotion Mr. Jha came back home. Now he had reached the top echelon of his company so the workload minimized subsequently. He had more time now to relax than before. At home the children too had grown up. Almost everyday the children enquired of their mother. Mini was mostly disturbed and became a recluse. Rahul returned home after school in staggering times excuses being involved in extra-curricular activities after school hours. Mr. Jha realized their feelings, but took everything in his strides.

Instinctively the children too learnt to adjust themselves in the absence of their mother to the adverse circumstances and challenges of life. They became more attached to their father. In the beginning they grumbled but soon realized their father had all the ingredients and qualities of love, affection, care, companionship and understanding. Mr. Jha took very special care of his children's education and in extra-curricular activities. Every weekend he took the children to the club and played Tennis, golf and swimming in the club's pool. They all missed Mrs. Jha at times. But nothing could fill the void; she was so far away in the wide world. The Heavenly Asylum was in doldrums. Life went on without its charm, but it went on.

"When will our mother be here?" Asked the children to their father regularly.

" She will be delayed a few days, I presume." Mr. Jha had the answer ready for the children.

"My friends make fun of me" Rahul said to his father one day.

"What do they say?" Mr. Jha asked him in return.

"They say she has eloped with her sweet heart and she will never come back." Rahul made his father know the precarious situation that he was in.

"I'm rather shocked to hear the opinion expressed by your friends about your mother. Tell them she had gone abroad to study certain subjects related to her social work. It will enhance her knowledge on the work she had been doing here." A stark lie but Mr. Jha could not help it. This was the only way he could pacify his son.

"My teacher wants to meet Mummy. She has been assigned a piece of work in school regarding a project she has undertaken on social and humanitarian subjects which she wants to discuss with her." Mini asked her father one evening as he walked in to the house after the days' work.

Mr. Jha realized it was simply a ploy on the part of the teacher to confirm the rumor afloat in school and in the neighborhoods, of the whereabouts of Mrs. Jha.

" Tell her your mother has gone abroad with her parents to see an octogenarian ailing aunt of her. She is the eldest sister of her mother. She may come in the next month when your teacher can meet her." Mr. Jha tried to be reasonable to his daughter.

"Next month!" Mini expressed her surprise.

"Surely she has forgotten us." She retorted in painful submission to her father's false clarification of the topic for discussion.

After about six months sojourn in London with her heartthrob Mrs. Jha sent a telegram to the family suggesting a reunion.

The message read thus,

"Arriving on Sunday by British Airways."

The news was not actually a bombshell. Mr. Jha was expecting it to arrive any day. He delivered the news with alacrity to his children. But it seemed his enthusiastic outburst fell into deaf ears.

The children replied in indifferent tones.

Rahul said, "I'm representing school in the Olympiad Mathematics Contest on Sunday. I'm not available to go with you to the Airport to meet our mother. Dad say 'hallow' to her on my behalf."

" I'm taking part in the annual flower show in my school. I am one of the volunteers to show the guests around. Presumably I shall be out all day." That was Mini's concocted refusal for not receiving her mother on her return home.

"Never mind I shall go alone." Mr. Jha gave a mournful reply.

Mr. Jha made an elaborate preparation to welcome her home. The entire house was cleaned, every bit of the furniture was dusted, all the flower tubs in the balcony and portico were painted red and the plants were watered to add an extra glow to their brightness. The drawing room was given a face-lift. The new curtains replaced all the old ones. The kitchen was given the royal touch. New utensils, crockery and tableware were bought. Expert cleaners cleaned the carpets. The bedroom of the Jhas had a new decoration. It was painted with her favourite cream colour.

A day before her arrival Mr. Jha bought flowers from the market at an exorbitant price. In fact the front door of the house was decorated with flowers, streamers, inflated balloons and glossy crepe papers. The Heavenly Asylum presented a scene as if a newly wedded couple was about to enter the house for the first day of their wedding.

During her absence from home the children were rather depressed. They missed her greatly during evenings and mornings when she used to give them her company in every work they did for school or home. They could not see the reason why she should extend her stay in U.K. more than the stipulated three weeks.

At last the D-day arrived. The children had different alibi to avoid going to the Airport.

Mr. Jha went to the airport alone to meet her. The plane landed on schedule. He waved at her profusely as she dismounted from the DC 10 of the British Airways. She looked at him and waved back faintly. One could notice a great change had taken place in her personal appearance. She had lost the poise in her manner and gait in her walk, charm in her appearance and frivolity in character. The same enthusiasm she had shown before her departure was lost now. Her mind appeared to be over cast with gloom, sorrow and dejection.

Mr. Jha waited anxiously for her at the exit door of the custom cubicle. It took her an hour to get the clearance from the custom and immigration counters. During the long wait a genuine spontaneous smile was visible on his face. He even acknowledged cheerfully the greetings of some of his acquaintances that he had met at the Airport lounge. There was nothing amiss; he performed his act brilliantly and with dexterity. He looked like a teenaged lover waiting for his beloved on the first day of their meeting, full of expectations, possibilities and impatience.

As soon as she showed herself at the gate Mr. Jha literally ran to her with outstretched arms and enthusiasm.

Mrs. Jha hesitated for a couple of seconds, but mechanically flung herself into his ever-protective arms. They clung to each other for a few seconds and during that time he whispered into her ears,

"How are you, darling? The children and I missed you a lot."

A quick shudder could be felt in her body, she burst out into tears and said instinctively, "I too."

During the drive home he told her about their gaily-painted house in her favourite colour, the children, the aunt, his tour in foreign lands and the promotion. He lucidly described to her a particular tree that she had planted a year ago. Before her departure she watered, put substantial amount of manure and tended it so well that it has now grown up to be the most attractive tree in the garden. She would really be proud of it now when she had seen her handy work. It is the tallest, brightest and most beautiful of all the trees in the garden. He also told her of the rain a week ago that brought welcome relief from the grueling sultry weather of the summer months. He talked about the club, old friends, his business colleagues and associates. The only thing he avoided mentioning was the children in detail. Perhaps it was done intentionally to gauge her feelings towards her own offsprings.

All through the drive she did not utter a single word. Either she looked vaguely all around or sat very stiffly. They were hardly exchanging a glance at each other. No, it would be wrong to say that he was not looking at her. Each time he said something he looked at her but there was no reciprocal glance from her part to acknowledge the same.

The gate at the main entrance of the sprawling compound was flung opened by the guard but there was no one of her own to greet her. The children were in their own rooms pretending to study; the servants were either in the kitchen or had gone out to market. The aunt had already left in the previous evening to avoid confronting Mrs. Jha. Only a few pairs of eyes were prying through the shutters of the windows from the adjoining houses of their neighbors.

Mrs. Jha waited a minute in the drawing room expecting the children to emerge from their rooms to greet her. But the children remained aloof and would not come out to say hallow. Considering it's a discourteous behavior, Mr. Jha called for the children, "Rahul your mother is here. Come and greet her," said Mr. Jha as far as the norm of the civilized world was concerned. But there was no immediate reaction on the part of Rahul. He took full two minutes to come out of the bedroom and stood at the door only to stare at his mother.

" Say hallow to your mother." Mr Jha insisted.

Rahul uttered only 'hallow' inaudibly and bolted inside the room without much ado. The familiar scene of the affable, affectionate and intimate encounter between the mother and the son was missing at that moment of time which annoyed Mr. Jha greatly, but right now he was in different temperament and had to keep a balance in the family relationship. So he pretended as if nothing had happened. He called Mini in tandem to come out and greet her mother. Like a disobedient brat she remained inside her room. Mr Jha tried his best to call her out of her room but there was no response.

Instant reaction of Mr. Jha was to walk into her bedroom at without looking anybody. Mini emerged within ten minutes time after changing her clothes. She looked askance to her mother and said nothing.

On the next morning the children were at the dining table for breakfast. They displayed indifferent attitudes when the mother greeted them with a simple 'hallow'. The reply was half-hearted and cold.

Mr. Jha always rose to the occasions whenever a crisis of this nature cropped up. He anticipated a showdown between the mother and the children. After taking stock of the situation he collected all his wits together and said

"Come on Rahul, say hallow to your mother."

"Hallow" was his short reply. He even shunned looking in the direction of his mother. Mini remained glued to her seat only to stare at her. Everybody remained silent at the table, excepting Mr. Jha. He first asked Rahul about his study so that his mother got up to date with regard to his preparation for the ensuing examination in school.

"So, so." He gave a very short reply expressing his annoyance of his mother's atrocious, inhuman and un-lady like behaviour over the last six months during her absence from home.

"What a lovely dress you put on today. Are you going to a party?" He asked Mini, silly though, only to keep her in humor. But all his efforts to make Mini speak to her mother went in vain. Mini kept mum all through the breakfast. In fact she only nibbled through the breakfast items without eating a morsel from the plate. The immediate reaction of her was to leave the table suddenly and disappear into the garden for solace.

That evening Mr. Jha thought of taking her to the club to remove all doubts of her elopement, a baseless rumor was doing the round and it was on the lips of every one and in the minds of the people known to them, closely or remotely.

After her departure it spread like wild fire all around the club. Although no one dared to ask him the cause of her disappearance yet it was evident in the minds of the nosey associates that something of this nature had happened. All the daylong he was beaming with pleasures for the return of the prodigal. So in the evening he gave the feeling all around the club of how happy he was at the reunion.

"Hey Mrs. Sonam Asha is back from her U.K. trip where she went to meet her ailing aunt. Now the game of flush will take a different turn." Mr. Jha said in a hilarious mood when they met accidentally outside the card room.

Mrs. Sonam was rather non-committal. She had a rueful smile on her face. She cast a skeptical glance at them before opening her mouth

"I don't know. Rita, Bina, Sheila have left the city. I am also about to leave with my family on a vacation to Goa." She replied without looking at them and disappeared in the other room.

They met Ranbir, the ace tennis player of the club and a close friend of the family in the lounge. He had an ironic smile on his face. He said only 'Hai' to Asha and discussed a few topics on politics with Mr. Jha and disappeared as quickly as he came there. But the familiar humorous conversations among them were missing.

Her bosom friend, Sharmila swept past them without casting even a glance. Mrs. Jha blushed at first and later on was agitated at the sight of her old friend's indifferent and unfriendly behavior. All old acquaintances of her seemed to be hostile and were trying to avoid her. Mr. Jha noticed the unfriendly behaviour of all their common friends. It looked as if old familiar faces were drifting away from them to the world of obscurity. In spite of all odds Mr. Jha remained unperturbed. He drank and ate alone in the company of his wife at the club. When they came back home they found, to their great dismay, the children had bolted their doors from inside securely and had gone off to sleep.

After this many days passed by, weeks rolled on and many months elapsed, but Mrs. Jha was unable to pick up the old threads of her lost glory. Half a year ago she reigned supreme in the Heavenly Asylum but to day she had been reduced to mere insignificant resident, a persona non-grata, sans power, sans respect and sans everything. The children had adopted an adverse attitude towards her, the relatives had stopped keeping any contact with them, the friends began to avoid them and even the servants discontinued taking orders from her. Her world shrank. She hardly could talk to anybody excepting her husband. Occasionally she picked up her knitting gadgets to knit or books to read. But she failed to concentrate. Practically the entire day she sat on the settee in their sprawling drawing room and gazed outside at the sky through the window. At times she muttered a few indistinct words on her own. The text was inaudible. No one could decipher what she said so everybody paid scant heed to it, excepting Mr. Jha.

One day she called Mini to her side and intended to talk to her. "How is school?" she asked her.

"Going as usual." Mini answered briefly.

"How is your study going on?" She tried to be more intimate. "Good."

"Do you need my help?" She opened her heart.

"No", a very curt reply. After this Mini got up from the seat abruptly and went to the garden. It was proved markedly that she abhorred her presence.

Asha was the sole architect of this sordid scenario.

The next moment she spotted Rahul and was about to comment on his dressed code.

" Mother I've grown up now and I can look after myself. I know exactly what is good for me. I would not like any interference in my life." He answered her indifferently without taking a scant heed of what she had said.

The curtain fell forever in her family life.

She now began to withdraw herself from everything around her. Her dresses began to sag, her hairs were disheveled, her eyes began to protrude out and her lips got discoloured due to lipsticks. Black colour encircled her eyes. She lost her appetite, began to thin down subsequently.

She was irked by her own children's passive attitude towards her. They maintained a staggering timing for their meals. They did it deliberately to avoid confronting her. As a result she was forced to have her meals alone. Mr. Jha was the only person who gave her company at meals whenever he was there. Then he related to her in great detail the events of the day pertaining to his subordinates and the directors of the company. But his superlative yarns fell on the deaf ears. His super jokes fell flat, yet he persisted. That ubiquitous smile was there on his lips.

Since her return from abroad only one question haunted her, day in and day out "Did I betray the man?" Mr. Jha never asked her a single question about her U.K. trip. Even after her return from abroad when the world went against her he had shown the utmost sincerity, deep love and care.

Soon after this she began to visit doctors one after the other to have the peace of mind. Mr. Jha accompanied her each time she went to see the best psychiatrist in the town. At last the inevitable fatal day came for which Mr. Jha had prepared himself for a long time, the day when the psychiatrist gave his final verdict, that she was a perpetual mental case. Mr. Jha took the pain of admitting her to the best mental asylum at an enormous cost.

For the first time the inmates of the Heavenly Asylum saw two golden drops of tears fell from his eyes.

Jogen Khan

2

The Waiter

Mohammed Hanif was my favourite waiter. From the day one of my visit to the covetous restaurant he charmed me with his sense of humour and affability. I never left the place without tipping him handsomely. He worked in the famous eating joint called 'NIZAM'. One could get here the cheapest and tastiest 'Sheik Kabab', rolled into a 'Parantha' at a nominal price. Every truant paid a visit to this popular joint for junk food, situated near the New Market at down town central city market complex. Hanif served them the wholesome 'KABAB ROLL' unparallel to any of its type existing in this Metropolitan City, with a smile.

"Would you like to have the salad with it?" He would ask me every time I ordered a roll of meat 'KABAB'. One nod and a quarter plate salads filled with sliced cucumber, tomatoes, onion and green chilly, a pinch of salt and pepper served with a dash of smile.

Hanif was a 'Bihari' Muslim, dire poverty, the typical trait of his birthplace, atrocious treatment meted out to underprivileged class of people by the upper cast gentry and endless land feuds among his own relatives forced him to come to Calcutta three decades ago. There was no dearth of jobs in

Calcutta for 'Bihari' migrants in those days. The menial jobs were found a plenty, as domestic helps, gardeners, chauffeurs and rickshaw pullers and more sophisticated among them were offered the jobs of waiters in restaurants of different standards.

In fact, a relative of the owner of the restaurant was prowling on the platform no. eleven of Howrah Station where Hanif landed with his meager luggage in one of those winter's cold mornings about thirty years ago, ill-clad, shivering in cold, hungry and dirty. The deputy manager of "NIZAM' grabbed the boy. Little did he know at that time that the boy would fetch him so much business. Hanif was engaged initially as a dish-washer and was paid a paltry sum of money. From the day one Hanif devoted his entire soul, mind and might to his work and served his master unflinchingly without paying much attention to the remuneration or the hour of work he had to work which every employer appreciated.

Hanif"s meteoric rise to the position of a waiter was due to his hard work. He had a perfect sense of time, acquired good knowledge of pleasing people, an honest disposition and pleasant look. The job of a waiter in a restaurant entailed a heavy amount of tips which every waiter in the hotel business desired to have.

It was during my college days when I was living in a hostel a class-mate of mine once mentioned the place. I was not a regular customer but made frequent trips during winter season when I earned a little extra money. In the other seasons I depended on my pocket money, which did not stretch beyond spending on necessary things, one needed to sustain a civilized existence. But in winter I joined the local Symphony Orchestra as a second violin player and two performances in a month would fetch me a substantial amount of money, a part of which I spent at my favourite joint. It seemed the way Hanif used to treat me that I was his favourite customer. Favouritism always would cost you more than what you expected to spend otherwise. As a young man I had always shortage of money but never was tight fisted and faltered to pay the tips since Hanif served me the best 'Kabab Roll' with a smile.

Each time I paid a visit to the restaurant Hanif would invariably ask me questions. It would speak of his wisdom and sagacity but reflected upon the darker side of his life, dominated by deprivation, illiteracy and poverty, yet there was an eagerness to learn.

"How many books do you have to study? How do you read these books?"

"Who has written these books, you or your father?"

"How do you store so many facts and figures in such a small head of yours?"

Some of these questions he repeated several times which irritated me immensely in the beginning, but later on I got used to them and avoided answering them by simply remaining silence. I was then studying in a degree college.

Hanif's mode of asking questions change as I entered a profession.

"Are you a bureaucrat? Which department of government do you work, Home, defense or foreign?"

Being addicted to the fashion of the time I dressed up as per the norm of the contemporary haute couture in the smartest and costliest clothes. Hanif was impressed and asked relevant questions.

"Can you get me a passport?" He asked me one day.

"Why, on earth" I was dumb-founded for a while and did not know how to continue with the rest of the conversation. A man of his stature, without having any financial support, sans worldly possession and without political clout to fallback on dared to dream of having a passport. The initial stupor changed into disbelief; the same changed into surprise after a couple of minutes.

"Why do you want it?" I asked him.

"I'd like to go to Dubai. They say I can get a good job in the Arab country. The waiters are well-off there." He gave his heart out.

"I don't know much about it, but I'm sure the restaurants over there maintain a very high standard of services, you've to speak good English and Arabic, dress up neatly and work very hard." I tried to make my points clear without hurting his feelings. As far as I knew it was a far cry for him to get a descent job in Dubai. He neither possessed an imposing personality or criterions to secure employment anywhere in the world.

"So you feel I have no chance there." Hanif drew the conclusion himself to a great relief of mine.

"Have patience. Keep the spirit up and have the faith in you. Something might work out." I consoled him and discontinued with the discussion on the subject.

After this I did not go to the joint for a couple of years. Pre-occupations and foreign travel kept me busy. In the meantime I tasted all kinds of junk foods in the States and in some of the European countries which I seemed to have liked immensely. I acquired a new taste for Burgers, Pizzas, Pastas, French fries, Lasagna, Pies etc. The native cuisine distasted to my reformed tongue temporally. But the old habit dies hard, especially with an addict of my type. After the last visit to the US, I felt the newly-acquired urge to visit my favourite eating joint increased.

On a Saturday afternoon as usual I occupied the same seat in the middle of the restaurant next to the main pillar. I scouted all over the place to spot Hanif, since, I presumed, he might have gone to the kitchen to execute the order of a dinner.

"What is the order?" a gruff voice addressed me. I turned instantly my head towards my left only to find a tough looking man, sporting a colonel type of moustache, staring at me. He stood like a statue, fixed his eyes straight into mine and was about to command me to execute my order.

"Yes...' I drawled the word, stammered and said in halting tone," I'd...like...To have... Two rolls."

Hardly I had completed the sentence he turned quick about turn and disappeared through the door of the kitchen. To my great dismay he returned at once with two rolls in a plate. His prompt action led me to think of two options. Either the rolls were the rejected order of a customer since he had discovered a contaminating substance in it or the fellow was prompt in executing the order as he was expecting a fat tip. Whatever might be the case, I did not go into a controversy so ate the rolls without relish. The rolls were hot but the ingredients- put in tasted insipid. It was not served with the genuine concern as Hanif did.

All through the meal I was itching to ask the man about Hanif, but hardly had time to do so. His mobility in the restaurant had frustrated me till the last moment of my stay there. Before paying the tip I got a chance to embark upon the question.

"Where is Hanif?" I would have hurdled a barrage of questions to relieve my anguish and inquisitiveness but refrained from it. The man stared at me once more and replied in a curt manner.

"He's not here. He's gone out for a walk." So saying he promptly disappeared from the scene.

I pondered over the issue for a while and realized, it definitely was a luxurious proposition for a man of Hanif 's stature to go out for a walk in the open maiden. It was an absurd pastime only the affluent, obese and senior citizens could indulge in such a lavish exercise. Hanif was a small fry, a day labourer, living from hand to mouth and had the responsibility of looking after a big family. "How could he afford time." I wondered.

A week later I dropped in once more for the hot, crispy and tasty rolls. Fortunately, this time, Hanif was present there. He had all smiles on his face as he welcomed me. I was elated beyond comprehension, spotting my favorite waiter.

"Sahib, what has happened to you? I'm not seen you for a long time." Hanif expressed his feelings in such an affectionate tone that it has choked my voice for a while. The same affectionate tone I used to hear from my dad. He is no more now, but, I thought I had a replacement.

"I was very busy with my work. I was travelling a lot, all over the country and abroad," I told him in one breath.

"Have you been to Dubai?" a simple question he asked and quickly turned away to go to the kitchen.

I sympathized with his obsession. But I had no power to implement it. In the meantime Hanif brought my quota of two rolls. One bite of it would speak of the heart and soul he put onto making the delicious rolls. I devoured the succulent rolls like a wolf. Hanif looked at me with satisfaction; the glee on his face would prove the truth of the fact.

"Sir, can I ask you something?" innocent as he was, Hanif had no hesitation in asking for another favour.

This time I was a little surprised. I noticed something different in his movement. He was very polite in approach, spoke in subdued tone and went beyond his way to oblige me. I felt he was aware of the presenoe of the other waiters all around the room. A couple of waiters were watching him from the beginning of his entry into the dinning hall. Something they wanted to remind him of. Their eyes were revetting at intervals and pointing at me. Hanif, too, wore an extraordinary smile in his face. It was sign of complacency.

"What is up Hanif?". "What do you want to ask me?" being confounded I blurted out.

"Could you give a tip?" he said with confidence.

"What tip? Do you want to go to Dubai still? But that is impossible. I have told you already one has to be upto the mark in every sense."

"No I'm not talking about the Dubai trip, but I'm asking to give a tip of the next horse race at the maidan."

I was stunned at the remark and for a few seconds no voice came out of my throat. What did he think of me? Am I a gambler or a punter? I was about to burst with anger for identifying me wrongly but the inner council prevailed on me.

I smiled and said to him, "Hanif I am not what you are thinking of. I am not the man who runs horse races. I have got nothing to do with it."

"One of the waiters had seen you at the race ground a month ago. He told me to ask you for a tip. It's a great favour." Hanif said innocently.

"Hanif, I was in Delhi all this time, before that I went abroad, your friend couldn't have seen me anywhere in the city." I expressed my inability to help him.

The crux of the matter was that, of late, Hanif had fallen pray to the evil men of no consequence. He had been influenced by the other waiters in the restaurant. They were involved in nefarious activities. His frequent visit to the maidan had induced him to get involved in horse-racing, betting, and gambling with cards, ludos and Chinese checkers and chewing tobacco. Only redeeming factor was that he stayed away from smoking and drinking, as a true follower of Islam.

Fortunately this was just a passing phase in his life. Being away from home and family for a long time, gave rise to loneliness and over-burdened responsibility to maintain a large family forced him to earn an extra cash by fraudulent means and so he plunged into the fray in real earnest.

On my next trip a couple of months later I dwelt upon the same topic and tried to find out more about his latest fancy.

"Hanif do you still want the tip?" I tried to make fun of him."

"No, No, Sir. I have given up everything. Those cheats have drained out all my money. The little savings I had in the bank for the rainy days have gone. I'm a pauper now. I do not know what happened to me in those days. Perhaps I was overcome by the Devil."

Hanif put his hands up and continued saying, "I promise in the name of the Almighty that I'll not mix up with those wicked people any longer." To assert his point firmly, he pulled his ear lobes, twisted the rib of his nostril and made a clucking sound with the protruding tongue. His repentance was genuine that I discovered from his face. A sea of change had taken place in his personality. In shame he put his head down.

I had no words to express my happiness at his transformation. Vicissitudes of life at time either made a man substantially strong or reduced him to an ignoble state. One had to discreetly keep a balance.

"I'm so happy to hear the good news. The Almighty has blessed you." I wanted to carry on with my sermon but Hanif left the table abruptly and went inside the kitchen to execute the order. I could see streaks of sparkling tears rolled down his cheeks. He was carried away emotionally.

This time he took rather long to serve the delicacy, the reason was obvious. He needed a few minutes of isolation. When eventually he brought the rolls I took the opportunity to be cordial and intimate.

"Hanif, where is your family? Do they all live here?"

"My family is staying in the village in Bihar. I have a small family. My parents do live with us. This is my second wife. My first wife died of cholera. Nafisa, my second wife, is a divorcee. I married her five years ago. She has three children.

"This is not a small family!" I quipped.

"Traditionally the married women in my village are not supposed to keep their wombs empty. Till the age of forty they must bear children, otherwise they will be looked down upon by the rest of the village folks as barren. I will be suspected of being imbecile and lost my virility. Having a minimum of ten children is very common."

I felt he was very proud of his family and the village tradition. Innocent as he was, he never knew in a developing country like ours such large families would cause population explosion.

"How do you manage to make both ends meet for you and the members of your family? Don't you feel it's burdensome?"

Hanif's philosophy of life and that of his compatriots in the village was beyond my comprehension.

"When do you see them?" my inquisitiveness wetted my appetite to know more about him and his world.

"Every year in summer months I go home. It is very hot then in Calcutta. The business is dull so that the owner allows us to go home."

"Why don't you bring them to Calcutta and keep them with you?"

"No, No, I can't do that. Firstly, the little land I own in the village will be taken away by the partymen or the relatives of mine will devour it in my absence. Secondly, this city is too expensive to maintain a family of my type. The house rents are disproportionately very high, the jobs are scare, moreover, people here are all cheats."

"It is not the case always." I could well imagine the plights of the people in the metropolitan city. Everybody is hard hit. People like me, for instance, earn our livings by the sweat of our brows. Hanif's sagacity and the perfect logical conclusion of the city life moved me greatly.

On my next visit to the favourite eating joint, I asked him more intimate questions.

"Hanif, how do you spend your days besides working in the restaurant? You must have some leisure hours besides the tedious days' work here?" as I was gormendising the savoury placed before me I asked him the question.

Hanif presented before me a vista of a vivid picture of the scenic beauties of his surroundings and the human passion and his love for natural elements.

Hanif's working hours stretched between six in the morning, when the Restaurant started functioning and eleven in the night, the time it was to be closed. Food was on the house. He slept on the floor of the restaurant at night. A few faithful waiters had the privilege.

Only recess he had during the day and between his busy scheduled working hours was from four to five. It was a golden hour in his hectic day.

Clad in his favourite blue coloured 'Lungi', a half-sleeve discolored shirt and off-use 'Gamcha' on his shoulder, Hanif would go out into the close-by Maidan for a leisurely walk during the golden hour! While trudging alone on the lush green Maidan, he never forget to smash a big pinch of the dried tobacco leaves between his palm till it grounded into powders. After adding a dash of white lime, he very dexterously parted his lips and holding the lower lip with one hand, he plopped the content into the parted lip and quickly closed it. Every third minute of the walk, he spat on the ground to get rid of the excess saliva, intake of which would give him headache and nausea. He felt elated when stepped on to the soft green grass with bare-foot and the lush green trees beckoned him for Camaraderie. Those vendant lush-green foliages kindly offered him protection from the glaring sunlight of the summer months by casting their shadows. In spring and autumn the rich blossoms painted the atmosphere with yellow, violet and red colours. The panoramic view was nostalgic. It brought back joys in his heart and reminded him of his youth spent in the village in the identical atmosphere.

Once Hanif related to me the experience of his solitary walk he had everyday in the maidan. He loved to watch the children in colourful dresses, running helter-skelter all over the green field in the company of the 'Ayas' or grandparents. Some ran after small balls, some hauled up their own friends, some chased the old parents, but they all followed each-other in the pursuit of fun and frolic.

The youths wandered about in the open field to give vent to the pent up energies. The cooped up energies found avenues in giving expressions to their talents through various games. The most popular one was soccer. The unorthodox methods of the local version of the game pursued thrilled Hanif beyond measure.

The goal posts were made out of their discarded clothes placed disproportionately on two spots ignoring completely the established rules of the game. At least ten games were played simultaneously on a field suitable for three conventional soccer games. The areas were not marked and none conformed to the right measurements according to FIFA rules.

The acquisition of the field, whether large or small, depended on the brawn, brain and priority. Small skirmishes over the rights of possession of the field were the matters of daily occurrences. No dress code was followed, player's age was no bar and the rules and regulations depended on the principles of 'might is right'. The boundary lines were not demarcated but calculated mentally by players on the basis of sheer imaginations. The most astounding sight of the game was that each one of them respected the other's right after a certain portion was occupied by a team.

Hanif ambled through the spaces left between the team non-chalantly. Since no side lines were clearly visible so no one stopped him for trespassing their grounds. Occasionally a few upstarts passed caustic remarks at him of his physical appearance, his elongated forehead and his unorthodox and odd dress. But most of them got used to him since he was a regular visitor.

At times some stray balls came his way and at once Hanif would swing into actions. He kicked it usually along the path of the direction of the ball to the utter disgust of the pursuer.

On some occasions he tripped over the ball and fell down head long on the spot, which evoked peel of laughter from all and sundry onlookers. Once, it's so happened the 'lungi' went up above the waist when his left foot slipped in the process of kicking the ball.

This caused almost a riot. The youngsters all around him screamed, hooted, booed and danced wild dances to ridicule him.

"He's a rustic Bihari fellow, a joker. The fellow is a nut, a dirty pig and a shit of Maradona."

All these subsequent remarks annoyed him, but having a good, forgiving soul he took everything in his stride.

Winter was the best time of the year when Hanif enjoyed the walk most. The bracing climate of the months of December and January rejuvenated his soul and filled his heart with joy and happiness. Now cricket replaced soccer. Hanif prolonged the walk a little longer to enjoy nature's bounty abundantly found all over the maiden and reflected through the creative works of God. The number of players increased, multiplied by three times. In every nook and corner of the extended field the young players were bubbling with enthusiasm. The age groups of the participants ranged between ten and forty years. The number of players in one team was not fixed; it varied between four and twenty in each team, depending on the resources. Each player impersonated and imagined himself as one of the contemporary great players dominated the current scenes in the country. The strokes, styles and bowling capacity determined who was who. A short, stocky player, good with bat thought himself to be a Gavaskar or Tendulkar. The all-rounder called him Ravi or Kapil and successful bowlers, even if he bowled in an unorthodox manner, was called Zahir or Kumble. The opponents were given the alien names as Tony, Steve, Imran, Lara etc.

The one astounding fact was that they all followed the dress code strictly; the white uniforms were prescribed by the ICC. Most of them used the standard cricket balls, barring a few teams, who used the soft ones. As it was in the soccer games, the fields were not marked but imagined. The makeshift cricket pitches crisscrossed, one overlapping the others. The remarkable part of it was that no one interfered with the games of the other teams. At times it's so happened one fielder caught the ball of the neighboring team or stopped it in time to save fours or sixes from the imaginary boundaries. The scorers of them got hurt in the process, yet all the games, on all holidays, from sunrise to sunset, went on unabated. Hanif felt the spirit of the game and the love of it were expressed through the enthusiastic participation.

Hanif too had his share. Quite often he stopped the balls drifting from imaginary boundaries. Many times he intended throwing the ball in front of him, but ended up hitting the chap who stood behind him. Since the gripping of it was not exactly as he held the 'Kebab' plates in his hands. A barrage of abuses followed, some even threatened him with dire consequences for touching the ball, but Hanif was not thrown off balanced. Once he showed me a cut mark on the right upper lip of his mouth. A stray ball hit him hard there. He bled and two stitches did the work to hold the parted skins together. He also showed me the permanent swell on the left eye. A ball hit him there in last winter season. He stopped to catch the ball moving towards his direction at a great speed, but suddenly it touched a stone in front of him and rose to the height of his forehead. His eyes did not reflect quick enough to prepare him to move ahead, and the ball hit him straight on his head. It left a permanent mark on his face forever.

"Why don't you see a doctor and operate on it?" I suggested without thinking of the cost it would entail.

"I am not in a position to do it. In my village such accidents are daily occurrences. We administer the local medicines; we crush the leaves of a local plant and apply the juice on the wounded part. The cure is inevitable. Moreover, doctor will cut through my nose for nothing." Hanif replied with a huff.

Realizing argument would produce no result; I said to him,"Hanif, I think it is a permanent beauty spot." To this he chuckled and said nothing.

Now over the years I had established an intimate rapport with him which forced me to return to the spot more often than before. On my next visit I found him morose and a little ruffled. .For a few minutes I restrained my curiosity and held back the desire of holding a conversation. I liked to respect the dignity of silence in a man's variable moods. It spoke many things of the nature of thinking power. I could deduce from the silence the storm was brewing up in his heart. Only a genius like poet Wordsworth could guess the probable themes and the content of the songs of 'The Solitary Reaper.'

But no one could prolong his silence forever. At one stage he had to blurt out and speak. Normally the sympathiser or the listener try to break the silence. According to the latest theory the psychologists propounded in the US that the former should make a sufferer speak and he should listen. I did the same. Remained silent and provoked him to speak. I assumed his heart was stirring and it was about to burst.

"Do you know the reason of my silence?" he looked into my eyes and asked the question.

I could see the beads of precious tears in his eyes. I presumed it definitely was a sad case about to be revealed before me. A loss in the family, bankruptcy, loss of money in betting, getting a sack or the news of the death of a dear one were all one could guess in the present circumstances but the incident he related was of a different nature. The great human feelings of love, care and concern for each-other, irrespective of social status, religious conviction, economic power, affluence, caste, creed, went with it.

Hanif was very fond of watching the movements of the multitudinous vehicles in various shapes, colours and qualities moving on the streets, encircling the Maidan. The most attractive mode of transportation among those was the Tram - Car. As a new comer to this city in those days he was overwhelmed by the sight of its two elongated boxes, attached to each-other with a chain, moving along the two parallel slender lines steadily' with an antena like rod protruding out of it, also tied to an overhead wire. They called it a Tram-Car in which scores of people, jostling with each other for a vantage position, screaming at each-other in abusive languages, hanging outside the body of the car for lack of enough space inside the car travelling from one part of the city to another. He noticed and wandered how one man with two hand devices made the tram-car move. Two men also were there to sell tickets and guided the passengers to alight and board the car. An electrifying sock ran through him whenever a tram-car passed him by.

Watching the graceful movements of the tram-car for several years, Hanif developed a love for the same car. He admired its majestic movements, swayed in fancy manner defied the approach of the other cars, specially the smaller version of it. The assorted advertisements displayed all over the car, both interior and exterior fascinated him immensely. The multiple animated figures of man and animals in different colours, shapes and sizes dazzled his eyes and transformed it into the world of fantasies. One particular advertise thrilled him to a great measure in which an ant held the four legs of the mighty elephant and was about to hurl it into the air, advertising the power of the medicine over the particular disease and its disastrous effects. He liked the signs of big M (Macdonald's), bearded chef serving fried chicken, the smiling baby fed with a spoonful of milk etc. he abhored from the core of his heart an advertisement of the female bust covered with half clad undergarment, but did not mind to look at the masculine body of a man in his scanty garment on his person.

Quiet often he was shaken at the sight of the approaching tram car and tried to justify the strength and energy it held. His small mind often compared it with the power and strength of the Almighty God. He always felt the tram car held the secondary power, God had the supreme one. He literally worshipped the man-made mobile machine.

The amazing part of it was the incredible power it possessed. How could those two boxes carry so many people he wondered. The trams were overcrowded in the late afternoon when Hanif took the stroll-the office goers were returning home and the boisterous youngsters hanging outside the foot board and jostling on it for a foot-hold were the sight he liked to watch.

Sometimes the upstart commuters travelling in the tram cars hurled abusive words in his direction without rhyme or reason, especially on those days the professional soccer matches were held on the maidan. The supporters of the losing side made Hanif their target to express their grievances:-

"You babbon, return to African jungles."

"An odd shaped monkey."

"A son of a gun. Look at his head."

"A rustic 'bihari,' the face of a mammal."

The scores of unsavoury remarks were passed at him almost everyday by the young commuters hanging outside the tram cars. At least eight to ten of them stood at the foot board, their feet were hardly touching the floor, some of them even rested their feet on the others and the entire bodies of these hangers were suspended in the air. One slip of the foot, the disastrous fall was inevitable. Hardly anyone bought a ticket.

Hanif felt sorry for them and could never imagine himself to be in their places.

The illegible jargon used by these scums went far above his head, but he could guess their meanings. He had been staying too long in this city.

Hanif's physical appearance stirred all the commotions in the hearts of these devils. Traditionally clad in a blue 'Lungi', sporting a white 'Fatua' (an odd shaped T-shirt) and slipping in pair of the cheapest plastic chappals, he used to go for his favourite pastime, the stroll in the maidan. In summer he threw a 'Gamcha' on his shoulder ostensibly mopping the sweat from the brow, but in winter he wrapped himself with a squalid discoloured shawl and equally dirty and out of shape pair of sneakers. Two beady eyes embossed on the oval shaped head, quiet similar to the rugby ball, crowning the diminutive figure of an oddly dressed up man, prowling besides the tram cars evoked laughters from the onlookers. He became their ultimate target. Injustice but the human nature was such, particularly the youngsters were prone to get embroiled in such obnoxious actions. Hanif paid scant heed to their booing, jeering and sneering.

"I'm a creation of God. He has shaped my figure according to his wish. Who am I to point a finger at Him? He definitely has a purpose behind my presence on the earth." He said to me once in the defense of his creator.

I simply nodded my head in the ascent. I could neither revoke the dictate of his creator nor was in a position to defend him against the onslaughts of his detractors. I could only show sympathy as one human being should do to the others.

Hanif had a golden heart. The sad incident he related to me on that evening spoke vociferously of the man and his mind. He spoke to me in a depressed tone.

"A couple of western origin, middle-aged husband and wife, used to walk the length and breath of the maidan, pushing a perambulator alternatively between them and holding long conversation in a strange dialect which was beyond his comprehension, presumably in English. They came to the maidan at a particular time everyday. Sometimes the man missed the walk but she was there regularly. While pushing the pram alone she was musing and talking to the baby alternatively. Hanif tried several days to have a glimpse of the baby but was unsuccessful. One day he collected enough courage, went near the pram and had a glance. It was a bonny baby. He failed to determine the sex of the child but what mattered most was that the baby smiled at him. The meeting of four eyes, of occidental and oriental origins, thrilled him beyond measure. He was greatly satisfied and its brought a meaning to his flagging soul and enhanced the urge to live a worthy life. Simultaneously Hanif saw another eight pair of eyes beckoning him. He out stretched his arms to draw them near him. But in the next moment he came to his senses and found the baby was gone. Henceforth, Hanif hovered round the pram daily to have another look of the beautiful and innocent creation of God. Initially the lady got suspicious of his motive and even suggested her husband to find out a solution of the menace, soon realized the man's intention was good so left him alone. For at least three months Hanif had the opportunity to go near the pram. In each encounter, he looked into the pram, saw the baby either sleeping or sucking its right thumb. The child always welcomed him with a smile.

It was early March. The weather was warming up. Hanif realized the visit of the baby would be few and far between. Every day he went there early, least he missed the moment, but was greatly disappointed. The couple stopped coming.

Suddenly one day in spring on a Monday morning in the middle of March he spotted the pram. The lady was pushing the pram and stealthily moving towards the tram lines to cross. Hanif was thrilled to the core. He thanked God for the dual views, both had become the part of his life. He closed his eyes and saw the other pair of eyes, calling him from the distance.

But all on a sudden there was a scream. He heard the tram car came to an abrupt halt a few meters away from the pram. The mother pushed the pram in front of him, as if to indicate a safe custody, and ran to the tram-car. The people all around the place were running helter-skelter, some of them even shouting.

"Help"

"Get the Ambulance"

"Get the person out from underneath the tram-car"

"Call the police No.100"

"Don't let her go near the body. She will faint."

There was a real commotion with the fifty yards from the tram car.

Hanif witnessed a couple of ladies were holding the baby's mother in their arms and were consoling her. The pram was standing before him in which the baby was fast asleep. He held the handle of the pram securely, imagining the baby was left in his care.

The police, fire brigade and para-medical people arrived. After a strenuous effort they were able to extricate the body from the tram car. At first the mangled body of a foreigner was difficult to identify. They took the body in an ambulance to the nearby nursing home. Hanif handed over the pram to the mother and was about to go. Before going he happened to ask a bystandard. "Who was the man? Do you know anything about him?"

The man gave a curt reply, "Don't you use your eyes? I see what you see. The 'ferengi' was perhaps the husband of the lady with the pram". The identity of the man remained obscured to Hanif.

The European gentleman was the pastor of the nearby Methodist Church. His ministry was credited for doing the pioneering works of looking after the slums in the eastern part of the city in addition to the pastorate works. He was tall, lanky and had the imposing personality. He was an active member of the local choral group and was in great demand during winter season when the major musical shows were held. He had the best baritone voice in the city. Last winter, before Christmas, he took part in the musical play entitled "Amahl and the night Visitors" depicting the influence of the nativity on a crippled boy. He sang the part of Melchoir, the second King. The local newspapers gave rave reviews of his performance.

The priest had come to the maidan regularly with his wife and the baby during winter season. Of late he was busy in the other parts of the country where he often visited in connection with his social works. Being the chairman of the organization, he was away to U.K. for a week to attend a crucial meeting of fund raising cempaign there to woo the benevolent doners for the philanthropic works done in this part of the world. He had returned on that fateful afternoon just before the accident. From the airport he went home, deposited his bag and rushed to the field to meet his wife and the baby. His wife spotted him from the field as he was about to cross the road. She hailed him from the distance and decided to meet him half way near the tram line unmindful of the danger lurking in the vicinity of their meeting place. She did not notice a tram car was approaching the spot in full-speed and wanted to cross the lines with the pram. The driver of the car also noticed the lady with a pram. He shouted at the top of his voice to warn the lady of the imminent danger. It was very difficult for him to put the break at once to a running car, the result would be fatal. In the meantime she had pushed half of the pram on the lines of the speeding car. She saw the tram car, approaching her and the baby, lost her nerves, her feet became dead. She stared at the car, transfixed and was about to be fainted. Realising the catastrophic danger lay ahead, the priest sprinted and jumped towards the pram and pushed it out of the way of the running car. He was successful in saving the lives of his wife and the baby but in the process he got entangled in the mud-guard of the frontal portion of the car. The body was dragged along with the tram car twenty feet ahead from the spot of the accident.

The entire European community of the city, particularly his co-religious activists and social workers kept vigil in turn for over twenty four hours outside the intensive care of the Woodland Nursing Home. On the second morning after the day of the accident he succumbed to his injuries and was buried in the local cemetery.

As the luck would have it, I happened to drop in to the same Nursing Home to visit my ailing boss on the same evening of the accident. I was aware of the entire episode of the accident and its aftermath but was ignorant of the link it had with the sordid phase in Hanif's precious life.

Hanif missed the rendezvous. Two contrasting countenances, the smiling face of the baby and disfigured body of a white man, perturbed his soul for a long time to come. He wandered the field for many days to get a glimpse of the pram but there was no sign of it. Ignorant as he was, he never knew the relationship between the baby and the wounded man. Only memory lingered on in his mind was the protection he had rendered to the baby during the commotion after the accident. He held the pram tightly and wouldn't budge an inch even for his dear life in the face of any onslaught. The serene face of the sleeping baby and the anguished mother, the contrasting pictures was looming still fresh in his mind.

Now even after a week of the incident Hanif was ruminating over the accident. Slowly and surely he was trying to forget the matter, but only this morning someone told him the connection the baby had with the man. The news intensified his sorrow even more.

I had no word to console him, excepting that the passage from the great writing of the sages in the pristine glory. I quoted to pacify him,

"God gives and God takes away. Our earthly sojourn is for a short while. We are no one to refute His judgment. Behind every birth and death of all living objects He has a design. We'll have to obey His command."

I said this as he deposited the plate of succulent, hot and smoke-wafting 'Kabab' rolls in front of me on the table of my occupancy.

"I totally and unquestionably accept His verdict. We're very small against His mighty power. But human souls are vulnerable. It is natural that one soul cries for the loss of another, irrespective of social status, caste, creed and religious conviction, which separates one from the other. Hanif's philosophy and logical conclusion of his religious belief stunned me. He lacked any kind of academic knowledge but his wisdom and discretion of differentiating between good and evil were characteristic features one had to reckon with. Nature, a true representative of God's aesthetic design and great teacher imparted its impartial, unflinching and informative knowledge to an illiterate, ignorant and poverty stricken person like Hanif was the great cause for adulation. I doffed my respectful hat off to Hamf and his creator.

Inspite of the fatal accident Hanif's fascination for the tram car did not diminish, in fact, it had increased in many folds.

"I wish I was a driver of the tram car", Hanif expressed his secret wish, perhaps the most stunning one, to me on my next visit to the restaurant after a lapse of six months.

"Why do you say that? What is wrong with the present work? Are you not satisfied?" I quipped.

"Oh! No, I'm very happy with my present job but the tram car fascinates me. The majestic run of the cars on those two sleek steel lines is unparalleled to any other vehicles a man could invent. Who has conceived such an idea, I wonder! The drivers press the buttons and the cars come to life. They sway to and fro sideways and forwards at the command of a single man. He is the most powerful person amongst all creations of the Almighty. He rings the bell and the commuters move out of it's way. He is the lord of the roads." So saying he sauntered out of my sight to serve in another table.

A simple remark of this nature made by an innocent folk would move any sane person. His philosophy of life, illiterate though he was, would put any scholar in an embarrassing position as it was filled with goodwill towards humanity. It had a universal appeal of love, care and concern for the fellow human beings.

Soon after this my visit to the restaurant became less frequent. On reaching the naughty age of forty one became aware of one's health. In the mean time the standard and quality of food in the restaurant deteriorated. The ownership had changed hands. The old man was dead and the son lost the grip, the administration lapsed. Hanif was in a quandary. I too stopped going to the joint for sometimes.

After this a year or may be more passed by, suddenly, I felt like having a roll so visited the place for a quick bite of my favourite 'kabab' roll, I missed Hanif. On inquiry I was told he had gone out for his usual stroll in the maidan. I did not wish to miss him, the substitute was rather an uncouth and arrogant fellow. On my second visit, a fortnight later, I missed him again. Finally when I visited the restaurant six months later I was told he had just left for his customary stroll.

That was the last time I tried to establish my old connection with my faithful, philosophical and philanthropic waiter, a great soul who had impressed me beyond measure as a perfect human being almost non-existence in the contemporary world of ours.

Next day I read in all the leading newspapers of the city the following reports.

"A man was run over by a speeding tram car in the middle of the maidan on the spot, where a Christian priest met with a fatal accident a couple of years ago. His limbs were severed from the body. The police could not identify him as his face had been smashed beyond recognition. He had a blue 'Lungi' and a 'Kurta' on his person. A 'Gamcha' smeared with blood was found near his dismembered and mangled body.

From the clipping of the news item I could figure out who the man was. He was no one but Hanif, my most favorite waiter of 'NIZAM' restaurant. An invisible plaque would have been read thus :-

"This was the man, who loved his fellow human beings and considered them as his own. May God rest his soul in peace".

3

The Kanchenjunga

With a clang, bang and thud the rickety old railway gates fell at the level-crossing to stop the flow of traffic on the dusty village road, penetrated through the massive parallel iron bars, that were laid down to allow the trains to roll over it. The falling of the gate was a prelude to the arrival of the on going trains, East or West, and between the falling of the gate and the appearance of the train, the short period of ten minutes forced the traffic, going to and from North to South to come to a standstill on both sides of the lines. The loaded trucks, long distance buses, two wheelers, carts and the pedestrians all came to a sudden halt. The drivers waited patiently at least for fifteen minutes before the train passed. During the short span of time some exchanged greetings, some looked aloof, some pressed tobacco leaves in between palms, mixing it with a pinch of lime and some cursed at the obnoxious system as they were getting late. All these people were strangers to the place, just passers by.

The people lived around the spot were the villagers. They were having a stagnant life. Be it winter, rain or summer they were there. Only in winter, the harvest season, they were rather annoyed since a lot of time wasted at the level crossing, which could have been utilized more effectively on their farms. They were both amused and astonished at times. The giant mobile man made machines was fascinating too. They looked at it in awe and with reverence, knowing fully well that their shortcomings could not match in any way with its great prowess. The frequency of movements of these mobile giants increased rapidly over the past decades. Now at least ten pairs of trains - mostly passengers - some expresses sauntered up and down the two lines, causing vibration in the surrounding areas, resulting in heart throbs among the onlookers. Innumerable good trains passed through the crossing and rattled the ground around the place. However, it was the part of life. The villagers got used to them.

Every day just few minutes in the afternoon, Hassan stood diligently at the railway crossing when the giant Kanchenjunga Express passed by him majestically. Dusts flew, leaves fluttered on the branches of the nearby trees, the ducks waddled off hurriedly, the cows bellowed and ran helter-skelter and the children danced with joy, full of glee. Hassan stood there transfixed. He wondered whence cometh this, and whence goeth. It appeared in the northern horizon like a speck, developed into a dot and later changed into a shape of a gigantic monstrous machine. It flashed for a couple of seconds in front of his eyes and then disappeared in the reverse order in the southern horizon. Almost everyday he counted mechanically the bogies attached to the engine. The carriages danced in front of his eyes like quick moving shutters. Some days he counted sixteen, some days eighteen.

The numbers alternated, which thrilled Hassan immensely. He took mental bait on the number of bogies and most days he won. One day the train did not come. Hassan was upset. He missed the short rendezvous at the level crossing. The rumour spread like wild fire that the train plunged into a swift flowing river resulting in spot death of all the passengers. Hassan thought it was an absurd idea. The truth contained in the fact that two bogies jumped the rails at a place called Alubari, subsequent result was the cancellation of all the trains till the mess was cleared.

Hassan wondered at the enormity of the mobile man-made iron giant. Who could have conceived such an idea as to build a train? According to him it could devour ten villages in one gulp-its people and houses all. He gazed and thrilled. The more he gazed the more he was mystified. At quarter to twelve, he stood at the crossing punctually. Heats of summer, rains in monsoon and the icy cold winds in winter could not deter his spirit from wondering. Often his father Abdul got annoyed with him.

Hassan was a village boy, about eleven years old. His father Abdul was a day labourer. He inherited a small plot, but lost it to the local landlord due to indebtness. To make his both ends meet he took up to the profession of a hired labourer. Of late, on account of ill-health and abject poverty, he lost all bope of living a normal life.

Hassan did not go to school, as his father could not afford the fee. He was unable to work like his father because he was under-nourished. Only opening he had, to work as a child labourer, but he had none to hire him.

"I wish you were dead along with your mother. A good for nothing fellow", his father would say to him everyday in desperation.

"You have a big mouth to eat but small hands to work - a big head but no brains," he would continue.

Scolding of this nature was a daily occurrence, which was casual to little Hassan.

"I wish I am as powerful and strong, as speedy and gorgeous as the giant express", he would say to himself. The only solace he found amidst agony, torture and reprimand was at fleeting view of the express train.

Abdul lost his ancestral land a decade ago. Since then, he had been working on his own land as a bonded labourer. He could never pay back the immense debt he had incurred, therefore stayed on his land to bear fruits for his master. The consequential wrath and indignation fell on little Hassan. The bare sight of his son infuriated Abdul to such an extent that he first used his malicious tongue to lash him out in incivil language, which would cast a shadow on civilisation. Then he would hurl things at him indiscriminately with anything he could lay his hands on within close proximity. Nothing would touch Hassan as he had learnt over the years how to dodge his father with dexterity. Some days his anger had no limit and Hassan was chased out of the house. While Hassan ran out for his dear life, his father would stager behind him.

One day it surpassed all limits and norm of parental love. Abdul chased his son with a knife in his hand. Poor Hassan ran. He crossed the courtyard in front of their house, ran beside the small pond where the ducks flew in fear and got entangled in the hyacinth plants, crossed the small grocery shop where the local maids made their meager purchases, sprinted along the tiny hovels where the local school was held and he could hear the boisterous students reciting the multiple tables at the top of their voices and then to the open field. At last, he came over the railway crossing, his father at his heels. Both were exhausted, but Abdul's madness overcame his tiredness. He was determined not to give up. As he was about to catch him, the giant express train came in between them. Most of the bystanders screamed in unison "watch out". They took it for granted that the boy was crushed under the giant wheels. However, it was a miracle. The boy crossed the lines just in time, went over to the other side of the lines and the father stood still on this side of the tracks. The express merrily puffed away between them.

Abdul was dumb-founded. He presumed his son was dead. Within a second, his anger disappeared and he was transformed.

"Alla, forgive me. I do not know what overcame me. I acted in a stupid manner. If only I could get my son back, I shall remain grateful to you all my life", he cried out to Alla in full throat after he had knelt down on ground. His eyes and hands were raised to the sky and tears rolled down from his eyes.

The express took thirty-second to cross the level crossing. He could hear the all-clear bell in the guard's room. It sounded as if the Angel Gabriel was singing into his ears a melody that was enchanted by the "high land lass" in the Scottish Highlands many years ago. The moment he opened his eyes, lo and behold, Hassan was standing near the other gate surrounded by bystanders. And that was the end of the persecution.

Since then, Abdul began to treat his son differently. His affection intensified, the persecution diminished, but his economic condition deteriorated. Recently, the landlord even threatened to serve him with eviction notice. The inevitable should occur and the only way out was to take to the streets. A respectable but poor Abdul would be reduced to a beggar.

Hassan realized his father's predicament. He vowed not to annoy him anymore. Henceforth his demand for anything to substantiate his sustenance lessened. He even determined to forgo the only meager meal of the day. He wore a patchy short to cover his groin. He remained bare-bodied, as there was nothing else to cover his chest. The ribs had no flesh to conceal them. The rickety thin arms and legs were symbols of impoverishment and dirt all over the body showed neglect and indifference.

Abdul tried in many ways to earn money so that he and his son could have a decent living. However, his physical indisposition of doing anything worthwhile stood in his way. He was unable to work on the field. Moreover, it paid no dividend. The land did not belong to him. Only worldly possession he had, the hut. That too was mortgaged to the landlord. Recently,Abdul started getting enteric fever. The onus fell on the shoulder of little Hassan.

Hassan never went to school, he never learnt the alphabets, but he had a sharp memory. Nature was his teacher. He saw the sunrise and sunset, day in and day out, he heard the melodious strains of the seasonal birds, he watched with keen interest the blossoming of the various wild flowers all through the year, he smelt the odour of the sun burnt soil after the first shower, he watched dusts flying on the sticky and murky afternoon, he saw the rivers, ponds and wells dried up in summer and the water receded at the lowest level only to rise again in monsoon. He watched with pride how men and women of his village and in the adjoining villages adapted themselves to their surroundings, infected and influenced by natural phenomenons, he saw all these and marveled at man's tenacity, perseverance, adaptability, common sense and eternal faith in nature's whims. At times life appeared to him to be an enigma.

"Open the door", a thunderous voice woke him up one morning. It ushered into his heart a kind of warning that a great disaster would befall. Abdul was unable to move. The fever had shot up again to 105 degrees Fahrenheit. His father's indisposition compelled Hassan to rush to the rickety door. If he were late for a couple of seconds to reach the door, a second knock would have opened it automatically and, perhaps, the roof of the hut would have collapsed simultaneously.

On opening the door he saw the orderly of the landlord was standing on the other side of the threshold twitching his oily serpentine moustache.

"Where is Abdul?" Demanded the orderly in a gruff and imperative tone.

"There he is", Hassan pointed his finger to his ailing father to the monster.

"Why is he lying there? Is he not going to work?" the orderly reiterated the demand.

"He is sick", retorted Hassan.

"Sick my foot. He does not want to pay back arrears, so he is pretending to be sick. Tell him if he doesn't bring the money by this evening, you both will be ousted from this house", so saying the monster departed with thumping feet, twitching his serpentine moustache.

He might be young, but Hassan knew the meaning of the summon. Abdul was ill and there was no money to buy food. How could his father repay the debt? Their very existence on earth became difficult, as he found no way to earn money. Although he had started vending wares in a very small way to supplement the family income, it was not adequate. His paltry income was a drop in the mighty ocean. Hardly he brought Rs. 1.50 each evening after selling seasonal fruits, which he collected from the gardens of well to do, clandestinely. Half eaten fruits like guavas, berries, dates and mangoes were found everywhere scattered in the gardens, the bounty of the over-fed birds.

Going to the 'durbar' of the landlord meant persecution. Abdul would be thrown into the dungeon for torture till he had paid all the debts or would be forced to sign a document, relinquishing the entire claim on his property. In an occasion such as this, the local police remained silent spectators, the erudite lawyer would lend his prompt service to execute the deed and the *panchayat* leaders, and the elected administrators of the local self-government heaved a deep sigh. Hassan was on the horn of a dilemma.

"Why do you have to go to the landlord?" Hassan asked his father.

"Shut up. Do not ask me any questions. I am exhausted and famished", Abdul spoke in a weak tone, yet authoritatively.

Abdul was desperate in concealing his pain from his son. He did not want his son to be the partaker of his sorrow and suffering. But Abdul was not able to do so as the streaks of tears rolled down from his eyes. Hassan never missed the moment. It emboldened him further and he asked. "Please tell me father, what is the trouble?" He begged, cajoled and threatened. At last the father relented.

"I owe Rs.500 to the landlord. Unless I pay this amount he will either send me to jail or requisition my hut. I have already lost the paddy field where I am working now as a bondman. If this goes, where will we have the shelter. I have taken time till today to pay of the debt, (its being the last day of May). My body is burning with fever. Today I cannot go on any account. Tomorrow his men will come and burn this hut. You and I will be on the street", he paused for a while to take his breath back. He began again. "I feel like committing suicide. Let the mighty Kanchenjunga crush me under its giant wheels".

"Don't father, please don't say things like that", Hassan screamed. In an ordinary situation, such a sound would have evoked curiosity in the minds of the people in the neighborhood, but the sight of the visit of the landlord's orderly to the hut kept them at distance. They preferred not to meddle.

"I will go to the landlord and catch his feet and ask for remission", Hassan told him in desperation.

"You can try my son, but to no avail. The landlord is adamant". After this Abdul turned his face towards the wall and plunged in deep silence.

Hassan rose from the ground and left the hut quietly. He walked slowly through the village and pondered over the incident. 'Why does my father want to fall under the mighty Kanchenjunga? He once told me that the Kanchenjunga is the name of the grand mountain peak of the great Himalayan Mountain. It is the abode of the Almighty God. The express train originates from there. The lord God sends his trusted angel, Gabriel in the train to study people if they still loved him. He travels from Darjeeling to Calcutta to gauge the depth of human frailties'.

Hassan walked aimlessly for an hour in the scorching sun of the pre-monsoon period. The heat was unbearable, particularly at this time of the year. He felt suffocated. At the same time, he knew it was just the preparation for a heavy cyclonic depression and subsequent downpour. Some boys from his immediate neighborhood saw him but avoided him like plague. In the village everybody shunned the fellow who had been visited by the landlord's orderly. It predicted bad omen. After a couple of hour's walk, Hassan decided to go to the house of the landlord to plead with him on behalf of his father for the remission of the debt or to secure time for repayment.

The landlord's house was a palace. It was a grotesque ancient building. The walls were curved with many attractive figures of damsels in dancing postures, men in hunting paraphernalia's and other living creatures of nature. The rooms were wide, spacious and airy. The doors and windows were decked with different figures of Gods and Goddesses. A spicy aroma from the kitchen filled the nostrils of the boy, which increased his appetite.

Hassan approached the palace, slowly with measured paces lest he trampled something valuable and drew the attention of the coterie of the landlord. He wished to see the landlord alone immediately, hoping to have a positive reply of his request. Urgency of the matter emboldened him to a great extent.

"Hay, you scum, what are you doing here?" a thunderous voice reverberated in the atmosphere and shook the boy to the bones.

"I - I - I wish to see the landlord" Hassan stammered in fear.

"Why? Who are you?" the voice demanded to know.

"I am Hassan, Abdul's son" he replied.

"What is this noise all about?" a second voice interrupted.

Being a simpleton, Hassan came straight to the point and said, "My father is having very high fever. He cannot come here today", he hardly could finish the sentence when the first voice yelled "what audacity".

The next moment the boy felt a heavy thrust upon his neck and he fell headlong on the ground near the feet of the second man, at least ten feet away from the place where he was standing. His face was dumped on the dust and it smeared all over his sweaty face.

"Stay there you fool. How dare you lift your face to His Excellency", said the first voice in a gruff tone. The landlord, a stout, fair-complexioned, well-fed potbellied tall man in his middle age stood before the boy. He heard the sound and emerged into the courtyard from the rest room; where he was reclining on the sette, surrounded by a group of village idle gossipers-friends and well-wishers. When he saw the dark skeleton, in a loincloth prostrating before him, somehow he felt pity on the boy.

"Get up you scum. What is your problem?" the great man asked him.

"My father is indisposed. He is not able to come today. But Sir, if you kindly give him one more day, tomorrow he will come at your feet". Hassan said this without raising his eyes.

"Go away now. Come tomorrow either with your father or bring Rs.500, or face the tune".

Little Hassan came out of the landlord's palace as an experienced person. He learnt many facts of the intricacies of life during the short visit to the palace. The ordeal he faced for half an hour matured him to an extent that only a youth in his late teen achieved such a feat normally. He walked on aimlessly in the scorching sun for half an hour, hungry as a wolf but found no solution. He loathed facing his father again. Simultaneously, almost the same thought came into his mind, to lie down on his body under the wheels of the mighty Kanchenjunga. He wanted to run away from home, his village and his father and wished to become a part of nothing. So he proposed to God to take away his soul, but the Almighty God thought about him differently.

In the meantime dark clouds was seen in the North - Western corner of the village. It was lurking behind those verdant trees in the horizon like a small bundle of freshly cut stocks of plants. Soon it got enlarged and spread all over the sky just above his head. It was ominous. A weather expert could predict its significance. A mighty storm was bound to develop followed by heavy rain. A little after mid-day a dust storm arose, exactly from the Northwestern corner and moved towards the village. The storm accompanied by hails lasted only for fifteen minutes but its devastating effect left an indelible mark on the normal lives of the village. The tin roofs of several houses were dislodged, thatched roofs of scores of huts flew away in the adjoining paddy fields, about 100 yards away. Many mud walls collapsed, tiles broke, trees uprooted, bullock carts overturned, cows fled, and men, women and children ran helter and skelter for protection. The normal life of the entire village was disrupted and eventually collapsed like a pack of cards.

Hassan saw the big cloud overhead before the storm blew the dusts away and knew at once that nature had a purpose behind it. He ran straight to the mango grove of the landlord and stood in the middle of it. There were about one thousand mango trees in the garden. Each tree contained approximately fifteen hundred mangoes. Half of them were half-ripe and the rest were green. The velocity of the wind was so strong that the trees could not hold all the fruits long. Every tree dropped at least 20% of its fruits. With the first drop of mango, Hassan swung himself into action. He was fully aware of the golden rule of the landlord - that one could collect any amount of mangoes dropped on the ground due to natural calamities like rain, storm and hail - but no one could pelt stones or climb the trees.

Hassan collected mangoes to his hearts content. He was the first to arrive at the garden, which was hardly a few stones away from the railway crossing, so was the gainer. Before others came, he gathered about two thousand mangoes. No kind of rain or storm could dampen his spirit. He hid all the mangoes behind a tilla. He ran between the tilla and the trees about thirty times. At first he felt it was easy to run but soon his legs gave away. Yet he went on running to have the maximum benefit before the others joined the fray.

"What shall I do with these mangoes?" he asked himself. If he had sold them in the market, he would hardly get a return of his hard toil. It could be sold for Rs. 3/- a mound, hardly 20 to 25 paise per Kg. He had to carry the entire load on his shoulder as the transportation cost was beyond his reach. No *'rickshawala'* would carry them free of cost.

Determined as he was, Hassan was not made of such stuff as to cow down to any kind of eventuality. It was one blessing the creator had bestowed upon the poor. They never give up. He had suffered a lot already.

Looking around, Hassan was lucky enough to find a broken basket. The gardener, being worn out, discarded it there. In spite of its wretched condition, the basket could hold only thirty big mangoes. He picked up the two dozens of half-ripe mangoes dumped them in the basket as sample and briskly walked towards the market. It was well past two-thirty in the afternoon. The rain had just stopped but the destruction it caused was discernable in every aspect of life all around.

It annoyed Hassan greatly to find the rickety Iron Gate at the railway crossing was down. He thought it was unusual. The UP Kanchenjunga Express should have passed the crossing four hours ago. That was the scheduled time. He wanted to hurry to the market. After he had sold a few mangoes, he could buy some *chapatis* and *gur* to fill his stomach. He wished to buy some food for his father as well. Medicine, of course, was not within his reach.

At first, he thought of going through the gate. He even tried to put a foot through the broken bars of the gate but a sudden yell of the gateman alerted him of the impending danger.

"Don't try to cross now, you fool. The train has reached the crossing" the gateman cautioned him.

Hassan retreated from the gate in nick of time. He leaned back and perceived the mighty engine of the Kanchenjunga express slowly puffing out of sight. The engine crawled at a slow speed and to his great surprise the giant train suddenly stopped in front of him unexpectedly with a jolt. Hassan was astonished and could not believe his eyes. He had witnessed the train passed him by, but it never stopped there in his living memory. This was the first occasion the train had halted at the crossing. He looked and looked. A kind of strange fear overcame him. Fortunately, his stupor disappeared in no time. Next moment he began to admire the express. His inquisite eyes began to search for the Angel, who had been regularly traveling in the train.

"You chap, what are you carrying in that basket?" asked a stout man from the compartment which stood in front of him.

Hassan was suddenly awakened from his reverie. The presence of the giant manmade complexity emboldens him and he said in an authoritative tone.

"I'm selling mangoes, Sir".

"How much?" the man asked.

"50 paise a piece", Hassan replied.

"Damn cheap" remarked the genial-looking stout middle-aged man. Come here and give me a dozen".

Hassan ran to the window and handed over one dozen mangoes. The man did not have any change nor did Hassan. He, out of sympathy gave him away a note of Rs. 10/-.

His co-passenger on the train could not resist his temptation and bought another dozen from him. The third person bought the rest with Rs. 1/- a piece.

"Do you have any more?" enquired the fourth passenger.

"Yes Sir. I have plenty more. Shall I bring them?" Hassan replied triumphantly

"Go on, fetch as many as you can. The train is full of passengers. They are all hungry. We have no food with us here and are unable to buy any in this deserted place. Let us be satisfied with these half ripe mangoes," he suggested further.

"I don't know how long this wretched train will stop in this godforsaken deserted place", commented the fifth passenger.

Being encouraged and realizing the prospects of making more money, Hassan ran to the tilla and brought another basket full of mangoes. He sold each of them at Rs.1/- a piece. He made twenty trips altogether between the train and the garden and sold about thousand mangoes at the same price. After he had sold the last mango, he simply dropped down on the road to rest and saw the train was pulling out slowly out of his sight. The express train stopped there for two hours before the signal was finally given for its departure. As the train got a new lease of life, Hassan looked at the Express inquiringly and was trying to figure out in which compartment the good Angel Gabriel was traveling.

Today a well-stocked grocery shop is doing a brisk business round the clock near the railway crossing. The passersby can read the sign board hanging on the roof. The name of the shop is written in bright bold letters, **'The Kanchenjunga'.**

4

The Favourite Tourist

Section-I

Suresh waits at the station dutifully everyday to transport the incoming passengers to their respective destination. Be it winter or summer he is there with his two wheelers, daunting the heat of summer or the mild winter season of Goa. It becomes worse in monsoon as the incessant torrential downpours continues days together, forbids him to go out to the station regularly. But he tries to be there everyday since he is the only bread winner of the family of four, his wife and two small children. Recently he has been working very hard to pay back the loan, incurred to build the small house for the family. The thirty years old man is honest in his perception, dutiful and hard-working. A very difficult proposition to remain steadfast and upright in today's world where dishonesty, incompatibility and human greed play a prominent part.

He is a typical middle-class Goan, a free-lancer and god-fearing person. He will not budge an inch out of his house in the morning without offering his prayer to the domestic Goddess of Wealth. Honestly, he works and honestly he wants to earn his living by the grace of Almighty God.

It is the ritual he followed everyday. Winter is the season when the foreign tourists flock to the innumerable sea beaches spread on the western Coast of Goa. The days before and after the Chrismas and New Year have to be celebrated with fun and frolics. The tourists happen to increase the prices of everything. There is a mad-rush for finding a suitable shelter. The sky-rocketing prices are beyond the reach of the ordinary tourists. The affluent people who can match up with the affordable prices are welcome, the rest will wait for the off season rates when it falls to the lowest unimaginable prices.

Suresh has a moderate range of income all through the year. He does not discriminate between the foreign and Indian tourists. He will carry anyone on the pillion provided he pays according to the rates fixed by the transport department. Obviously he prefers foreign tourists to the Indian. The former are the good pay masters, the latter bargains and tends to cheat. But Suresh is a hard-nut to crack. He demands only a justifiable fare and his imposing personality will stand him in good stead. Everybody pays his price.

Once it's so happened that a middle-aged foreign tourist hired his service to transport him to Colangute Beach, the most sought-after beach in Goa by both the occidental and oriental tourists. It was the peak season. The man moved around the entire length and breath of the beach on the pillion of his bike, knocked on every door of the resorts, dotted on the sea-shore and enquired about someone from every person, but it was a wild goose chase. Suresh, initially was in the dark of his intention, due to language barrier, but soon realized he was in search of somebody who might be very dear to him. It broke Suresh's heart when the man broke down and cried like a baby, after meeting his compatriot belonging to the same country that the man came from. Before leaving the palace, Suresh asked the desk-clerk what could possibly be the reason for this show-down. The man explained to him in native Konkani language that the tourist was in search of his only beloved daughter who had eloped with a young man, one of his adversaries, to this place. The girl was here till morning. The couple had left in a hurry to the other part of the country, presumably sensing his arrival. Suresh was reluctant to accept the money he offered for his labour and time, which was quite substantial. On second thought he decided to accept the money as his life did not depend on charity but hard, sincere and honest labour. The entire episode moved him greatly.

Recently one afternoon a young man of 22 years of age engaged Suresh to transport him, as usual to the Colangute Beach, the Mecca of all fun-loving tourists. He said he was from Mumbai, wanted to relax a couple of days or more here. The city he belonged to was polluted with not only dust, human excreta and polly bags, but also with excess population almost choking the life of any nature-loving human being. In the jargon of the youngsters he had come there to 'freak out'.

"What about your other friends?" asked Suresh inquisitively, "All the guys are busy with their exams. The female ones are all flirts. I have no time for them. They are after you only to fleece you out of your money and empty pockets. I consider them as plagues and production machines", he replied.

Suresh was flabbergasted at the words he was using to describe all female creatures of human kind. For two days, almost the entire days, he accompanied him to different places. His ear lobes got pierced with the acrimonious sound of adverse qualities of the female species that he abhored to. He has shown no respect for womanhood. Nevertheless Suresh was paid handsomely for the services rendered to the young man.

On the third day Suresh was asked to stand in the usual meeting place at the specified time. He waited for the man for over an hour, but there was no sign of him in the near vicinity of the place. In the afternoon he tried again to meet him. It was in vain. The next day, the fourth, he came again but was disappointed. Assuming he had gone, Suresh tried to forget him. But, on the sixth day, lo and behold, to his great surprise he saw the young man walking hand in hand, with a beautiful girl of his age. They both were smiling and submerged into their own world. Suresh thought, perhaps the pollution free great sea air has tremendous influence on the fragile human souls. It worked as an elixir to the immature young mind and converted him to a Romeo who found his Juliet on the pollution free Colangute Beach.

Then, in 2003, on Boxing Day he met him. Suresh was on his bike as usual standing near the exit gate of the station. He scrutinized all the passengers that came out of the gate, called them aloud to pronounce his profession and objective. A local young man was the first to appear, followed by a few local gentry with families, trailed by a crowd of chattering young students. Then he came. The man with hairs half greyed, a slight protruding pot-belly, dressed smartly with clean and a well-pressed trouser and a bush-shirt, carrying a blue 'NIKE' bag on his shoulder and holding a 'GIVO' hand bag in his hand. The bespectacled person came straight to him and without bargain sat on the pillion of the bike.

"Could you take me to Mapusa? I believe the place is close by". The man said in a whisper. 'Yes, I could', replied Suresh.

"How far is Colangute beach from here?" The man asked him next.

"It is beyond Mapusa, where do you want to go? Mapusa or Colangute" Suresh simply enquired.

"I'm undecided, but I prefer Colangute to Mapusa. I'm here for a couple of days, alone", the man said.

There was no conversation between them for a while after this.

Suresh rode on the bike with his passenger, driving along the narrow, undulating turf road which according to the man was incredible to find in Delhi. The scenic beauty and the mild-cold air blowing from the Arabian Sea smoothened his soul and helped him to recover his tiredness.

"I like these small ancient houses of the Goan people. They are fascinating. Those seats placed in front of the door, meant for gossip and after lunch Siesta, mostly in the summer season reveal the Goan simplicity and the way of life. The newly-built multi-storied houses dotting all over the places are eye-sores". The passenger spoke in monologue.

Suresh was astounded at the knowledge of the man about Goa, but remained silent. "This is not my first visit to the place. I keep coming here, off and on, to ease out the tension and fatigue of the urban settlement, my permanent dwelling-place", the man continued.

Suresh was unperturbed, the reason being that the subject for discussion was beyond him.

After a solid 15 minutes ride they were about to reach a wide cross-section of four roads when suddenly Suresh opened his mouth. "Where do you want to go Sir, Colangute or Mapusa?" "I really want to go to Colangute. In the event I do not get a place there I'll come back to Mapusa. Can you help me to find out a place?" The man asked and paused.

There was a silence for a few seconds, when perhaps Suresh was thinking and trying to gauge the inner-self of the man. Is he honest or an imposter?

"Yes, I can do it". He answered in affirmative after a while.

So they rode on, at a moderate speed in a dark road running through the open wide vast field of wasteland. Sporadically a car or another two wheeler will cross them from the opposite direction with burning head lights. Occasionally a local bus will block their ways and emit forcibly endless black smoke to the great discomfort of the riders.

"That's an imposing hotel. Look at the light. A barbeque has been arranged. One can discern from the smoke and smell whirling in the air of the roasted meat and "paneer" "I wonder what could be the rent of one room" the man rattled off noticing the lonely three star hotel in the midst of the wasteland.

"It is expensive on ordinary days, but it is more now. They will cut your throat" Suresh retorted.

"I see, I need a place to stay at moderate rates-between Rs. 1000/- and 1500/-" the man said finally.

In the meantime they reached the beach of their destination. Suresh ran from pillar to post in vain. There was not a place to be found in the whole of the beach. Each nook and corner of all resorts, hotels, private places, guest houses and hovels were fully occupied. It was a tourist boom. Finding no place in the tourist heaven they decided to look for a place in Mapusa, a commercial hub in Goa. In the centre of the city stands a vast market place, well-reputed for the quality of goods sold here.

Two or three hotels disappointed them. One was sub-standard, meant for, according to Suresh, the drivers of passing trucks and commercial vehicles, the rest were full. The man quietly admired the tenacity, perseverance and discerning judgement of Suresh. Eventually Suresh found one place. It was only for the night the man could get shelter there. The man's intention was to spend three more nights in Goa. Before giving up hope Suresh tried the last place he could think of. The hotel that he went in just to enquire about, found a room still unoccupied, the very last one.

The next morning Suresh came promptly at 10 A.M. to shift him to the other hotel. In the afternoon of the same day Suresh accompanied the man to the beach. In the evening he dropped him to his hotel. On the next day Suresh carried the man to Panjim, the capital of Goa, where he spent an hour at Mira Mar beach. After shopping a few articles for home the man desired to come back to his hotel.

The Penultimate day Suresh took him to Colangute Beach. The beach was crowded beyond capacity. Its being 31st eve, Goa was preparing itself for a big show. All five star hotels were full to the brim. The bars were stocked with the latest brands of different kinds of killer drinks, meant for affluent extravagant and frustrated men and women of society. The destructive power of alcohol, both physically and financially, does worry Suresh from time to time. Being a teetotaler he does not seem to endorse the view of scores of the revellers on the beach and around it who were running from bar to bar for drinks and fun, "why not you go and earn a few quick bucks. This evening has created an opportune moment for all the drivers of hired vehicles to earn", the man suggested.

"I am against the principle of such atrocious behaviour of the young people who throng this quiet place once in a year in great numbers and desecrate the sanctity of our native land", Suresh retorted.

"They are simply enjoying themselves with friends. They are also helping the exchequer and the ordinary people to enhence the coffer and purses respectively". The man said. "I do not want their money. The extra money earned by unscrupulous means will land me nowhere. It comes in fraudulent means, it disappears in the same manner", Suresh said. The man was a little surprised. He could not understand the mind of the man. Usually people of his class indulge themselves in all kinds of anti-social activities, submerge themselves in cheating. Here is Suresh, quite contrary to what the world thinks of the struggling labour class.

The picturesque and panoramic view of Goa beaches on the eve of the New Year present a different scenario. The domestic tourists from all parts of the country throng the shores in multitudes. The opulents, the middle class and the poor people - the proletariat and bourgouis alike merge into one and form a great mass of revellers. The male tourists plunge in the undulating waves in one piece of loin cloth which covers their modesty. A few female protagonists venturing into the water, clad in complete outfits, being conservative, were more exposive. The wet clothes stuck to the bodies and became transparent. The concealed parts of the female physique, all its curves and creveses are more pronounced than in dried conditions. The beach is dotted with the people gambling with three round blocks, two in black and one in red colour. One has to bet on the red one by dropping minimum one hundred rupees which is shifted very frequently at a great speed. Whatever amount of money one drops become double, otherwise it is forfeited. The man was astonished to see the ordinary people got addicted to the gambling.

"I saw those poor people, clad in ordinary clothes, shapeless profiles, sad countenances, and demure eyes dropping those big notes to the table. A few are winning, but a majority of them are the looser, leave the arena in tears". The man confided Suresh later on.

Thousands of fun-loving souls will converge on the beach and a few more will emerge and join the merry group as the evening progresses into night. There will be erotic dancing, unnecessary fighting, useless conversations, gossips and uncontrollable fake laughter, teasing and indiscriminate use of fingers, eyes and bodies on female tourists. The female revellers are the center of attractions and also the victim of circumstances.

The affluent young couples fly from one bar to the other, spending lavishly unaccounted money to get drunk and intoxicated so as to earn maximum pleasures. They must be seen among friends in different places with the best beaus in their arms to proclaim their class. The middle class couples buy a couple of beer bottles pretend to be intoxicated. The poor people gaze at their wealthy counterparts and wonder and question each other of what mettle they are made of.

The man coaxed Suresh to go and join the mainstream of the festivities "Go and take the people from place to place. You can charge those revellers there; four times more than the regular fare. I shall wait here. Tonight is the night of the devil. Everything that is evil will have a fair chance to shine," the man said.

"I do not want to join the band wagon of the devils. I am extremely happy to serve you", Suresh replied.

"So what will you do after dropping me in the hotel? The night is still young. The lure of extra income is still there". The man was trying to read his mind.

"After dropping you at the hotel I shall go to my mother-in-laws house to meet my wife and two kids. Thus I shall spend the New Year Eve in the company of my own dear ones" Suresh replied.

"God will bless you for being a loving father to your children and a faithful husband" were the parting words of the man to Suresh.

The last night, in the hotel the man spent in agony specially at midnight. The new year was ushered in with church-bells, the honking and hooting of car horns and wild and monstrous shouts of the revellers. The latter were most boisterous in their behaviour and vociferous in speeches perhaps the influence of addicted drinks affected them extraordinarily. The forces of the law were inactive, the elders kept mumb, it being the conventional night of pleasures of the revellers.

Suresh was quite pleased with the money he received daily from the man. Next morning he appeared promptly at 9:00 A.M. at the reception desk. The man was surprised to see the sense of duty and integrity of the bike rider. Suresh being very kind also carried his bags down to the loby from his room. After placing the big bag on the petrol tank he rode on cautiously and dexterously. He never speed up and maintained the speed below forty all through 12 k.m. journey from Mapusa to Tivin Railway station. The undulating paved road carved in many places. Some narrow loops in the road to the station they met with devout Christians returning from morning mass. It's a must for all Catholics to attend the morning communion services on the first day of the year all over Goa.

"It is nice to see the devout people of God in communion with their maker on the first day of the year". The man commented as they passed by the families walking down the streets in their best attires.

"It is a common sight here on every morning. It intensifies on Sundays and on special occasions such as this". Suresh replied.

"I do not find any young man in the group. What has happened to them?" The man enquired.

"They were busy last evening in sundry ways. Perhaps some of them attended the services during mid-night", Suresh replied. "It is a common sight everywhere. Only in the big places the men turn up. Affluency shows its ugly sight in the big places of worship where hypocracy, exhibition and power reveal themselves through the presence and physical appearance of the worshippers".

The man was impressed by his sagacity, simplicity and wisdom. He's not an ordinary person, must be a genious, he thought.

"You seem to be very knowledgeable. How far have you studied?" The man asked.

"I was born in a poor family. My father was an ignorant farmer. Since we belonged to a low caste family I was denied of any kind of formal education. Finding no option my father wanted me to be a farmer like him. Instead I've become a two-wheeler driver. Right now I feel this is my vocation. You see there in the distance where the Western Ghat mountain has sloped down, is my home." Suresh slowed down the vehicle, for the man to have a glimpse of the place.

The man had a good look of the Railway tracks of the Konkan Railways built along and parallel to the hills, nestling besides it the house, nay a hamlet of Suresh, the two-wheeler driver. The rocky land with sandy soil can pose a lot of difficulty. For its ragged nature is inaccessible to live in, but Suresh has an invigorating nerves to overcome the difficulties.

The small house in the midst of wild ragged-hills is an example of men's insurmountable energies to accept nature's whims and fancies.

"This is my brother. He is a dissolute, drunken, disreputable rogue. Always indulging in nefarious activities. He does nothing at home but drinks. My parents have disowned him of their property" Suresh expressed his grievances. Pointing out to a slim under-nourished man.

"How does he earn his living?" The man asked.

"He does masonary works. Just a helper" Suresh replied.

"Where does he stay?" the man asked.

"He stays around this area, sleeps in the railway platform at night".

A perfect contrast the man found between the two brothers. "The divine and the demon are occupying every conceivable space on the earth". He told to himself. "They need a Messiah once more to come and clean the earth which is full of prejudices, false ideologies, sinful acts, betrayal, terrorism and covetousness".

The man cast a quick glance at the skinny and dirty man walking ahead of them from the pillion of the motor-bike. In the fleeting moment passed by he could discern how the chap would be living a miserable life.

"He's not married. I don't think he has any chance to have a wife, does not posses any quality to rear children. His only aim in life is to get drunk" Suresh expressed his view on the subject. "He'll die without experiencing the joy of enjoyment of life on earth," he added.

"There are scores of rehabilitation centers spread out all over Goa. He can get easily cured. You must take him to one of those centres," the man suggested.

"It's no point. He's incurable, moreover, he has no hope of living a normal life", Suresh said in disgust.

"No, Suresh you're wrong. There is hope in every person to live a Godly life provided the person in question effects a radical change in the personality. It is the realization of ones own mistake and getting rid of the anomalies of life, judicious and proper guidance from experts is the wisest way to rehabilitate one self. You must try to involve him in various activities. An alcoholic body is poisonous one. It can sting anyone to ease the pain", the man concluded.

"I see, there is logic. I'll try once more to rehabilitate him. Suresh said to himself. "It looks like we've reached our destination. I can see the railway station ahead of us". The man said loudly.

The grotesque and panoramic view of the newly-built Tivin Station on the Konkan Railway line is both fascinating and breath-taking. To reach the station from Mumbai the train passes through fifty-five tunnels. The construction of the Railway tracks and the tunnels through these ragged mountainous terrain speak volumes of the ingenuity of the planners, engineers and workers who have toiled more than a decade to build an edifice of modern structural wonder. The trains glide on the tracks at ease without bounces bringing relief to the passengers, particularly those traveling in the unreserved compartments, perched on the uncovered benches, where every conceivable space is occupied by the commoners, the outstanding camaraderie of the commoners have no parallel in the history of any travel document.

"I was given the best seat beside the window on the right hand side of the compartment by a very dark-looking, unassuming, bespectacled young man from south

- The passengers never fought over the space
- They conversed in a language, Greek to me, as if to prove they knew each other so well. In fact each one of them was a stranger".

"I booked a ticket in the sleeper class. It was not confirmed. I was 36 wait listed officially before the departure of the train so entered the ordinary compartment. The reserved compartment got emptied in Ratnagiri junction and I went there to get an empty seat, but the man next to the empty seat was a liar and so nasty. I decided not to occupy the seat in fact I got disgusted with the man. The man commented sporadically while sat on the pillion during his stay in Goa.

"Who is this man?" Suresh will ask himself during the journey.

The steep steps leading to the platform could pose a problem to the man but Suresh out of courtesy and admiration carried his two bags to the station platform. They bid each other a quick farewell as Suresh felt it was no use lingering on here with the man.

"I have to go and wait for the passengers coming in the down train from Mumbai" Suresh said as the parting words.

The man saw the down train emerging from the last tunnel in the distance and was astonished to find the sense of duty imbibed in his favorite two wheel driver of Goa.

Section-II

The train happened to be a lucky one. Suresh transported an affluent tourist on his bike to Panjim who tipped him heavily beyond imagination, from Panjim he reached another passenger to Colangute Beach. In the afternoon and late evening he carried several passengers and earned a substantial amount. It went on for several weeks after this and Suresh's earning multiplied several folds.

"I wonder what could be the reason! There are thousands of two wheeler divers like me, most of them complain always that business is dull, but look at my fortune, I have no time to rest. I am going to buy another piece of land in the heart of Tivin and build another house by the end of this year." He confided to his wife one night.

"Your lucky star is favouring you," she just added to the conversation.

"Yes, it is true" Suresh replied in relaxed tone. "What could be the reason for your prosperity and you have such big hauls everyday?" His wife asked him one day.

"I don't know exactly, but my luck turned, it seems, after I met that man on Boxing Day. He used to pay me Rs. 300/- a day, a big amount, irrespective of the hours I drove him across. He told me he would be here in the last week of March" he said as a matter of fact.

In March that year he attended practically all the trains puffing into the Tivin Station from Mumbai in the hope of meeting the man. But there was no sign of him. Again in monsoon season when the incessant rains make life miserable in Goa, as a result the inflow of the tourists thin down, but it never deterred his spirit, Suresh went to the station, soaked to the marrow but heart is full of anticipation for his arrival, the meeting was providential as his heart was longing to express his gratitude and thanks. He was completely disillusioned.

As the days went by he become more convinced 'it was the man', perhaps a divine one who favored him in his own divine way and thus effected his prosperity. The myth soon turned into conviction. A kind of faith developed on the believe he had formed of the appearance of the man. He began to imagine illusionary figures which he could not explain to his wife. He saw images of nativity, the birth of a child, the baby is growing into adult-hood and dying a valiant death on the cross to save mankind of their sins. The innumerable Churches, the figures of saints, the family members and the master himself, curved or built as statues to remind the worshippers of their conviction and faith. Suresh had seen those statuettes carved or embossed on the outer walls, arches and rising steps of the churches. He could never interpret their implications in human lives. The symbols help a sinner to concentrate on the subjects and speak to God to their heart's content.

Suresh circumbulated several Churches, jenuflexed in front of the deities and prayed to the alien God. The subject of his prayer was an expression of gratitude and thanks. He ardently hoped to meet his benefactor in the days to come as he had promised but was disappointed.

The parents got suspicious of his strange behaviour. He hardly talked to them, even spoke seldom to his wife. The family members developed a kind of weird feelings towards him. Normally in an uneducated family in this country the people are swayed by the evil and unwarrantable thoughts, blaming it to the tradition and a divine wish dictated by man, specially the preceptors. Eventually they consulted a quack secretly for the remedy.

"What is that worrying you? Of late, I have noticed you do not show any interest in the household affairs. You do not listen to the cry of your children any more. Someone told me the other day, you sit hours together in front of the station gate expecting the arrival of a valued passenger", his father asked him one evening. "Are you loosing interest in life"? It looks like you're drifting away from our ancestral religion and preparing yourself to succumb to an alien religion."

"No Dad, do not worry about me. I am O.K. I am looking for someone who has promised to come and meet me sometimes in the near future. Am I not doing my household duties, performing daily chores and going out of the house to earn our livings?" Suresh said with a minimum of words he could gather at that ostentatious moment.

His father had to beat a hasty retreat since he could not face such powerful tone. He wondered what could be the reason? He thought of his son who is an illiterate person, never went to school. "I made him a farmer after my own fashion but he has turned out to be the wisest creature I've ever known of. In my living memory I've never heard of anyone in our clan as wise as he is, it seems. He told to himself.

"We will be outcast, socially ostracized, our tradition will die and the family will be ruined because of your arrogant behavior", his mother told him.

"Why are you worried about me. I'm not going to change, - my religious conviction is the same as before. I'm only searching for the man, once he had promised me to come. What you think cynical has no meaning. It is baseless to placard me. I'm grateful to the man. During his short sojourn in Goa in one Christmas week and my association with him has opened a floodgate of prosperity. Could you not see and feel how prosperous I've become now? It is his bounty" Suresh concluded.

Therefore, the family-members could never argue with him. His neighbours kept watchful eyes. Ironically they were regularly fed with acrimonious news by his alcoholic and estranged brother. He could never stand Suresh's normal behavior contrary to his abnormality.

Every year the local Catholic Church enact the crucification of Christ in the passion week. The programme start on Palm Sunday with the procession of the palm raising in the air and shouting slogans "Hossana in the highest and Rejoice he is come." A man seated on a donkey, is indiscriminately chosen from any community, specially from the Dalits like Suresh's family, rides through the streets of Tivin. The procession starts from the school compound, passes through the village, on its winding and undulating roads, with the cacophony of sounds, mixed with the whistles of the passing trains, brays of the donkeys, barking of the parier dogs and shouting of the local urchin children. The members of the parish, the core group of the processionists pose a solemn and somber looks while the others, comprise the tourists, on lookers and urchins, the later cause panic at some junctures, either to ridicule the show or to extract pleasures out of it, through the acts of demonic gesture and postures. The concept of religion is a great barrier it divides man from man, ignoring all that has been said about peace and harmony in various scriptures in diverse ways. After a circuitous run the processions terminates in the church compound where everyone is treated with some eatables and cold drinks. On Good Friday the cross is installed permanently on a pedestal for the devotees to pay their obeyances.

Suresh does not reserve any grudge or resentment against any religion, but being in Goa, surrounded by churches and cathedrals, observing the social and humanatarion works of the Nuns and missionaries to bring sucour to the poor, the suffering humanity he has developed a kind of respect for the Catholic institutions.

"I've seen the man in the crowd. Once, even I felt he was riding the donkey. I was following the procession with eager expectation hoping to meet him. But I was disillusioned. He was not there" Suresh told his wife the same night.

This statement of his did not ease the tension rather aggravated more to the contrary. She only sobbed quietly. On Easter day, Suresh was determined to go to the Cathedral in Mapusa, the place where the man worshipped on the New Year Eve. The four hundred years old Cathedral, reputed for its divine healing power have drawn the attention of all devotees irrespective of their religious conviction, colour-prejudice and silly sectarian caste or creed. The Catholics and Protestants alike the Thakurs and Dalits, Hindus, Muslims, Sikhs belonging to different denomination all like-minded people visited the shrine of our Lady of Holiness for its heeling power. On all festival days, holidays and sundays the place is over-flowing with people to receive His grace through her loving care and divine blessings. Suresh has dropped many tourists at its doorstep but never cared to enter the place. For him it was a place for weak persons lacking self-confidence.

"I've limbs, brain and heart, giving to me freely and graciously by my maker. Why should I depend on others for making my living? Divine grace bestowed upon me because I work hard, deligently, intelligently and dutifully. Only the people who lack self-confidence, indolent and shirks duties run to the saints for divine grace" Suresh said this many times to his co-drivers.

But today is different from other days. Today he is searching for a man who is residing close to his heart since the day after Christmas.

Suresh reached the Cathedral in the wee hour of the morning before it got jam-packed of the worshippers. After dipping his second finger of the right hand to the holy water he made the cross sign over his chest like the others. He jenuflexed on the pew at the far end corner of the house of worship, closed his eyes for prayer. His prayer comprised only 'Thanks to the Almighty' for raising his status from poverty to affluency, multitudes of graces bestowed upon him in sundry ways and bringing peace to his heart. He prayed for his estranged brother for bringing back sanity in him. He prayed for the people of all the nations so that they all live in peace and harmony. At the end he requested the Divine one to reveal Himself and show his face to him once more.

After the prayer he opened his eyes to look up to the cross but, lo, and behold he spotted the man standing close to it and smiling. Next moment he realized the man beckoned him with spreading arms. Suresh rose from his seat and moved towards the cross to meet his most favourite tourist. It was like a dream; he moved closer and almost reached the cross when suddenly he saw the man was disappearing into the background from his view. He went close to the cross and held it tightly so that he could embrace him. He remained in that position for a couple of minutes thinking of his achievement when suddenly he felt a light pressure on his shoulder. He looked up and saw the pensive look of the divine one on the cross, blood dripping down from his forehead, heart and feet. A crown of thorn placed on his temple with a background proclamation, 'the King of kings'.

Suresh was a contented man. Henceforth he went to the cathedral on every festive day, looked for his most favourite tourist and came back home satisfied after he had crossed his chest with holy water, jenuflexed in the pew in the far corner of the house and prayed to the cross for over ten minutes, a prayer of 'Thanks giving'.

5

The Positive

It's a co-incident. This might be the third time the two charming human-beings bumped into each other. Each admired the other's guts, but refrained from coming close to each other. A kind of emotional trait was discernible on their faces whenever they met. The third and final meeting took place outside a call-centre on the outskirts of the city.

Abhijeet stood under the portico of the sprawling building where his call centre grew like mushroom a couple of month's age. After an arduous, pain-staking and tedious work at the centre, he always felt relaxed standing under the portico for a while. During this time he pushed all his thoughts, personal, social, economical and political, and actions during the eight hours of his scheduled working time that took place in a corner of his head. Those painful eight hours of the day or night, depending on the shift allotted to him, he had to face the most common place, irritating and unusual comments from the clients of the company for whose services he was engaged in lieu of a paltry sum of money.

"Hey, You ass hole, who'd given you the job? You don't know anything about the deal I've made with my client. I'd only like to know what percentage of profit I will earn." An irritated client of the company screamed from the other end of the world.

"Why don't you suck your ass hole, you mother f. — I need the divorce at any cost. I am only required to know what percentage of my salary to pay her as alimony to that unfaithful bitch. I don't want anyone to meditate in my affair. I hate that female character from the core of my heart." A divorcee fired him once in an uncouth manner when Abhijeet said,

'The best way to save your money is to compromise and settle the matter out of court. You have a little girl of three years old. Don't you love her, for her sake?"

At that moment the heaven let loose and all the curses a man can think of in the hour of peril, hurled at him.

"I want to buy a car for my son in installment. He takes immense pain everyday cycling through the crowded streets of the city. At times the traffic is so heavy on the short route that he takes; it compels him to ride a circuitous way to the place of his work. On those days he is late. Scolding and pay cuts are common; even he gets the threats of being fired. I want to buy the cheapest car in installment. Could you suggest me an agency where I can get the loan at easy installments?"

Ab. took a minute to find out the name of the company, where she could get the loan and the percentage of interest to be paid over a certain period of time.

She burst into a hysterical cry and murmured in an inaudible voice.

"O God, I shall never be able to pay that amount of money within that period of time. I rather give up the plan."

Ab. held the phone for a while thinking if he could console her in any way. But she cut the phone off.

"I think you don't understand what I am speaking. I wish to know what I can do with the million of dollars I've earned during my sixty five years of life. I am only asking you to figure it out what percentage of money I'm allowed to pay, according to country's law, if I bequeath it to the church, my children and some of my relatives, close to me."

Ab was stunned. He mused, "How can a man possess so much wealth!"

"Hey how old are you? I'm a student of the Yale University studying the Computer Science. I'm only twenty years old. The statistics of my biological anatomy is 34, 32, and 34. Would you be my pal? I'm desperately in need of your company." A female voice accosted him from the other end of the world.

"Excuse me madam. I don't think you know what you are talking about. I'm living almost two thousand miles away from you. I can't meet you, leave alone be a friend." Ab. said in his customary public school educated manner.

"I don't believe. I'm standing outside your office building. I will be waiting for you under the big maple tree opposite to the office gate till you emerge..... I'm desperate."

Ab. did not save the conversation in the computer. A young soul cried to another soul for genuine companionship, was rather rare in the west. Separation, divorce and betrayal were the fashion there, accepted by society as a normal day to day affair. It is picking up in this part of the sub-continent as well.

"Who's that dame? I hope she not the same one passed me by the other day. Is she the one is trying to be friendly with me?" He said to himself as he stepped out of the lift that evening.

At that point of time a girl of his age or might be a little younger than Ab. emerged from the second lift and boarded a waiting car that belonged to his rival company situated on floor above his office. He intended, for a long time to join the company, but never had a chance to step out of his office. It was believed in the corporate world the remuneration drawn there was much higher than any other company dealing with the same subject. The treatment meted out to the staff members is worth emulating.

The company in question was another call centre. It was a branch of the chains of call centers originated in the State of Ohio in the United States of America. The Co. followed certain moral codes, the first and foremost the treatment accorded to the staff members of the Co. was at par with the management. All new comers to the profession aspired to join the concern. But it was hard to come by a lucrative post in the company. The staff members of the Ohio call center always maintained a distance from their counterparts in another company, vice versa. The staff of the lesser group spied on them with contemptuous, malicious and vindictive looks.

Ab. missed the girl again on the second encounter. Today she was wearing a very tight black dress, could easily entice a man of his age to all kinds of weird thoughts and actions. He had only a glimpse of his posterior that had an electrifying effect on his mind. A shaft of lightning pierced through his body and he turned passionate. An urge for a female companionship grew in him.

"I must introduce myself to this girl as soon as possible. I've grown passionate about her." Ab. confided his secret thought to the man browsing through the net, sitting at a desk on his right.

"I, specifically not aware of the girl you're talking about, but I know there are many pretty girls employed in that concern. I wish you all the best for your pre-meditated plan and success thereafter." The co-worker encouraged him to go ahead with his plan, thereby fulfilling his heart's desire.

On the next evening Ab. stood firmly outside the gate of the building on time. In fact, his passionate heart forced him to come out of the center five minutes earlier than the scheduled time. He waited there for half an hour but was sorely disappointed. She did not show off. He waited there for half an hour more at the cost of missing the pool car, but there was no sign of her. He boarded a local bus and after surmounting enormous difficulty went home. He was mentally agitated and physically wrecked. Hardly could he sleep that night.

"I missed her yesterday. She did not come out of the call center. What could have happened, I wonder!" He said casually to the co-worker.

The friend was non-committal. He replied as a matter fact.

"This is the common feature of all the call centers. People come here for a short while and then go away as quickly as they had come. The young people, mostly the fresher from schools and colleges with a solid English background are lured to join these centers to avoid the stigma of being unemployed. They work here for a while and then look out for better prospects elsewhere. It suits the company well. There is no hassle about hiring and firing. I can attribute four reasons for her being absence. This girl of yours either left for a greener pasture elsewhere or she has been tired or she must be on a shift duty or sick."

"Then, how to find out the reason of her absence?" Ab's desperation to find out the reason surprised his co-worker.

"You have to wait or go to her office." The co-worker advised to ease the tension and remove the desperation.

Ab. could do neither. He was in grief, lost all hopes of meeting her. The same evening Ab. walked out of the lift casually, ambled through the reception room and stood outside the gate for his vehicle to arrive.

Lo and behold, there was she boarding her car which had arrived earlier than his car. She was dressed in a green coloured dress today. As usual he could see her posterior only. The rest of her body already moved inside the car. Her face was not visible at all. In spite of missing her entire figure everyday he still could guess her physical feature in its entity.

On the next encounter, a few days later he could catch a glimpse of her right profile, that made his soul stirred to a great extent.

"Who is she? I'm quite familiar with her face. Unfortunately I can not place her anywhere in my life at present." Ab. troubled his co-worker once again with his personal problem.

"Perhaps you're very close to unraveling your heart's desire. She is hovering very close to you to be grabbed." The co-worker said in an indifferent manner. Ab had already come to a saturated position on this issue.

Ab. thought, perhaps, it was wise to forget her. Let her dwell in the realm of obscurity of his fancies and forget about the whole issue.

"There are so many of them passed through my nose, this one is one of them. But she is very special to me." Ab. consoled himself with this utterance.

Ab. walked out of the lift in a hurry. He was late by five minutes. He knew unless he hurried the 'Qualis' pool car would leave without him. He could not imagine the trouble he had to undergo to reach his guest house.

At the same time the second lift opened and half a dozen people including the girl of his dream emerged on the scene. She was about to collide with him. Both stood an inch apart from each other and stared. They could not move from the place for a while. Their bodies got transfixed on the spot, feet glued to the floor, eyes met with curiosity, faces agape. The eye witnesses to the scene thought both were made for each other. The C.E.O.'s of the call centers where they were employed shot glances at each other. They were trying to gauge the situation. The female co-workers turned and cast their evil eyes at the pair, clucked their tongues and twisted and bit their lips in the most famine manner, a hall-mark of all human female species.

The male co-workers smiled subdued smiles mixed with sarcasm and appreciation. The frustrated ones looked sideways in contempt and said, 'Boo' the optimistic ones did not find anything wrong in it so said 'excellent'.

Ab's co-worker looked at him with satisfaction and contentment and said, "Thank God, he's met his match at last. I won't have to hear the monologue of his heart's desire anymore."

A few fourth grade staff around the place nudged each other, smiled sarcastic smiles and abused the pair. They spat on the clean floor of the building before uttering the word 'Sala" an expression of condemnation. The women folks of their counterpart covered their faces in shame, as if they had witnessed an act of savage expression of the human's inert feelings.

Ab. recognized her at once and said, "It's you? I can't believe it."

"What are you doing here?" She asked him.

"Why I work here. My office is on the first floor." Ab. quipped.

"I too work here. My call centre is on the sixth floor." Rani replied in a subtle manner.

Realizing the pair's familiarity the onlookers who expected a showdown disappeared from the scene. Only the co-worker of Ab's office stood a distance away to amuse himself out of this accidental meeting.

In those good old days Abhijeet and Rani lived in the same block, two houses apart in the R.K.Puram sector twelve. His father was a Major in the army. Rani's father was a bureaucrat, worked in the Krishi Bhavan as an executive secretary. They both attended a renowned public school together. Ab. excelled in extra-curricular activities more than academic subjects, but never failed in any subject. Rani was a brilliant student and won many prizes for doing well in academic subjects. She majored in English.

Initially they appeared to be strangers, although studied together in the same class from standard seventh. They had hardly bothered to talk to each other and avoided each others company like leach.

By nature Ab was an extrovert. He took part in all extra curricular activities in school and outside of it. He was keen in playing all field games. Cricket was his forte. His robust physique, handsome look and a photogenic profile of a gentleman stood in his good stead. In all dramatic performances he was given the leading role, in the game of cricket he was the star batsman and in sports he out played all the competitors in the school or out of it.

Rani was an introvert and never ever tried to do anything beyond the scheduled work of the school and home. She loved to dress well, read all sorts of books avidly and was a regular contributor of thought-provoking articles in school magazines. At the end of her school career she turned out to be a good debater.

While they were in class nine Ab. took notice of her. Sitting in the last row of the class Ab and three of his friends watched the girls in front rows doing their work sincerely. It irritated them to find the girls pursuing their studies so diligently.

It was a mixed class of boys and girls. The school authorities did not believe in the principle of segregation of sexes. Almost every class had fifty percent of both female and male students. But Ab's class teacher was a traditional, orthodox and benign lady in her mid forty. She believed the relationship between boys and girls would be so far and nothing in between, so she made the girls sit in the front rows and pushed the boys in the back rows in the class. A perfect line of demarcation conceived by her did not go so well with the boys. Each boy had a preference. Each one of them cast a wistful glance at the girl of his choice. Ab. took a fancy to Rani.

"Boys, please pay attention. Today we will have class debate". The English teacher announced. "The contest is between the boys and girls." She continued.

The immediate reaction of the class was a mixed one. The boys vehemently protested against the impromptu debate. The girls supported it whole heartedly.

The topic read out by the teacher, was the traffic snarl in Delhi streets mostly at peak hours of the day.

Almost all the students chipped in. The girls as usual scored higher than the boys. The teacher asked Rani to conclude the debate briefly in favour of it and Ab. against it.

"The traffic snarls are common features in the streets of the capital due to lackadaisical attitude of the civic bodies of the area. The infrastructure of the city is not planned in the practical sense of the term, the streets are narrow or occupied by the vendors, the commuters are not disciplined, and the motorists flout the traffic rules, the traffic policemen manning the area are not efficient," were the few comments she made to defend the motion.

"In a big city where the population is increasing in a geometrical order, the numbers of cars growing and becoming double day by day, the potential owners of the cars are growing, the traffic snarls can not be avoided" Ab's defense of the positive aspect of the motion did not carry much weight.

The motion was carried in favour, but it had an impact on both Ab. and Rani. They had the reckoning of the class. But there grew no intimacy as such between them. They just came to know each other like the others. They were not in that advanced age where a deep intimacy could grow between them.

The class picnic of that year left a permanent mark in their lives. This was the only day the boys and girls were allowed to mix with each other freely. The line of demarcation between them went overboard. Each boy had his favourite girl seated beside him in the bus during the bus journey to the venue. Ab. sat beside Rani and for the first time they opened their mouths. "You spoke very well in the debate" Ab. complimented Rani.

"You did speak well, too." Rani returned the compliment. No doubt, it was a lie.

"No, I did not speak well. I'm not used to impromptu speaking. Moreover I am a sports buff. Cricket is my favourite game." Ab. spoke in one breath. "Do you like a piece of chocolate? I've got one from Germany. It's a gift from my aunt who lives in Munich". Rani offered him a slab of milk chocolate.

"You said Munich" Ab. asked her.

"Yes Munich, why that name strikes a note of recognition?" R. asked him to prolong the conversation.

"Munich Olympic still is a slur in the annals of human relationships. In 1972 eleven Israel participants were gun down by the terrorists. It is an example of the highest point of human foible." Ab. would have continued the discussion further but a sudden jolt made him lean on Rani. A black cat suddenly appeared in the middle of the road, winked and sprinted on the other side of the road. The driver being obsessed by superstition forced the brake to the utmost limit in panic. The teachers got furious, the students loved it. Ab. and Rani benefited the most. They came close to each other.

The picnic was the turning point. It provided plenty of mirth, fun and jollity. They ran all over the open field, played endless cricket in an unorthodox manner, fought makeshift fights, and ate all kinds of delicious dishes brought by them from home and established intimacy beyond permitted limit, ostensibly enforced by the school authorities.

For the first time Ab. and Rani felt a natural inclination to be in close proximity with each other. In multiple dreams that each one of them dreamt, the figures of both of them appeared pre-dominantly. They met very often outside school, not as sworn lovers, but as good friends.

"We will be going to Goa for a week's holidays with my parents." Rani told Ab.on an autumn morning."

"What a surprise. It is co-incidental." Ab. replied.

"What do you mean? Are you going too?" She asked.

"Yes, we are going too." Ab. replied.

In Goa Express in coach# 3A the two families met for the first time. Rani's father was an executive secretary in the government department. Her mother was a socialite. She kept herself busy with Kitty parties during the days. Her evenings were spent in innumerable clubs. The man was an introvert, well-read and impeccably dressed. He shook hands with Abhishek's father. The later was a Major in the army. The grip was so strong that effected Rani's dad's spinal chord to churn and the sustained mild pain later on made him uncomfortable for a long time to come. He assured himself to refrain from such courteous social norm for sometime, especially in the company of army personnel.

Ab's mother at once showed her true amiable nature by extending an invitation to Rani's mother to seat beside her. A prolonged gossip on topics of different nature, ranging from the domestic tit-bits to the world outside the ambience of home including fashion, movies and exotic foods dominated the gossip.

Ab. and Rani shared every bit of food served to them.

"Chocolate is still my favourite sweet." Rani gave out her secret.

"I'm not very fond of sweets but I like food. My mother is the best cook on earth." Ab. said proudly.

They had a rollicking time on the sea shore. They plunged into the water together, ran on the beach in ankle deep water and held each other's hands. Ab. pushed her into the sea water and held her in it for a while till she was out of breath. He too stayed under water for sometime as a reciprocal gesture. During day and in the evening both the families stayed together, had their meals together, walked together on the beach and reclined on the beach in close proximity of each other. They shared all the expenses together.

On the last day of their stay in Goa the families became more intimate than the previous six days. Ab. and Rani swam, ducked, plunged, splashed and dived in the salty sea water in each others company. Once his swim suit went down his waist line, but he retrieved it quickly. Rani was the sole witness of the scene. She was embarrassed, the others missed it.

Traditionally the girls of her age were not allowed to wear swim suit like the girls do in the western countries. Rani wore indigenous dress. She had a pink coloured suit on when she dipped into the saline water. After two dips the suit turned soggy. It stuck to her body exposing the vital statistics of her physical structure. Ab. looked at her with hungry looks, off and on, to avoid being detected of his intention. It was a mere feast to his eyes which he would cherish for a long time in future.

The parents of the duo got tired after an hour's work out in water. So they left sea for shore to recline on the sands, to savour cocoanut water and rest. The two protagonists stayed in water for a while within the ear shots of their parents, but not for long. They wanted to venture out, to see more of the expanding horizon where the endless water meets the sky at far end of the world. The friendly pair drifted into the Vagator Beach, inch by inch, feet by feet, from Arjuna, ignoring the stern warnings from both the parents not to go beyond their beach to be on safe side.

The Vagator Beach was ear-marked exclusively for the foreign tourists. The alien men and women visited here believed in living with nature in natural conditions. They indulged freely in all kinds of activities with regard to human relationships which were morally, ethically and socially avoided and religiously banned in this country., considering such acts as unclean and a mark of degeneration of Indian Society.

The duo were stunned to see about three hundred men, women and children roaming on the beach naked, holding each others hands, kissing, hugging, girls sitting on the laps of men. Quite a number of couples were in passionate moods, lying on each other in erotic positions.

The innocent, tender-aged friends suddenly turned romantic, looked at each other with passionate eyes and craved for each others company more intimately than before. Ab. looked at the frontal mounds and swelling posterior of Rani and felt a jolt in his body, an electrifying effect over-powered him. He was mesmerized for sometime and could not talk.

Rani looked down at his groin and noticed the swelling shaft of his creative cell was about to burst, in fact, she felt, she was being mocked at. Ab. was a little surprised at her abnormal behaviour. He looked down and realized the reason for it. He pulled Rani close to him and was about to kiss her when he was interrupted by a sound, calling his name in the distance. It was his father. Finding them missing from their part of the beach the parents got panicky. They began a frantic search for their children, at first around their own beach, and then moved into the creek that separated Arjuna from Vagator.

It was an awkward moment for both of them. The climax of the moment did not materialize at a crucial point of time. They got disengaged, walked to their parents.

"What on earth you two are doing here away from us." The Major asked in his customary military way.

Ab. took a couple of seconds to search for the right words to reply.

"We were lost." He gave a shy reply.

"We thought you have gone before us so we walked up to this place in search of you." Rani rose to the occasion and gave a convincing reply.

The matter ended there as abruptly as it started. They walked back to their hotels together in silence. While walking Rani's mother wrapped her body with a towel which she carried along with her. Ab. felt a little embarrassed at being ill-clad. He went down the waist deep water of the sea to cover his modesty while the others walked on the beach in parallel line with him.

The return journey was smooth and interesting; Rani looked out of the window of the coach of the train into the sky, musing at the latest incident that took place at the beach. Ab. was slightly perturbed and regretted at the un-fulfilled desire which could have been accomplished if the parents delayed their appearance on the spot a fraction late. Henceforth, their minds were occupied with the thought of incomplete desires; two-folds in nature became an obsession with them.

One day after school they met in a park, expressed their heart-felt desires to co-habit about which they learnt a lot from different sources, especially from their co-mates — all precocious brats.

"How are you? Ab. asked her in subdued tone.

"I'm fine. You, how are you keeping?" Rani also asked him the same question.

"I'm keeping well. What about that thing?" Ab. asked her.

"What thing?" Rani retorted.

"We're about to do in Goa." He said.

"No, not here. So many people around us watching each movement of ours" Rani protested.

"Then, when and where?" Ab. was exasperated.

"Come to my house tomorrow after school." She suggested.

"But your parents will be there." Ab said.

"No my father is out on an official tour, my mother will go to a kitty party. The party is thrown in honour of the Chairperson of the group. She won't be back before eight in the evening. So we will have the hell of a time." Rani concluded with a positive note.

Ab. was in seventh heaven. He dreamt of a glorious afternoon. He would have a sensational experience of his life, unprecedented, un-called for and perhaps it was providential.

Next day he hopped, skipped and jumped in glee on the way to her house. His joy had no bound. As he came near the house of Rani his heart beats increased, breath faster in quick successions and perspired even in the winter season. Just outside the door he stopped stock and listened. A peel of laughter of mixed voices greeted him from inside the room.

'Perhaps she is watching a film of Govinda, the king of comedy in Indian film. Johnny Lever, the shadow of the great actor must have cracked a joke which has enthralled the guests. I will join her. Together we will have a profitable afternoon'. In anticipation of an exciting moment of his life, Ab. knocked on the door. He had to wait an agonizing full minute before the door was flung opened.

Dev, a classmate of his stood on the other side of the door. He straight way stared into the eyes of Ab. Dev was dumb-founded and could not believe his eyes.

"What are you doing here?" Ab. asked him.

"I'll ask you the same question." Dev replied in a curt manner.

"But she called me alone in the absence of her parents." Ab. said.

"Oh man. Abhi. Come inside. Don't fuss." Rani called from the drawing room. She drawled and her voice sounded as if she was in an inebriated condition.

Ab. slowly and stealthily moved in her direction. He never expected what he encountered there. Rani was lying on the sofa, her head resting on the lap of Raj. And her feet being massaged by Rohit. All three boys shared the rear row of the class with Ab.

"Abhi sit down on the chair. I was expecting your arrival when these boys came. I'm sure you know them all. They are your friends too." Rani introduced all three boys to Ab. It was a mark of dishonesty and a breach of trust. Rani was not in her natural self. Her dress was in shambles, hairs disheveled and voice wobbly. It seemed she had an alcoholic drinking bout in the company of these 'Three Musketeers'. The mere sight of the place, its vitiated atmosphere and the presence of his friends angered him to such an extent that he beat a hasty retreat from the place.

On his way back he was narrowly saved being spotted by Rani's father. He just parked his car in front of the door of the house. After opening the door he ducked to collect the office files that he brought home for unfinished works to be completed. His coming home at that point of time was not expected. Fortunately Ab. passed him by in the nick of time and avoided detection.

"My God, I escaped detection. Let me stand aside and watch the drama to be enacted in the house." Ab. stood behind a pillar and kept an eye on the door of Rani's house. Within a couple of minutes the sequences of events unfolded itself. The wrath of Rani's father fell squarely on the boys. He pushed them out of the house after administering his peace of mind. The three boys walked passed him crestfallen, their eyes on the ground and head drooping in shame.

Ab.'s world of fantasy was receding into background. He dreamt of a sensational event but was rebuffed so resolved,

"I will not talk to her again. What business she had to invite those ruffians at the same time when she called me?"

On the next day in school he completely ignored Rani. She cast a few lusty side glances in his direction but finding no reciprocal affectionate return she withdrew from the sight entirely.

In tenth grade they were busy with the preparation of the forthcoming final examination. Ab. always cherished a lurking desire to have an intimate relationship with Rani or anyone of the female characters to get cracking into the business of mutual, cordial human companionship, but it never came in his way. He was quite upset with the atrocious behaviour of Rani, but there was no way he could stop liking her, perhaps nature would take its due course eventually.

Rani felt rather miserable after the unexpected incident. She really wanted to have Ab. exclusively at her place on that fateful afternoon. She made all kinds of preparation. Unfortunately as things would have it those three ruffians appeared on the scene unexpectedly and forced their way into the house. They brought along with them three bottles of beers which they purchased locally from the government outlet by fraudulent means. Rani tried her best to get rid of them, but they overpowered her. In the end she gave up and danced to their tunes. The incident would remain a secret forever to Ab.

At the beginning of class eleven Ab. got a jolt. Rani's father got transferred to Pune. His separation from Rani after that cursed hour did not diminish his passion for her. In fact his inquisitive mind became sharper and appetite grew for an intimate human relationship with the opposite sex. But such personal trait could recede to the background over the passing time. It was the building of his career that got priority over the other things.

In grades eleven and twelve Ab. was a loner. He lived almost a secluded life, but dedicated his time for studies.

The teens in every where in the world went through this phase of transformation in their lives. As they stepped into the adulthood in twenties they looked for companionships outside the family ambience either in the opposite sex or among their pals. They feel an acute need of sexual fulfillment. Their physical feature change from boys to developed young men, voices change from the melodious soprano to hoarse contralto or bass. Minds enter the realms of foppish pomp and glory.

"Hey Ab., you have dropped a book. I found this under your desk." A female voice drew his attention from behind in the school one afternoon. Ab. turned mechanically to grasp the situation and saw Sonali, his classmate and a friend of Rani as well.

"Thank you. It slipped of my hand. I was not aware of it." Ab. replied hesitatingly. Later on he expressed his surprise to his male friends in school. "I am at my wits end. How daring and bold these girls of today?" At the same time it stirred his soul, the natural characteristic of every human child. He felt, perhaps, the void created after Rani's departure could be partly fulfilled by a girl whom he did not care much previously.

On the next day Ab. took the initiative of meeting the girl outside the school gate. In fact the opportunity arrived when there was a mad rush to board the bus for home. During the run for freedom, the students turn insane. They scream - an expression of rejoice, they push and pull each other — a sign of gregariousness, effecting pains by kicking, pinching and hitting each other-a sign of animal instinct in them, but they show a fraternity of different kind - the hallmark of the tender youths was discernible in every step they took after the final bell rang to declare the end of the six grueling hours that preceded it.

Ab. stepped out of the gate, crossed the road and stood behind the Ice-cream box, a pre-planned spot where Sonali would locate him easily.

"Hi, how's the day?" Ab. greeted her with a few words.

"The day was good. How was your day?" She also answered briefly. "Fine. Will you have an ice cream?" Ab, asked her.

"No, thank you. I have a bad throat." She very reluctantly refused the offer. "One ice cream won't do any harm." He insisted.

"O.K. I will have one." She relented in the end.

Ab. rose to the occasion in spite of financial constraint. This was the beginning of their friendship which in time turned into close intimacy.

They met everyday outside the school gate after the classes were over for a brief period. Soon the meeting period increased, spilled over to the adjoining park in the neighborhood. A mere friendship had consequential effects. They got emotionally attached to each other.

"Do you still remember Rani?" Sonali asked him one day. It startled Ab. He cherished quietly her image in the core of his heart, she being his first burning flame, a live inferno very difficult to extinguish so easily.

"Yes, I still remember her face vividly. But I have no knowledge of her whereabouts." Ab. replied with alacrity.

"I believe she is in Pune. Her father is the deputy manager of the ordinance factory there." Sonali delivered the latest information about her.

Their clandestine meetings came to a sudden halt a fortnight before the final examination. During the month long final examination they went through an ordeal of mugging facts and figures, punctuated by questions and answers. They spent many sleepless nights in preparations for the examination.

Ab. and Sonali did not care much for each other. He made good use of her company to fulfill the vacuum created in his heart after the sudden departure of Rani from his life. It was but natural that he sought female company. Sonali never thought that she was worthy of filling the vacuum in his heart.

They met in the local Mall after the first Sunday of the examination was over. Ab. was surprised to see the dress code followed by her in that occasion. It was quite contrary to the one followed in school.

She wore a skin tight T. Shirt to cover her bust. The bottom of which was raised to expose the neat naval ring. The shirt hardly covered her breasts. The V. shape cut in the middle revealed the vital part of her two precious life giving mounds. Short sleeves of the T-Shirt showed the half of the breasts from the sides. The low slung blue jeans would reveal the neat border line of the posterior once she bent down. Her eyes were painted neatly with black colour, the eye-brows drawn symmetrically matching the eyes, the lips parted like the first bite of an apple. Her hairs were fluffy emanating the odour of the use of a strong shampoo and a pungent smell of a body spray hit his nostril.

Ab. could not resist the temptation. He pushed her in a corner of the park, held her close to his body and kissed her. The action lasted for a minute. Their tongues twisted and turned, saliva dripped, the shaft swelled, the crotch parted. They were hungry for intimacy, but nothing had happened further. It ended then and there.

Ab. experienced the first intimate relationship with Sonali in a Party. Ranen, a back bencher in school had thrown the party in his farm house to celebrate his eighteenth birthday. It was a freak out party where the youngsters meet to ease out the pent up energies. Intoxicating drinks were served in unlimited quantity in spite of statutary warning and the revelers being youngsters to make the event colourful and enjoyable. The elders normally stay away from such gatherings for fear of being out of place.

Ab. was well advised by his parents and well-wishers to stay away from intoxicating drinks and female companionship as both were considered immoral, unethical and damaging to ones reputation. The former would destroy his nerves the consequential result was insanity. The later would invite endless trouble in human relationships.

"Will you dance with me?" Sonali asked Ab. when the D.J. struck the first note on the music system.

"I do not know how to dance." Ab. gave her a modest reply.

"You need not know anything about it; just move your body with the rhythm of music." Sonali suggested.

"I'll try, but don't laugh if I make mistakes." Ab. said.

"No one present here knows how to dance." Sonali pulled his hand. "O.K , I'm coming." Ab. consented.

A dozen pairs of dancers were on the floor of the drawing room. Half-clad, gaily painted and in hilarious mood they were dancing the most erotic dances to excite each other for the inevitable moment, the climax of all desires.

It was the first time that Ab. felt the soft touch of the female skin. The odour of the female flesh entered his nostrils next and finally he felt an inward urge strongly. His mind wavered, appetite for carnal desire intensified and discretionary power receded into the background.

"Shall we go for a walk? The room is stuffy and filled with cigarette smoke." Ab. suggested.

"Yes, I'm getting suffocated. Let's go out." Sonali agreed to the suggestion.

They slipped out of the house, walked hand in hand for a while, then settled down on a bench in the dark corner of the garden.

It was natural they were drawn close to each other. Subsequent result was an intimate affair for which they were not prepared.

Ab. felt guilty of a crime which might spell disaster in the days to come. The ecclesiastical leaders would consider such an awful behaviour an act that break a religious and moral law. The elders of society where he belonged to would curse him for his debauchery, the young men and women would turn their faces away from him as if they all were sinless, his peers would say 'it was a matured act' and the girls known to him would have a mixed feeling of both, hatred and appreciation.

There was no bond of love, no concern for each other, no social stigma; only an insatiable physical hunger for each others blood and flesh bound them together.

Ab. and Sonali met very often clandestinely. Both of them extended their meetings with many other like-minded youngsters ignoring the norms of society, disregard in the social behaviour conceived by the sensible individuals through interaction with each other over the years.

Ab. father smelt the rat. He noticed the behaviour pattern of his son, from a normal human being; he turned into something unacceptable to the society he belonged to.

"Son, we are very worried about your future", he told him one day after dinner when Ab. was almost at the fag end of his class twelfth.

"Why, Dad, what's wrong with me?" Ab. almost challenged his father.

"Your outgoing nature and free mixing with the female counterparts make both of us a little worried", his father came straight to the point.

"But dad it's an 'in' thing. All my friends and young people around us are indulging in liberal life. If I do not toe the line, I become an outcast".

"Camaraderie among friends is one thing and the close intimacy is another issue altogether. The former is healthy, forges you to go forward, the later is harmful unless utilized judiciously"

"Dad, I understand what you're aiming at. I am extremely careful of my dealing with the female friends".

"I'm sure you have matured enough to understand the intricacies and implications of such irretrievable and inveterate behaviour"

"Yes dad I am" Ab. did not like to prolong the discussion.

A drunkard knows the taste of good drinks. He helps himself without restraint. Once he gets addicted, there is no way to come back. . It gets into his system; he forgets the world and his family. His ears are always close to advices, turns away from religious practices, ignores the family ties, overlooks the welfare of children, and eventually loosen discretionary power and common sense.

Ab. met many friends after this and indulged in countless awesome affairs. In the eyes of his young friends he was a hero, but the elders in the family and society condemned him, a maniac they used to say.

The years went by; from school Ab. entered college, the august house of higher studies. The advanced age was the sign of growth and maturity. Diverse characters and of different natural youngsters assemble here to sharpen their brains and achieve their goals. The ultimate result would be to build a career. Physical and mental development reached at their peaks during youths, added to it was the hunger for knowledge.

Ab. was determined to curve a niche in the academic world around him. He attended classes regularly, took down the notes and mug them up at a reasonable speed. Hardly he visited the canteen, a place for the young academicians, the Mecca of all social camaraderie among them. Here the students get divided into groups as per their natural endowments. Some adhered to strict routine of the institution so did attend classes regularly.

Some were flamboyant upstarts, did care only for their egoistic nature. A few smart persons stayed put in the limelights of all games and sporting events. The 'would be' politicians led the students to form unions and get involved in everything anti-campus activities and anti - administrative dictates.

"I'm not a loose type of person who indulges in the nefarious activities in the august institution of ours." Ab. told his recently acquired friend Joe.

"See, all our friends are addicted to some kind of intoxicating stuff. It's not out of place but an 'in' thing." Joe advised him.

"I don't agree with you. I like to spend my time in studies and build my career." Ab replied in real earnest.

Unfortunately it was not so. His heart was willing, but the flesh was reluctant to stay away from evil practices. A temptation is an evil enigma. It breaks all resolutions of doing well.

"Who is she? I see a familiar face shining in the midst of a group of my Classmates" Ab. asked his friend in astonishment.

"That's a new girl just joined the college. Her father is in the govt. services, got transferred here recently from Pune". The friend informed him.

"It rings a bell in my ear. I must find out. I hope she is not Rani".

Abhishek did not get a chance for a while to have a glimpse of her profile to clear his doubt. Then one day as he emerged from the library in a hurry he collided with the girl who eluded her identity for so long.

"It's you? I can't believe my eyes". Ab. said in an astonished manner.

"I can't believe my eyes, too." Rani replied as a reciprocal gesture.

Ab. was surprised at her lusterless reply. In fact Rani had spotted Ab. earlier. She was eager to meet him, but was in double minds. She was not sure of his intention. "Will he be interested to resume the old tie, I doubt."

Ab. was now in a quandary. His heart was willing to resume the old tie, but was in doubt whether the old flame of his would cause his heart to burn for fidelity. For him the old adage, 'absence makes the heart grow fonder' made its impact felt in tandem. On the other hand Rani felt a jolt in her heart. Her perturbed soul could not reconcile with the tragic departure from the school where she left her dear friends in a jiffy. In the new school at Pune she made acquaintance with a couple of boys but they had left no mark in her soul.

It was winter months. At the dawn of the season all educational institutions organized sporting activities. The athletic sports were considered an event of the year where all the budding athletes participated. Abhishek was an ardent sports lover too. He hopped, sprinted and jumped in all events. Even took part in fast running races. He won couple of first prizes and a few second and third prizes. The sporting committee of the college declared him the valiant sportsman of the year.

Such a feat attracted attention of all people, especially in the student's community. Ab's classmates hailed him as a hero, the senior students took cognizance of his feat and female counterparts, both seniors and juniors stared at him with lustrous look as if to devour a living human creature made of succulent flesh and sweet hot blood.

Ab. began to receive secret letters from all quarters.

"You are my only hero."

"Would you like to go out for a drink with me sometime?"

"I'm really fascinated by your remarkable feat, would you oblige me by being my permanent buddy."

"Hey man I'm in love with you. I'd like to have a close intimacy with you. Please oblige."

"Abhi dear, I dreamt of you last night, from the pit of the long jump, you took a long stride, sprinted and fell on me. I was so delighted in the morning."

"I'm crazy about you. I'd like to bear our children for you."

"It was fascinating, especially the long jump, I wish u all the best."

The last one was from Rani, otherwise compliments of the above nature poured in incessantly aftermath of the conclusion of the sporting events. Endless invitations to freaky parties followed.

After a lot of deliberation Abhishek went to a party in a not so wealthy farmhouse in the remote part of a certain village on the outskirts of the city. Here every man had to bare his torso and the girls had to put on minimum tags on their chests to cover the modesty. Dry white powder of murderous kinds and of various quality and alcoholic drinks flowed in profusion. Erotic dancers in unorthodox postures and gestures took the centre stage. The culmination of all these behaviour ended in close intimacy. Abhishek had his share too. The hostess, a female classmate of his kept him busy during the party.

"It's, in fact, in honour of your brilliant achievements in sports field I've decided to hold this party" she said while dancing and holding each others hips tightly, lips touching, scouting for pleasure, at times tongues rotating in their mouths for that extreme disposition. The long night ended in the nook and cozy corner of the garden.

The next party was in a pent-house in down town area of the city, a posh locality where affluent youngsters showed their ugly faces in diverse occasions, in awkward dress codes, in social nuance and in awesome manners. The young people had too much to spend, too many things to buy and indulged in too many activities in pursuit of pleasures. The type of get together held here could disturb the peace in heaven,(where spirituality of life were expected in the creation of God on earth). Every unethical, anti-social activity showed its ugly face in the name of 'modern trends', 'in thing' and 'the hype'.

Abhishek, the hero of the elite group in college received an invitation card from the only daughter of Mr. Finch, the widower. After the sad premature demise of his wife Mr. Finch brought up his daughter single handedly with affection, love and care. In his younger days he held many coveted posts as CEO in multinational companies and amassed a lot of wealth by sheer hard work. Now, in his mid-forties he left everything in the hands of his beloved daughter. Rebecca exploited the situation and misused it. He spoilt his daughter by giving excessive of everything, love, care and concern. He had fulfilled all her worldly desires. The net result was that she turned a precocious brat. Her physical growth was something to cherish as the blossom of flowers in springs, but the mental capacity was as low as the winter temperature in artic circle. Her life was given to pleasure and entertainment.

Rebecca was proud enough this week to throw a party to her close friends. Her father being away in Canada in connection with a conference of the GI 4 countries, she had the whole world free before her. The guest list was not long, only a couple of dozens of co-educationists from her class and a few from the neighborhood colony and clubs were the privileged ones to be invited.

They were like-minded souls and the true followers of her ego. The students matching her own caliber were invited to the bash party. They had to take solemn oaths that the get together was an exclusive party where anything was done unnatural, unobtrusive, not-conforming to the traditional convention of society had no social stigma was attached to it, would be accepted with free mind. The excessive alcoholic drinks, surfeit of drug consumption and erotic behaviour in the name of 'kicks' , 'trend' and 'in' things were allowed without any constraint. Ab. was only an exception. He was shown favour because of looks, satiable appearance and Rebecca's urge to satisfy a lustful appetite.

"You must come to my party." Rebecca invited him verbally. She was boarding her car at the outer gate of the college where Ab. met her.

"I am not so used to this kind of party going culture. Who else will be there?" he asked inquisitively.

"Why, they all will be there. All your pals." She gave a quick reply.

"Will Rani be there?" Ab. shot.

"Why, is she very special to you? Yes, she will be there. You can have all the fun. My party is well-known among our friends." She said and boarded the car.

The prospect of Rani being invited to the party was an added incentive. His lustful appetite enhanced. He promptly accepted the invitation without hesitation.

The party was to take place in the penthouse atop the multi-storied building, but the spot was changed from there to the drawing room. A small place was preferred to a big one as the later one was not quite fit for the type of intimacy that was expected to be maintained among the couples. The room had a very few furniture, no decoration at all. The lights were dim; only one lamp shade of 40 watts bulb in it was placed in a corner close to the bar, improvised one though. The makeshift structure would disappear next day.

Ab. stepped into the house half an hour later than the scheduled time of the start of the rendezvous. He was received at the door by no other than Rebecca herself. Ab. could not take his eyes away from her for a while. She was stunning, wore a provocative negligee, no under cover was used, and hardly could hid the erected dual mounds, two black-berries embossed on them. Below the waistline, Ab. could see transparent white underwear under the cover of a nylon skirt and the V-shaped cut was taunting him for not asking a favour.

Rebecca pulled him inside the quasi dark room, near the drawing room, where the drama of a weird kind would be unfolded to the view of a youngster who was bound by tradition and culture to lead a life of celibacy, till he tied the knot in matrimonial alliance. Ab. could not see anything inside the room, excepting the silhouette figures of a few characters moving inside the room in unsteady manner.

"This is Ronita." Rebecca introduced him to a girl whom Ab. could figure out in the dark, stark naked, swaying to and fro under the heavy influence of a substance known to them as 'Ecstasy'.

"Hello-o-o-o-o." she drawled and protruded her right hand for the cordial hand shake.

"Hey you, hairless dame, why did you leave me?" A male voice came after her from a closed room.

"This is Saby, the son of Mr. Ram Gopal". Ab. was familiar with the name, since the man held a prominent post in the cabinet at the local government.

What embarrassed him the most was that the young man was standing before him in his birthday suit!

Ab. greeted him with a semi-hand shake and said, "Nice to meet you."

"It is not nice; you're not a civilized man. Look at us; we're all in our natural self. Be like us." He tugged at his shirt. Ab resisted but was powerless. At least six people surrounded him and twelve hands tugged his clothes off. In no time they made him nude as a new born baby. The valiant act was performed by the like minded people whom Ab. could not see in the dark and never knew the people who they were.

Ab. protested vehemently against the uncalled for act but there was no one to listen to him. He could not find his clothes either; it all disappeared in the dark room. Rebecca stood there as a mere witness to the whole proceeding. It seemed to him, the entire act was stage rehearsed, performed on helpless guys in sundry occasions in the past. Since no help came forward, the hostess was in league with the perpetrators, the motive was crystal clear and the purpose of the ugly desire was fulfilled. Ab. began to guzzle alcohol to drown his sorrow.

The intake of the destructive powder, better known as cocaine, and also some 'L.S.D.', which was available aplenty there, began to tell on him. In his semi-conscious state of mind he felt Rebecca was pulling him to the sofa which was placed in one side of the room. He was pushed onto the sofa by Rebecca where he laid on his back, breathing heavily. Soon he found a soft warm body of a female descended on him. She smelled nice and provocative. In his semi-conscious state he found there were a lot of actions on his person. Rebecca was licking him, biting him and sucking the nectar out of him. Later on he was inundated by more female species, repeating the same actions as if to satisfy their long lustful desires. Initially he too reciprocated but as the time wore on the pressure mounted, one person followed the other and he felt exhausted. He finally fell of to a deep sleep.

Early in the morning he was woken up by Rebecca with a cup of tea and an innocent smile on her face. Ab. got up from the sofa with a start, looked around the room in the light of the day. An exquisite place, gaily decorated, attractive furniture, assortment of choicest seasonal flowers, carpets of oriental fabric rolled all over the floor.

"I hope you enjoyed the party last night." Rebecca asked him the very first question as soon as the stupor disappeared from his face.

"What happened to me last night?" Ab. asked her while still in the state of shock.

"Nothing much. You drank too much, then fell of to sleep." She replied in jest.

"I see. Who were those people I met last night?"

"They all were your friends."

"But they misbehaved with me."

"No, what they did was according to the norm of the party. They enjoyed themselves to a great extent. Everything was done with the consent of the participants."

"Not mine. I did not have a clue of what was going to happen." So saying Abhishek got up from the bed and then to his great surprise, he discovered he had no clothes on, only his underwear saved his modesty.

"Was Rani here last night?" he asked as he was about to go out of the door.

"Yes she was here for a while, but left before you had come." Rebecca gave a curt reply. The door was shut with a bang on his face, immediately after this.

Ab. stood on the pavement in front of the house, took stock of the situation. He felt miserable.

"I'm no good as a human being. All those stooges used me to satisfy their carnal desires and I could not do anything about it. I vow to take the revenge."

'How?' he could hear an echo in his heart asking him the question.

"I give up drinking, taking drugs and stay away from female companions. Every male youngster had to encounter three stumbling blocks in his life. I will help anyone who gets trapped unknowingly in the intricate web of his circumstances."

The tall promises and the determination to stay away from evil practices did not last long. The hunger for physical appeasement, the female companionship and indulging in intoxicating drinks and drugs recurred in one's life as natural habits, Ab. was no exception. He met Rebecca several times after this in college, at her residence and in private places. He always longed to meet Rani, his heart throb, privately, but there seemed to be no chance to fulfill his hearts desire.

"Son, I don't find any seriousness in your day to day activities. You don't study hard enough to secure better position in the class; study should be your prime concern now. It would help you to build a solid career." His father told him one day, observing his lackadaisical attitude towards daily activities.

"Dad, don't worry about me. I know what is good for me. Building of a solid career is of prime concern now. Trust me, I will do well." He assured his father.

"A man with a solid character is the most successful person in life. Indulging in too much of free mixing may cause trouble, both physically and mentally. The former could contain a deadly contaminated, serious disease which may develop into an incurable stage. Once afflicted by a serious disease, you will regret."

"Dad, we are living in the twenty first century. Medical science has developed to an unimaginable extent. Life span of human being have increased, the young people are conscious of their rights and duties, pseudo-social restrictions on lives have relaxed, free mixing of both sexes is no more a taboo. Let me tell you dad, we youngsters are more aware of our circumstances than our predecessors."

"I doubt." The father held a pessimistic view of life. He was skeptical about his son's optimistic view of life. He confided to his wife one day, "our son has joined the mainstream of the present day life. The youngsters are depending more on themselves, relying on the trends set by a few people, trendy clothes by designers, upbeat livings imitated from the film personalities, extravagant livings beyond the limited income have become the fashion of the day. He indulges too much in personal activities of no consequence; of late he has adopted an attitude towards anti-social, anti-religious and anti-family policies."

"What can we do? Put a restriction on his activities, we loose him. Allow him to have his own way destroys him. We should follow a policy of watch and wait." His wife expressed her view on the matter.

Ab. felt uncomfortable at times of all the things that were happening around him. In spite of all adverse conditions he remained steadfast in his own conviction.

"I am right of all the things I'm doing. I move according to the present trend in society. My dad is traditional, orthodox and religious minded. I do not endorse of what he thinks about me or the way he wants to mould me. I'm an exclusive person, a separate entity. I follow the dictates of my mind. Let the whole world go against me. I am what I am."

In spite of living a riotous life where debauchery played a dominant part Ab. was quite steady in his studies. The young fellows at times become aware of their future, so work hard to carve a niche in the academic circles, so did Ab.

In the meantime Rani too had a disorderly life. She mingled freely with the young upstarts of the male version.

"Remember you are a girl. Troubles of various sorts are looming around you. Living an unrestrained life will cause you a lot of pain in future, physically, mentally and socially." Her mother said to her one day.

"What are you hinting at Mother? Is it all about me and how I spend my life in the company of my friends? Mother, I'm no more a kid. I know what is best for me. I have the power of discrimination between good and evil. We, young people are living in a fast world where we learn everything from our surroundings and from our peers. The young men around me are the most potential entity with whom I inter-act daily. The free-mixing of the young men with girls are considered in today's society as healthy, educative and natural. Please don't stop me from being with my male friends. It will have an adverse effect on me. You'll regret afterwards."

Such a strong dose was not expected from Rani. The mother felt her daughter was representing the true picture of today's society girl, living in a different pragmatic social fabric with queer outlook, in contrast to the society; she was living in the days of yore. She decided to quit interfering in the private affair of her daughter and allowed her to live a contented life of her own.

Rani spent many nights with friends of both sexes in parties and in their residences. Her secret mission with the boys were very well guarded with concocted stories to study together, exchange of notes and solving intricate problems after trials and errors. The parents did not like the idea at all. Their daughter was having such a glowing of time, but could not help it, thinking of the adverse effect.

Rani spent her first night with John, the macho man of her college on the pretext of being with Latika her best female friend in college. She lost her virginity, but the night spent together with a man gave her a lot of pleasure and mental satisfaction at the cost of physical ruination.

The first clandestine experience emboldened her further and she spent many more nights with different men to satiate her inner feelings and youthful energies. She had no particular man as her true friend. She did not believe in staying put with one friend alone but a galaxy of them entertained her in parties, college outings and in educational camps. Each time she had a gala time.

But the adage,'all wells that ends well' did not prove right with the riotous life she was leading. On one occasion in a party she threw up.

"She must have had too much alcohol." One of her friends said in a 'conti' party.

"I have not seen her drinking at all.I coaxed her to have a sip from my glass. But she refused." The second friend chipped in.

"She must be sick." The third friend suggested.

"I don't see any reason of her being sick. She was perfectly all right when I escorted her in the hall." The fourth friend butted in.

"Then she must be pregnant." The first friend reiterate.

On the next day she went to see a gynecologist. In the afternoon she was a relieved girl. That spared her being tainted forever. It was a pleasant relief for her. Unfortunately she was nicknamed with a name not accepted in the social environment anywhere in the world. The friends called her a slut. In her sub-conscious mind, Rani felt a jolt. She regretted her bitter experience. What she thought previously natural and right turned out to be nightmares. Rani stage-managed everything so well that her parents remained ignorant about their daughter's secret affairs for ever.

The vicissitudes of life affect all of us, in certain degrees. We change from the normal and ordinary state to an abnormal state, vice versa. Today's child grows up to tomorrow's youth, with physical and mental changes occurring simultaneously. The economically poor transform into an affluent one. Adversely healthy child growing under the parental care develop into a diseased person due to pamper, undisciplined and un-cared for type of life spent during youth.

Perhaps the chance meeting of Ab. with Rani at the threshold or the call centre building was the ultimate concern of both of them. They preserved the secret wish of their hearts for many years in the past. Now both had decided to the fullest, if possible, end up in marriage.

"What a surprise. We never had chance like this ever to come so close to each other." Ab. told her in one breath.

"It is indeed." Rani gave a short reply.

"I missed you all these years. Whenever I became serious about you in the past, I found you had gone." Ab. expressed his regrets briefly.

"I felt very bad when I left you in class 11. My dad got transferred to Pune." She just reminded him.

"I too felt very dejected and morose. Can we meet someday, somewhere and ruminate over the years gone by." Ab. suggested.

"Yes, I don't mind." She approved of the suggestion.

"We'll meet this Saturday evening at Priya Complex near the entrance to McDonald's outlet. Are you free?" Ab. expressed his sincere desire. "Yes, I'm free." Rani replied nonchalantly.

Next couple of days they both felt elated. The reason being that at last they were free to meet, away from their other friends, close relatives and detractors. They both prepared themselves mentally for the day when a new deal would be struck in their relationship. It was long due but deprivation blocked the way due to adverse circumstances.

They dressed up like the young couple meeting on their first date. For both the stylist haircuts, body spray with the choicest eau de cologne and elegant dresses cut according to the fashion of the day were common. Rani had the briefest top dress with plenty of exposition of her vital statistics of the torso, tightest trousers showing her swollen posterior and thin eye-lashes all that went with the fashionable society girls of the day she had on her person.

Ab. was first to reach the place. Rani followed suit. They went to Bacchus, a Bar cum Restaurant, frequented by the young buddies. Mr. Bach, the friendly manager welcomed them cordially and directed them to a corner table, meant for two. Ab. ordered drinks, Beer for himself and Sherry for Rani. Initially they felt very shy, but after a couple drinks began to talk.

"Look at that girl. She must be older than the boy who is accompanying him." Ab. pointed at the couple under discussion, occupied a seat near the window.

"We all are subject to our likes and dislikes. Taste of a thing differs from man to man. Perhaps, they feel they are made for each other." Rani defended the couple.

"What would you like to eat?"Ab. asked.

"I don't like to eat anything at this moment." She replied.

Ab. asked Rani to dance with him after a minute's silence.

With the sound of off-beat tune struck on the disk player the other couples stepped into the dance floor to express their rustic talent. Ab. and Rani followed them in real earnest.

At first they stood apart. Next they held hands. With the next item they came closer and put their hands around the waists. As the intimacy grew stronger and understanding of each other's feelings increased they held each other's grips tightly. Hot airs gushed out from their nostrils and the warmth from each other's bodies enticed them to have a conjugal relationship. Rani stayed in Ab's arms for as long as the music lasted. The DJ. prolonged the music till they felt tired of staying in each others arms. The other dancers stood around them viewing the prospect of intimacy of the two as an everlasting one.

"At least one couple here knows how to love". One voyeur said to the other.

"They are perfectly matched for each other." The second man chipped in.

"I wish them all the best." The third reveler expressed his pleasant view.

Two remained unconcerned of their surroundings for a while.

They did not stay at the restaurant for long, since they both had to go to work early in the morning next day; they parted for the time being.

But they made it a point to meet at the foyer near the main Reception Hall for a ten minutes chat everyday. The outcome of the meetings made their hearts grow fonder. The thought of settling down got implanted into their hearts. They began to dream of founding a home where the couple would live along with their children, a boy and a girl, an ideal family.

"I will call her Mekhla. She would fill my heart with her beauty, feminine touch and million dollars smiles." Ab. expressed his anticipated love for his yet to be born daughter.

"I will name our son Sameer. He should be an idol for all young people when he grows up. His robust physics, exceptional nature and interaction with them will move even his detractors." Rani proved herself no less imaginative than Ab.

Another day in the Koina Bar Ab. elaborated his thought on the dwelling place, owned exclusively by them,

"We'll build a small cozy house on the bank of a swift flowing river. A part of which has to be extended on the river itself. The soft murmuring waves of the river has a free access to roll down underneath. On the platform of the balcony we will have enough room to recline on deck chairs and to catch fish on holidays with fishing rods and long lines. In the evening tea will be laid on the veranda for us. A panoramic view of the undulating hillock on the other side of the river, the setting sun at the back of the mountain, lush green trees through which the shafts of the dying sun rays are penetrated, we will savour while munching hot 'pakoras' with blended Darjeeling Tea. The house will be named 'Heavenly Abode' where peace and tranquility will reign supreme. Darkness will swipe the light every night and envelope the atmosphere which proclaims the end of the day and promises at least ten hours of sleep."

"I want our house is being built on top of a mountain on a secluded corner of the cliff. The sound of streams, rivulets and rivers passing by will make their present felt. The chirping of various multi-colored birds, the cacophony of wild feline species and the howling and roaring of bigger animals in the distance will fill the vacuum of the sound missing from the world of human beings. The flower garden around the house will be filled with blossoms of the assorted seasonal flowers, the butterflies flying from flower to flower for nectar, the bees buzzing during the day to proclaim their presence in our midst, occasional intrusion of the deer calves, invasion of Jackals at night, all these natural elements will keep us busy all the day long. I will grow vegetable, tender flower pots and build nests for the birds." Rani supplemented the thought propounded by Ab.

At Mayank Bar they stayed embraced all through the stipulated hours of dancing assigned to the bona fide participants.

They drank some choicest drinks intermittently. Its being the happy hours the supply was of double quantity. It made them high. Rani lost her balance and rested on Ab' s arms all through the second hour of the dance. AB. had to carry her home in the end to face a barrage of questions from her parents. Fortunately it was a Saturday so they could rest on Sunday and restore their senses.

On Monday they met again outside the call centre. Both of them delayed their lift cars for a while but did not cancel them. The exasperated drivers cursed them profusely in endless abusive languages and made stumpy remarks at their friendship.

It became a topic for discussion among the uncouth, illiterate and un-cultured people, trooping around a leader. The protagonist, a self-imposed man, had the advantage of being stout, flamboyant and forthcoming in action. They all pressed the indigenous tobacco between their palms, added a pinch of edible white lime, made a ball and plopped it into their mouths, safely perched between the lower set of teeth and the bottom of the lower lips. The immediate reactions were to spit on the spots where they were standing.

Such intake of intoxicating substances was the moral booster; invoke awesome feelings and arouse emotional traits which inspired them to stay put in one place hours together (in rain, hailstorm, summer heat and winter's bitter cold) all seasons.

They coined a few new words to describe their targets. Eventually it became a usage added to their jargon of obnoxious words to pull down a person and stain his identity.

"Look at that 'Maal' (an expression to denote the inferior status of a girl) doing all 'nakhra bazi' (expressing herself cheaply)." The leader commented at the friendly appearance of the two kindred souls.

To this there was an uproarious laughter from all expressing their assents.

'Sala', a good word is used to describe ones brother-in - law, degenerated into an abuse, directed to the boy. It was said by one of them and spat on the road which just missed an innocent passer-by hurrying to his work place.

Ab. and Rani now got used to such erratic abuses from different unknown quarters, from the people who would never understand the minds of the couple, their involvement and inner feelings. In fact such unfriendly comments from all and sundry people brought them even closer and their friendship grew from a mere 'Hi and Bye' to a dream of a future, a relationship that would bind them together forever.

The relatives, friends and neighbours were divided in their opinions. The most liberal ones felt it was high time that they bind them in matrimonial alliance according to religious rites and rituals.

The moderate ones felt it was the most suitable time they spelt out their heart's desire to each other. It should be now or never.

The detractors felt the couple should spend their youths in merry-making and jollity. The sacrament of marriage was designed for the rustic and illiterate elements living in rural areas or in un-cultured and uncivilized society.

The parents hoped their children should go through the normal social life as it was prevalent in their society.

In the meantime both Ab. and Rani felt for each other in the strongest term. "I have had so many girls in my life and used them in the greatest possible ways, but I could never manage to have any kind of interaction with her emotional, physical and sexual activities" He spoke from his heart to his co-worker in the office one day.

"That's because you're afraid to say or express your emotional feeling." The co-worker replied.

"That's not the case. I don't want to use her temporarily. She has ingrained, an indelible mark in my heart. From my school days I knew her and cherished a lurking desire always to establish a permanent relationship with her. Perhaps the day is in the offing when we will tie knot for an everlasting bond between us, Ab. said emphatically

"I wish you all the best." His co-worker said nonchalantly.

Rani was having nightmarish dreams for over a week. She dreamt of some weird figures from the realm of the evil spirits beckoning her to join the merry group. Some celestial beings hung around her house day and night to tease her forbearance, steadfastness and uprightness.

"I am very concern about your future. As a girl it is your prime duty to settle down in life," her father expressed his anguish one day during dinner. "Yes, dad. I'm also thinking about it." She replied promptly to avoid the issue to linger on. But she could not stop the discussion, her mother butted In.

"We're getting old. Someone has to look after you once we are gone." The mother retorted.

"We've no objection if you have chosen your man, not a Man Friday, but a life's partner" The father was sarcastic. It revealed his inner thought. Perhaps he was aware of Rani's secret life-style.

Rani kept her head down and said,

"I agree with your wishes and am willing to marry a boy called Ab. You know him very well."

"Where is he now?" The father asked Rani.

"He works in a call centre near my centre." She replied without hesitation. "But the call centers are not permanent establishments. Will he be able to support you permanently?"

"I'm also working."

"But you can't work forever. You're to look after your family." The mother had the final say in the matter.

Once more the parents of both families met in Rani's house. A sumptuous dinner was thrown in, at the end of the discussion. No dowry was demanded. Expenses sorted out amicably, not a lavish reception, but a reasonable friendly relationships with them, but none, according to her, and could have been chosen as her life partner. Her old flame was the right choice for her to spend the rest of her time on earth together.

The engagement ceremony was fixed on a full moon day. The ceremony would take place in Rani's house a fortnight hence. It was a Sunday, convenient for the duo, since it was a weekly holiday. Rani had applied for a couple of days leave before the scheduled engagement. Prior to this they mutually decided to reduce their regular meetings; even if they had met accidentally it was brief and cordial.

On a Sunday, a week before the grand ceremony Ab. decided to give his heart out to Rani and tell her all about the illicit relationship he had in the past with a few female friends, including Rebecca and the incident associated with and the crime enacted in her presence.

"Perhaps Rani will also tell me how she had spent her days in college and later on in the company of her male companions." Ab told the co-worker at the call center.

"You'll be surprised to note. The girls never open their mouths in spite of all hazards faced by them. The secrets buried in their hearts will never see the light of the day. Rani is no exception to it." The wise co-worker replied him. "But it is only fair that we discuss our relationship with the opposite sexes to clear out all doubts of our integrity, commitment and smooth relationship in future." Ab. said in reply.

"You can try. But it will be a futile attempt." The co-worker said and turned to press buttons on the keyboard of the computer.

Ab. resolved to meet her on Monday outside the gate of the call center and ask her directly the question of her involvement with the other boys in the days of yore.

He went down in a huff a couple of minutes early to catch her at the gate on time so that he did not miss the moment. She did not come down at the scheduled time. He waited there for extra ten minutes and faced the wrath of the car pool drivers who spat incessantly on the clean surface outside the gate to express their empathetic attitudes towards Ab. and his consort.

He called in her mobile no but there was no reply. He tried several times after this but met with the same fate as before.

"Shall I go to her house?" He asked himself the question.

"No. It is not appropriate. The custom and tradition of society do not allow us to meet privately before marriage. So I will not call her today. It may be tomorrow. I will try to contact her again."

On Tuesday Ab. fell ill. Of late he too was having mild fever off and on. But today it was rather severe. Simultaneously he was having stomach trouble. He went to work on Monday unwillingly just to meet her and discuss the crucial point pertaining to their lives. Tuesday he stayed back at home. On Wednesday he tried half-heartedly to attend the call center. He could only go as far as the road to board the pool car. His co-travelers in the car dissuaded him from getting in the car. They had spotted black marks on his face. Thinking they were marks of small pox, a severe contagious disease of the tropical countries, they advised him against his intention of going to the office, instead, he should go and see a doctor immediately.

Inmates of the hostel where he was lodging forced him to see a doctor in the afternoon. Firstly he checked for small pox virus in him. The physician tested his blood for the small pox virus in the next morning. He was found clear of the disease. With renewed vigour, Ab. embarked upon a new plan to forge ahead in the professional pursuit. So far as his personal life was concerned he lost contact with Rani. Neither could he contact her in the office nor to her residence. Her mobile phone was inactive.

Ab. stayed in bed on Friday and Saturday, thinking it was a common fever afflicted by the virus which was afloat in the atmosphere. He felt 'crocin' was the answer for his fever. On Sunday he collapsed. The boarders called an ambulance and accompanied him on a stretcher to the AIIMS Hospital. In his sub-conscious mind Ab. felt he saw Rani also was being carried in a stretcher for a check up. It was rightly so.

The doctor's at the prestigious hospital checked Ab. thoroughly. First for viral fever, next for the contagious small pox and in the end for Aids. It was evidently clear Ab. was suffering from the last kind of lethal disease. His blood was contaminated with the HIV Positive.

While in the secluded ward of the hospital, Ab. was virtually escalating into his doom, he came to know about Rani. She was in the early stage of AIDS, but there was every possibility for her to recover with proper medical care.

The engagement ceremony was cancelled. The parents felt miserable, the friends were upset, the relatives were stunned and the detractors decided to stay away from the condemned family.

"I did not have the clue that my son went astray." Ab's father told all the relatives. His mother was inconsolable. She only blamed her fate and said. "I've lost my son forever."

"He should have taken all precautionary measures to avoid a disaster of this dimension." The co-worker of the call center confided the comment to his colleague in the office.

Ab's. Friends could not believe his association with the female friends was so serious as to call for such a disaster.

"He should have taken all precautionary measures to avoid a disaster of this nature". His co-worker at the call center commented.

"He sometimes freaked out without constraint." The hostel inmates said in sympathetic tones.

"How can a well educated young man like Abhishek who had a wide knowledge of the complexities and intricacies of life be so careless and ignorant of his personal welfare?" His boss wondered at the call center.

Hardly any friend came to see him at the hospital. His parent made it a point to visit him once a day. During their stay at the hospital, the father only stared at his stupid son; the mother shed tears quietly and prayed to God for the cure of her son. The close relatives dropped in once in a while only to add to the misery of Ab.

A couple of medical research scholars also came to see him in hospital and asked him irrelevant questions on his relationships with the female friends during his salad days.

"Who was your favourite female friends?" asked one female doctor.

"So many of them I met in school and college and interacted with them. It is a common practice every where. What is so great about it?" Ab. replied with an irritated voice.

"But surely you had definitely one female friend on whom you have showered all your love and feelings." A male young doctor asked him in jest.

"Unfortunately, the one I had in mind for over a decade, my betrothed, one whom I was going to marry before this monstrous disease afflicted me, is also down with fever for a long time. I hope she is not suffering from the same disease as I am!" Ab. answered in remorse.

"Rani is safe. She is recuperating in a nursing home after an attack of severe chronic viral fever." Ab's mother whispered into his ears in one of those visits to the hospital.

"I'm glad to hear it, mother. What has the doctor to say about my illness? Am I not going to get cured?" He begged of his mother to say something positive.

The mother kept quiet. She had nothing to say about the cure of the illness.

She only sobbed incessantly.

Ab's father was outspoken. He could never keep quiet.

"A Youngman living in today's world has multiple choices of activities offered to him by open, free and pragmatic society in which he lives in. Religious activities, humanitarian works, acquisition of knowledge from the vast resources lie before him, numerous sporting activities, not only help one to develop physically but also offer economic gains in sundry ways if taken seriously. Multiple business propositions including expansive I.T. programmes and the last resort of a scoundrel, the political life are some of the options open before him. He can chose anyone as hobby which may turn into his profession. I wonder at my son's short-comings and short-sightedness. May God help him now?" The father's philosophical outbursts irritated the mother, but it had its solid point too.

Ab. was admitted to a special ward of the hospital. His father did not spare any money including his savings for his cure, but the disease had spread into his system like the tentacles of an octopus. So far no medical treatment was invented which the doctors' could administered on his cure. A hefty, handsome body gradually escalated into a thin, lifeless embodiment. He lost appetite; energy thereby lost the will to forge ahead. Ab. parents ran from pillar to post, consulting various doctors at a premium. He met many religious heads, irrespective of sects, denominations, and positions. Nobody could find a solution to ease the hearts of the desperate parents, eager to see their sin's recovery. But it was in vain. Ab. was convulsing on the day Rani came to the hospital. She was not allowed to enter the ward to see Ab. She peeped inside the room through a glass window, saw the skeleton figure of a man, bereft of youthful glow, immobile figure of a human being, sunken eyes, inactive arms and legs, appeared to be out of place in human society. Rani burst out in grief. She was inconsolable. She sobbed and uttered, "Why is he alone the victim of his circumstances and not me?"

The founder of Young Man's Christian Association (Y.M.C.A.) was a visionary. Two centuries ago he conceived a unique idea of establishing an organization in which the youths of the world could involve themselves in various sporting, cultural and social activities. It keeps them away from mischief, anti-social activities and terrorist's outlook. Emphasis was given also to religious and humanitarian activities. If Ab. and scores of other young fellows like him afflicted by the killer diseases would have access to all the activities of Y.M.C.A., the world would have been a better place for them to live in.

As a last resort Ab's parents decided to take counsel of the preceptors of all religious denominations existing in the country.

First, they went to a temple to meet the greatest 'Tantrick' of all times. The sage in question studied his horoscope in detail, his date of birth, the influence of the celestial beings on his life, past, present and future, and surmised,

"Ab. is a victim of his 'Karma', the action, there is no remedy for it."

Ab's father consulted a 'Mulvi', the great preceptor of repute who only said, "Your son is not a 'Jehadi', so his doom is inevitable."

Lastly the parents went to a believers meeting in a nearby park. The man expound all religious thoughts printed in the Holy Book.

"Disaster of any kind is a part of our daily life. Be it earthquake, volcanic eruption, sunami, drought, hurricane, flood etc. all are part of natural phenomenon. We are helpless against such calamities. But knowing it fully well, the impending disaster, prevention of which could have been implemented and taken care of with the timely intervention. There is justification of Ab. plunging into the monstrous ailment is a mark of stupidity."

He quoted at random from the Old and New Books of the Scripture all the wise saying,

"Ab. must have faith in God. He should join the band wagon of the merry believers, then only he might get cure, being pushed down on the floor by one of the faith healers."

The Buddhist monk did not say anything of his own, but uttered the same stereotyped wise sayings, in fact, the motto of the religious order, "Remember the wise and the enlightened one; take cognizance of the great religion, its essence in your life and fall back on to the religious establishment of the Buddhist religious order."

The Jain 'Muni' kept mum and pointed out at the statue of 'Savanagola" for relief.

Ab's father was not relieved of his anguish of pain and sorrow. He witnessed the slow escalation of his son into the doom. He cried along with his wife and looked up to the sky either in condemnation or solace.

Abhijeet died peacefully. His friends, relatives and neighbours refused to carry the body to the cremation ground. Ab' s father and Rani's dad along with a few hired men, ignorant of the cause of this death carried the body to an unknown place, away from the civilized society for the last rites.

Jogen Khan

6

The Bond

The motorists passing through the crossing of Rao Tularam Marg and the Outer Ring Road near the West End Colony were surprised to see a novel gesture every morning by the driver of a Qualis Motor Van. The young man, probably twenty-six years of age offering a polythin bag to a beggar regularly without failures. The young man was definitely a driver of the car, which belonged to a wealthy person of Delhi. The beggar was a leprosy patient, a deadly disease that could cause death once afflicted unless precaution was taken in the initial stage.

The old beggar was seen on that crossing sometimes during the later part of the day as well. But his appearance on the spot in the morning could tell the time of the day to a regular traveler. The twain met there from Monday through Friday. The weekend the meeting was sporadic.

"It's a strange phenomenon." Said Mr. Kapur to his colleague Mr. Gupta, traveling in the same car to the same office where a multi-national foreign company employed both of them.

"I think the man is helping the beggar out of sympathy or for the atonement of the sin of his previous life" Mr. Gupta said on the ground of civility and not to annoy his friend.

"I feel there is a perfect understanding between them. The driver belongs to a notorious gang of swindlers. He has engaged the beggar to keep an eye on someone incognito who might be their dreaded enemy." Mr. Kapur said in jest.

"Let them do whatever their intention is, we haven't got anything to do with it" replied Mr. Gupta in a curt manner. "Moreover, it is none of our business. The responsibility lies with the protector of the law." He added further to discontinue with the topic.

Mr. Gupta was not that keen to stop discussing the plight of the helpless beggar.

"The beggar might be a police spy. The driver is the agent. The former watches the passers by, trying to detect the movements of the dreaded criminal, whom the police force is going after." Mr. Kapur wanted to continue with the discussion so that he did not have to hear the same stereotyped nagging story of the others wife's idiosyncrasies of daily household affairs.

"I shouldn't meddle with the affair of a mere beggar. The fellow has nothing to do with life so he's begging." Mr. Gupta expressed his irritation and hoped such a mundane topic should not be taken up by anyone who was having a social stature of highest degree.

"Begging is a social stigma. It should be condemned by all." Mr. Kapur said in irritation. "Why should we bother about it? It is none of our business. We are not beggars so it does not concern us at all." Mr. Gupta kept quiet after saying this.

"Look at that man. Why is he so interested in that silly beggar?" Asked a young executive to his college who happened to cross that way frequently on his way to work.

"I don't know man. Thank God we are not beggars". The colleague answered absent mindedly.

"I feel rather ashamed of myself to find wretched fellows on the streets of my city. There is no one here to get rid of the menace from the street of our beloved city," said the first young executive.

"He's a beggar under compulsion. Look at him closely he is afflicted by leprosy." The executive pointed his finger to his co-executive friend.

"1 don't understand how even today people suffer from such an incurable disease when the biological and medical sciences have advanced so much. All government agencies all over the world are spending so much money for the research work in this regard."

"The wretches sometime are not genuine. They pose and pretend to be afflicted. It's a ploy to earn money without working and putting in hard labor."

"They are so disgusting to look at. Their presence in the streets of the capital betrays the advancement we are making in all spheres of our life."

"The government and the civic bodies should pass stringent laws to get rid of the menace."

The young executives stopped their car at the red light everyday at the same time when the driver met the beggar and commented on the hopeless predicament of the man and suggested their remedial effects. The signal turned green and off they went to their destination.

The middle-aged foreigner, sitting at the rear of a chauffer driven swanky car, marked CD on a blue plate, looked askance at the sight and felt pity on the helpless beggar but at the same time quietly praised the driver of the Qualis for the benevolent gesture shown to him.

"My heart cries for the wretched condition of the man. I wish I were in a position to bring succor to the helpless creature of God. I am also glad to note that a lady has taken up the responsibility in our own time to look after the afflicted men and women. She had established hospitals and rehabilitation centers all over the world for them where the dedicated workers keep them busy looking after them. Her selfless work will soon earn her the coveted title of sainthood". He talked to himself every day as his car stopped at the red light for a couple of minutes.

Every evening he discussed the plight of the afflicted people with his wife.

"We must visit these people once in a while and see for ourselves what we could do to cure the poor people of the dreaded disease." The wife said to her husband who was really carried away by the incident.

"It is our prime duty. A human being should extend the helping hand to another human being when in need, irrespective of caste, creed and religious affiliation, but our hands are tied. We belong to the diplomatic core; therefore we are bound to follow certain code of conduct. Our movement is restricted. We confine all our activities within the premises of the Embassy building. We are not free to move like the citizens of the country."

"But we can help them through the missionaries who have vowed to work for the downtrodden people of the country" the compassionate wife of the diplomat suggested to the man who is sympathetic to the cause of the poor and diseased persons. On the next day he threw a hundred rupees note to the beggar as his car came to a grinding halt at the red light traffic signal.

The young lady put a scented handkerchief on her nose each time she drove through the way. She dipped it in the eau de cologne bottle, anticipating the odour of a dead carcass of an animal to hit her nose, as she appeared on the spot every morning. Rarely could she sail through easily when the green light was on. She prayed fervently for the signal to be in her favour, but that could never happen. Every morning her car stopped at the same spot when she could not help but turn her eyes on the scene. The wait gave her a couple of minutes to catch up with her make up. She dexterously gave the final touch on her face. Powdered it with the soft tender brush, eyelashes were given the final touch and the lips had the last coat of red paint before she went to work.

"What is the use of living a life of a beggar? Moreover, when one is afflicted by an incurable disease like the leprosy." The lady asked her female co-passenger working on the next desk in an MNC in Gurgaon.

"It's a mystery. We human beings are too insignificant persons to unravel the diverse mysteries of the world." The co-passenger replied to appease her.

The co-passenger's philosophy of life irritated the lady so she replied in the most fitting manner,

"I do not think one should live a diseased life as the beggar is living. He should disappear from the face of the earth and leave us alone to live a clean life." The lady replied.

"Who is going to kill him? The laws of the land will punish you as a murderer if you kill him. In the event you engage the professional killers, one day they will be apprehended and imagine your plight. Poison him; you'll be traced by the police. I don't understand why is the man appears to you a menace?" The other girl was rather ill at ease at her inhuman attitude and unintelligent remarks.

"He doesn't match my beauty. You know I mix with handsome young men. They are the perfect human beings. They dance, go to parties and walk with me. They keep me occupied all the days long." The lady said in agitated mood to snub her co-passenger and the philanthropic attitude of her.

It was rather a stupid reply, thought her co-passenger.

"Your beauty will not last long. In the days to come you will turn haggard. Then all those handsome beaus will leave your company. You never know, free and unlicensed companionship may cause Aids, the most dreaded disease of our time." The co-passenger got fed up with her irrational, bias and pessimistic concept of life, so turned her face on the other side of the car.

Our lady in question thought her companion a cynic and she had no jest left in her life.

The school children passing the way in swanky cars and buses always cast casual glances at the poor beggar. Their conversations veered round the topic in sundry manners.

"Why is the man so dirty? Doesn't he take bath?" asked a seven years old boy to his father, a Western foreign diplomat on the way to AES in Chanakyapuri."

"He's a beggar. A serious disease called leprocy has badly affected him. In our country the disease is controlled, but here the poor ignorant people suffer from it. You must remember the government and various other social agencies are doing a lot to bring succor to them in different manners." The diplomat replied in a lucid manner to his son's query.

"See how ugly that man looks. His skin has developed in a multi-color fashion.' A boy of class six standards said to his class-mates.

"He's a beggar. You see that man in white uniform. He's giving him food. The man must be very kind to him. I see him every day there doing a marvelous job." The co-mate replied.

"That poor beggar looks so out of place. I don't understand why he has been in the first place allowed to sit there. He is spoiling the image of the country." The first boy expressed his unhappiness at the sight of the poor man.

"He too is a citizen of the country. He has every right to be there. That is what we read in political science. Our social studies teacher has expressed her view on this subject more emphatically than on any other topic in the book." The second boy seemed to be more realistic and human in his outlook of life.

"I wish I go down there and forcibly remove him from there." The boy finally passed the caustic remark. His unsympathetic view disturbed the other boy to a great extent and he thought twice before he took his seat beside him in the bus on the next day.

"Hey, look at the hero he's sitting there again today. Look at the man in clean cloth. He brought something for him also this morning." A boy of class eleven standards passed the caustic remark.

His classmate also studied in the same class gave a reciprocal answer.

"Imagine him acting as the father of the matinee idol of today in one of those movies in Bollywood." The second boy replied in a curt manner.

"The entire film will be contaminated by the disease he is carrying in his person. The people will begin to hate the producer of the film. In the end it will be a flop movie." The first boy replied sarcastically.

"I don't think it is going to be a bad movie if the subject is tackled judiciously. In fact it may receive rave reviews from the audience with caring hearts." The second boy suddenly turned sympathetic and spoke in defense of the poor miserable person.

The lady teacher of the nearby public school spotted the leaper everyday on her way to school. At times, out of sympathy she threw a coin in his direction. She felt it was an act of penitence for all the sins committed by her, knowingly or being unconscious of it on the previous day. She boasted of her benevolent act of charity to her husband and children at home in the evening.

"I am sure I have been doing a great job in the way of offering a few coins every day. It is an act of God." She told the family one-day in the dining table.

"I'm sure you're doing your bit honestly. It is surely an act of God." Her husband repeated the last sentence spoken by her.

"Mummy blows her trumpet quite liberally." Her eldest son remarked while she went to get hot 'roti' from the kitchen.

"Of course, I do agree with my detractor that the amount of money I donate is nothing, but each drop of water makes the mighty ocean." She quipped after returning from the kitchen.

"I'm convinced what you do according to your mind's dictate. I am with you and would endorse your noble gesture." The henpecked husband said with a broad smile on his face.

"We must do something sister for that poor wretch over there. 1 think he is a beggar and troubled with the most dreaded disease. The young Nun just joined the convent at Vasant Vihar looked at the poor beggar and said to the Mother Superior who travelled along with her that way everyday.

"Sister Lucia you're very kind. Your sympathetic heart goes with the man. This is a Godly act." The Mother Superior answered her in a subtle way, as her profession would demand of it.

"We can take him to one of our many rehabilitation centers dotted all over the city." She suggested innocently.

"Sister, I must inform you, we have tried our best to accommodate him in our home for the lepers in Leper colony on the outskirts of the city. But he won't go there. His contention is that he earns his living in the city at ease. Begging helps him make his both ends meet. In fact with the money he earns here he is able to rent a small hut in the heart of the city. Of course it is in a 'Jhuggi' cluster but it is a place he can afford to pay. Only difficulty he is facing now is the disease he is suffering from. May God bless his soul?"

"Thank you Mother for making it clear to me with the information. My young heart gets troubled for nothing at the sight of the suffering of God's creatures. I am not able to bear the pain and sufferings of the fellow human beings. My heart is week and soul is feeble." The young novice admitted her frailty to the senior Nun.

'I'm sure you will learn in due course. There are more painful acts we encounter every day in this world than the good services rendered by our fellow human beings. You have to learn to live with it."

"Look at that beggar. The idiot has no place to go. He will die on that spot any day. I feel like literally kicking him out of that place. He's an eye sore." One Quails driver engaged in ferrying the call center employees told the passengers in the car.

"He is a beggar. I am in the least bothered about him." Said a young upstart who had spent smooth young days under the care of his parents and had seen very little of the world at large.

"The sight is gruesome. What are our civic authorities doing? They should get rid of the menace from the street of the city. I feel sick at the sight of the ugly man. The other man is offering him a packet is a fool. We have such idiots here encouraging these beggars to flourish. I wish they both are arrested and put in the jail for life for disturbing the peace of the civilized world." A girl of twenty years of age said to her friends.

Her outfits could cause palpitation in the hearts of the young fellows traveling with her every day in the same car. The one forth of the protruding breasts through her frontal V shaped shirt made the other young men traveling in the car hungry for intimate relationship. They cast their greedy eyes on her neat mound at the posterior and hoped to have a glorious light touch while descending from the car or embarking. The chances were slim.

"You're right. The other fellow standing next to him is an imposter. He is trying to be famous by offering him food. Look at the beggar. He is showing his gratitude with folded hands. I am sure sister you're right in your assessment of the man and the beggar." The young upstart remarked. This young man was trying to curry favour with her and was trying hard for sometime for an opening to meet her privately.

He had the chance of meeting her at a restaurant in the evening. His clandestine meetings lasted for a while after this day. Unfortunately it came to an abrupt end as quickly as it sprang. He realized that he was a part of a triangular gang of the kindred souls.

"I was taught in school by the scripture teacher that all men are the children of God. He had created all of us in the image of His own self. Don't tell me God looks like the old Beggar. Then we must have been created by the devil plagiarizing the handiwork of God's image." The third young man said to the others.

The immediate result of his caustic remark made everybody chuckle in the car. For the first time in the history of their journey together in the car the young dame smiled at him. The immediate reaction was the expansion of the chest of the man. It elongated a couple of inches. He was happy that she recognized him at last.

"We must not make fun of God. He's omnipresent, omniscience and omniscient. He was there at the beginning of the universe; he is present now in our midst and will remain with us till the end of the world. He has a purpose behind all His creation." Commented by a dark girl whom they all abhor, especially the boys, for her distorted profile and ordinary look. No one ever looked at her direction. Even the young girl avoided looking at her, being inconsiderate.

"What purpose does He have behind the creation of the leper?" The other girl shot at her companion.

"In the Holy Scripture it is mentioned that the Son of God has asked His followers to Love each other. Do well to the fellow human beings. For as much as we do to the others we do it for Him. Most probably the man is doing to the poor beggar what his maker wants him to do. He has extended his helping hands to comfort the poor wretch."

In the meantime the signal was clear and the driver started the ignition to set the car in motion for their destination. But before releasing the clutch he spat twice on the street either to express his indignation or to censure the beggar for his dishonorable living on this beautiful earth.

"Thank God for his mercy on me. I am not born as a leper." The last sentence was uttered by the unattractive looking girl.

Everybody was stunned to hear the true confession.

A few days later all the protagonists of the story read a stunning revelation in the local newspaper.

"A good Samaritan" was the caption written under a picture of the leper being helped by a young man. The news read as thus,

"The people traveling in the morning hours through the crossing of Outer Ring Road and Rao Tularam at the circle near the Central School are used to witness a scene of a beggar afflicted by leprosy is offered food packages every day at the same time by a man in white clothes.

In gratitude the beggar thanked him with folded hands, depicting a scene from the scripture when the Son of God voluntarily cured ten lepers but only one out of them came back to thank Him. It seemed the man was doing the job of the good Samaritan.

In the twenty first century when the world is running after glamour, amassing wealth to an unlimited extent, killing each other for monetary gain, fighting for power and position, it is an extraordinary feat shown by the young man.

The onlookers surely are of different opinions as to the identity of the man doing the job. Some think he is an eyesore. To a few persons it is a benign gesture on the part of the young driver. Yet some of them are of the opinion that the man is in league with the leper is encouraging the disease to grow so that he earns his living at ease. Some even blamed the civic authorities for their lackadaisical attitudes towards the poor of the city.

The latest stunning news received at the news desk of the press club was that the man was not to be found anywhere for the last two days. Even the beggar was not aware of his whereabouts. When asked about the man the beggar looked forlorn and pointed at the Sky. The scene spoke volume of the intention of God. "It is also observed that the leper is on the way to recovery of the dreaded ailment. The incident had a tremendous repercussion to the people who witnessed the scene daily. It shook them to the marrow."

The general readers of the paper thought it was a hoax. The regular observers and readers of the papers thought it otherwise. Everybody suddenly became eager to be there on the spot and see for themselves.

"Was it a miracle?" The thought was uppermost in the minds of those witnessed the scene daily.

Mr. Gupta and Mr. Kapur boarded the car silently. They even did not look at each other for a while. Of course in no time they reached the red light. To their utter surprise they found there was a terrible traffic snarl at the crossing. The reason being that a loaded truck upturned in the middle of the road when the drunk driver of the truck was trying to negotiate with the other trucks coming from the opposite direction a couple of minutes ago.

"It will take sometime to get the snarl cleared by the police." Mr. Gupta opened his mouth suddenly to make Mr. Kapur speak a few words.

"I see," was the small answer uttered by Mr. Kapur.

After a minutes silence Mr. Gupta asked him, "Have you read the hyped news in the newspaper yesterday about the leper and the young man. It seems he has disappeared from the scene of event permanently."

"Yes I too read in the newspaper the sensational news of the disappearance of the man, deserting the leper to his fate."

"I wonder what the poor beggar is going to do now."

"He will find someone else. There is no dearth of good men on the earth."

"I wonder who'd take the place of the benevolent man!"

"Why it is not you. You're so concerned about him" Mr. Kapur suggested.

"I am indeed. But I cannot take the burden alone. I need help. Why not you join me and together we can bring a little relief to the helpless condition of the beggar." Mr. Gupta said in excitement.

"Yes I will." Expressed Mr. Kapur with elation.

After that day the onlookers who happened to pass that way everyday at the same time, observed it when either Mr. Gupta or Mr. Kapur got down from the car and offered a box of food to the beggar with folded hands and bowed heads. Sometimes they brought clothes, medicine and fruits for the man of destiny. Then all the cars following their car came to a grinding halt in respect of the ceremony performed in the absence of the good Samaritan even though the traffic light had turned in their favour.

The diplomat dreamt a dream. He saw in his inward vision that the land of plenty was beckoning him with out-stretched hands. During his five years stay in the country he always wished that his next posting would be in Washington D.C. and elevated to the rank of the deputy secretary. Here he was the hot favourite with the top bosses in the Embassy. Deeply religious he prayed to God to bless him and fulfill his heart's desire.

"I would like to have a baby girl born to us while in Washington. Our son will have someone to give him company to play with." He whispered in his wife's ear while kissing her for the last time before retiring for the night.

"You hope too much. I am not the maker of our destination. It is God who decides what would happen to us in the next moment in our lives. We are insignificant before Him. Good night darling. You must be very tired after the day's hard work" she replied. On the next moment she could hear only a faint sound of "Good Night" as an echo. All was quiet after that.

The diplomat could not believe his eyes. There was a huge crowd gathered around the spot where he had seen the poor leper was placed in an improvised handcart. Regularly a man used to offer him a packet of food for which the beggar expressed his gratitude with folded hands as reciprocal gesture. Realizing the amount of time the policeman on duty would take to clear the jam the diplomat decided to go down and find out for himself the reason for such gathering. He stood silently at the rear of the crowd to ascertain the depth of the situation. He could only hear faintly the beggar was saying,

"I don't know who that man was. But he was like God to me. He fed me everyday with nourishing food, clothed me with clean, descent clothes and promised to find a shelter for me in the close vicinity of this place. My heart breaks at the sad news of his demise at the hands of unscrupulous men and women.' After saying this he burst into tears. The cry of one human being for another human being was inconsolable.

"How do you know that he is dead?" A man from the crowd asked them.

"I dreamt of his death last night in my sleep". the leper replied.

"Hello brother, the signal has turned in your favour. Go and occupy your seat in your respective vehicle." The traffic policeman shouted at the inquisitive onlookers.

The diplomat took the last look at the poor wretch before boarding his car. Their eyes met. A compassionate glow emanated from his eyes, which moved his soul.

" It seemed the man wanted to say something to me." He told his wife in the evening. "He was definitely expecting something from you." His wife said without showing any interest. She was slicing the roasted turkey for dinner.

"I wish I could give him a slice of that meat." The diplomat said while not quietly paying any heed to what she was saying.

"You've changed, darling over a couple of days". His wife rebuked him for wistful thinking.

The foppish lady danced last night at a local club with at least half a dozen young boys whom she considered handsome, affluent and full of resources.

"These are my dear friends. I really enjoy their company immensely. Life is too short to be wasted in doing nothing. It is full of mirth, joviality and entertaining. I am not a beggar like the leper who sits all day long in one place and begs. I keep my life busy with all sort of works."

"I'm sure you are very popular with the boys and rightly so. You're pretty to look at. You have an attractive feature. You dress well in the latest fashion. Moreover, you have no reservation as far free mixing is concerned. This is exactly what the guys see in you." Her co-passenger remarked at the end of their brief conversation.

"The signal is long to get clear. What could be the reason, I wonder!" The pretty girl asked her co-passenger while sniffing the scented handkerchief. She always turned her face away from the tramp as he appeared to her squalid, impoverished and an eye sore. As usual their car also stopped at the red light signal.

The unusual delay of the signal to get clear made her inquisitive, so turned her face towards the crowd.

"It must be the end of that wretch. Henceforth our eyes will not be focused on a miserable beggar whom I despise from the core my heart." Finding her co-passenger missing from her seat she talked to herself in a soft tone.

In the meantime the other girl returned from the scene where a motley crowd gathered to witness a supposed to be a 'happening' event of an unusual nature.

"Why have all the passengers gathered together around the leper? Is he dead? I shall offer a substantial amount of donation for his cremation." She was elated and her expression of hatred for an unfortunate creature of God's creation surprised all in the car, including the driver.

"You are not aware of the news that was published in the local newspaper. The beggar is being healed gradually. It is an unusual phenomenon. Never heard of such an incident in the medical history of the world. People are gathering there to witness the miracle. The news was published in all leading newspapers of the capital. You have not read it? I am surprised." She asked her with a look of surprise.

"I have better news to read. Who on earth will spend the precious time in reading such an ordinary affair." She said curtly and turned her face on the other side of the car.

But before leaving the place the girl turned her face towards the beggar. What did she see would remain forever with her in the days to come. The man's face was filled with smile, his eyes showed a compassionate glow and his right hand raised to heaven as if to bless all the inmates living on the surface of the earth.

She got a jolt.

The girl was disgusted initially, but soon a feeling of different sort developed in her mind. She began to perceive things in different perspective.

In the office she asked a few weird questions regarding living of a meaningful life to her co-workers which were rather fascinating and matured. It stunned the other girl.

"What has happened to you? You held a different opinion of life previously, biased, full of pride, hateful and intimidating. But now I find you have changed, perhaps for good." The co-worker said in a skeptical tone.

On next weekend she missed the usual rendezvous at the club. She ignored all phone calls and refrained from doing so herself. A kind of depression replaced her ever happy mind which was rather alarming. On Sunday she stayed at home and uttered a few incomprehensible words in silence. She prayed for the first time in her life.

In the afternoon she went out without any make up, glossy and attractive outfits. No costly ornament decked her body. She looked a simple girl of rustic sort.

The neighbors looked at her in suspicion. She purchased a few articles of domestic use. All kinds of material of fashionable sort were missing from her carry bag. In fact people observing her idiosyncratic behaviors were surprised to see her offering alms to the beggars. In the evening she paid a visit to the local temple and stayed in prayerful position for long. Instead of buying the roses she bought marigold flowers.

By the time the night fell she was completely transformed from a foppish girl to a moderately homely girl.

The school boys were unusually very silent this morning as they came near the scene of daily occurrence. The crowd gathered around the spot drew their attention. They all spoke simultaneously to express their stunning views.

"I think he's dead."

"The policemen are trying to vacate him forcibly."

"I feel sorry for the poor beggar. He has no where to go from here."

"I feel sorry for the good man who is trying to help him."

"He's a nuisance to be there. It is high time the administration swing into action."

The children uttered some unsavoury remarks at the scene of action.

"Do you know an article is written in today's daily newspapers about the leprosy afflicted beggars and the man, supposed to be his beneficiary? Here it is, please read." The teacher produced a Newspaper.

There was literally a scramble to grab the paper. In the process it got torn to pieces. Somehow the teacher was able to retrieve a few pieces from the remainder and read out to them. The immediate reaction was that they all began to sulk, not being depressed but à sense of guilt struck them for being rude and inconsiderate in their remarks of the good relationship the beggar had with the other man.

"We must not pass any caustic remark to anyone without knowing the true fact." The teacher said to remind them of their position in society.

"I think the other man was an incarnation of God himself." The first boy said remorsefully.

"How do you know that?" The second boy asked him being an atheist.

"You see the man has disappeared completely from the scene of action." The boy replied in a very convincing manner.

Henceforth, there was a perceptible change in the lives of those children traveling in the school bus, also witnesses to the miracle.

"I will not go to a junk shop anymore and spend uselessly, instead I rather donate the money to leprosy unit run by the Missionaries of Charity." The first boy told his father as they came to McDonald's shop in the Mall.

"I am surprised at your stunning decision." The father remarked observing his son's sudden change in taste and behaviour.

"My entire friends circle decided to keep away from extravagant expenses. We have formed a club where we have decided to donate every week fifty percent of our pocket money to the poor."

"Son, I am greatly pleased at your noble gesture. In a developing country like ours if all young citizens think in the same way as you are doing now, it will be a great country in the years to come." His father felt truly very proud of him.

The father of the first boy was greatly surprised at his son's epoch-making decision. He became more inquisitive to go deep into the matter.

"Our son has changed a great deal suddenly. It makes me very uneasy to see his recent behaviour." The father told his mother at bedtime.

"I don't see anything alarming. He's quite normal. He eats well, studies vigorously, plays with his friends and sleeps well. Only change I find in him is that he doesn't want to go out and spend money, instead he likes to donate the same for the poor." She whispered into his ears.

"It's a great quality in a boy of his age to possess. Only fear I have in my mind about his future. I hope he doesn't turn a monk and leaves us for ever. He's our only son. Our future is at stake without him." He expressed his obsessive view on the issue.

"Go to sleep. The future of man is not in our hand. God will show us everything in due course." After this she turned her face on the other side of bed and fell into deep slumber.

The inquisitive mind of the father could not stay at rest. He resolved to go into the depth of the situation for himself.

The father went from pillar to post, met his son's teachers, neighbors, local friends, close relatives and a couple of sages. No one could give him a perfect answer. Each one of them interpreted his version in his own way. The sages studied his horoscope, read his palm and consulted celestial beings, then pronounced a verdict, unfounded, indefinable and not viable. Then one day he gave a lift to a small boy who traveled in the same bus with his son. While talking to him on sundry topics he came to know about the beggar and his companion.

On realizing the cause of his son's transformation he also decided to do something good. "I'll donate one tenth of my salary to the poor from next month. My son has opened my eyes. It is better to give than to take. There is more pleasure in giving than taking."

His wife was, first got flabbergasted, but on realizing the present thought of his mind, she endorsed his sacrifice for a cause.

The second boy, a student of class eight, the only son of Mr. and Mrs. Oswal, the steel tycoon, lived in East End area of the city. Of late he had taken a fancy to travel in the bus with his friends. In fact, the bus in which they traveled to school was the property of the Oswals. When his father was at home the boy traveled in the red convertible Buick. His father loved to drive the classy car. They had another twenty two cars parked around the house, some were priceless. Last weekend he went to Australia to take part in a boy's cricket tournament at Adelaide. It was a day's affair. On Sunday night he was back to his own house. On Monday he witnessed the scene of transformation at the red light crossmg.

"We'll be going to a long tour of Europe during next holidays. It's only a fortnight hence." The second boy's father announced the good news to the family during dinner. He paused and waited for a wild scream from his son as it happened in the past. It surprised him a great deal for the morbid silence all around.

"Why son, are you not happy at the good news?" the father asked his heir to the unaccountable wealth he had accumulated.

"I am dad." The son replied in a simple sentence.

"No elation, no reciprocal gesture, no wild jubilation. I wonder what could be the reason!" The father said to his wife after dinner. "Do you know anything about it?" He further enquired.

"I am not very sure. But he had related to me an incident he had encountered the other day while going to school. Of course we read the incident of a leprosy afflicted beggar was attended by a driver of a Qualis car, generally believed by the onlookers his son who unflinchingly helped him everyday with food and other necessary things. He suddenly disappeared from the scene and soon after this the beggar began to get cured. Our son, all the other boys were the witness to the scene of action and the transformation of the man."

"It has a deeper implication behind the entire incident. I must find out its meaning soon." He said to his wife and went out to the lawn for a walk.

At night sleep eluded him for a while. After tossing and turning in bed for a couple of hours he got up and went to the room of his son. What forced him to go closer to him he was not very sure but he saw a glowing light emanated from the face of his son. It indicated he had turned over a new leaf. He was pleased to witness the scene. Soon after this he went to bed and fell into deep slumber.

Next day he drove one of his upscale cars, the priceless possession of the family to the scene of action. He looked into the eyes of the beggar and learnt the meaning of life. The beggar, as usual, wished him in folded hands, asked for alms and in the end thanked him for his generous giving.

A sea of change took place in his life. He built a place of worship in his sprawling bungalow where regular worship and study of the scripture took place in real earnest. He closed down his domestic bar, destroyed all the bottles of intoxicating drinks and broke all the glasses, which were a real prized possession of his. The children were made to toe the line. His wife followed suit.

The young Nun of the Anciliatory Convent in the Vasant Vihar area was in a quandary. She was opposed to the dogmatic religion practiced in the Convent which, at times suffocated her to the core. A kind of liberal and pragmatic religion would be the right answer in today's religious world hovering around her. She constantly sought for a change in her words and actions from deadly conservative ideologies of the sect to a liberal one.

"This convent runs on traditional lines. Here we follow the age-old practices of the church. Our liturgy for worship is based on the ancient Roman Catholic Church. Our life at the convent depends on three pillars of wisdom - poverty, obedience and celibacy. It's a disciplined order. Liberty of any kind, personal, religious and social are not tolerated here. We lived like this for two thousand years. If it does not suit anyone, she can leave the order. But before leaving the order one should think twice." The septuagenarian old mother superior said in a soft, yet stern voice.

The mother said this in the morning of that auspicious day when they all passed through the red light crossing where the beggar was slowly but steadily getting healed. The young Nun too got down from the car to witness the transformation that was taking place in the leper. The man smiled at her, blessed her with raised hands and in the end thanked her for the visit. The sparkling eyes spoke to her the mystery of God. She left the place filled with wisdom and Godly fear. She boarded the car silently. The old mother realized the change that had taken place in her heart.

"Yes Mother, I understand your defense of our faith. I shall try to emulate you and all our predecessors who have dedicated their lives to uphold the tradition of the church.

Henceforth a remarkable change took place in her life. She reached the prayer hall before everybody else. She said the prayers in the loudest voice and said "Amen" in a vociferous tone. She always volunteered her services to work among the lepers. Soon she became a popular figure among the sisters of the Missionary of Charity. Whenever she passed the crossing of Rao Tularam Road and the Outer Ring Road near West End corner she closed her eyes and prayed a long prayer of Thanksgiving.

Sister Fonseka of the order of the Nuns of Her Holiness formally inducted in the order and was sent to Mundi where they had a hospital for the lepers. She worked day in and day out among the unfortunate wretches, not exactly to cure them but to bring relief to their physical pain and mental agony with love and care. Her devotional services to the cause of bringing succor to the suffering souls was praised by all and sundry, even she got a letter of appreciation from no other than His Holiness the Pope.

Unfortunately Sister Fonseka lost her purity and got afflicted by the same disease for which she had dedicated her life being inspired by the leper whom she had shown sympathy in one point of her young life.

The young driver of the hired car that ferried the call center employees to Gurgaon from their respective home to the centers of their working places had the habit of spitting indiscriminately on both sides of the car after pouring a mouthful of harmful tobacco called the 'Gutka' in his mouth in the hope of getting a kick or to get relief from his otherwise tedious work. He did it also to get rid of the monotony of the job. He expressed his at the sight of the poor leper. On the day of revelation of God's infinite power of mercy and grace bestowed upon the poor leper, the driver became aware of his surroundings and took to heart the work of the divine authority that guide us in everyday activities. Immediate effect was that he changed overnight. The aura of divine light fell upon him. He began to dream of a better days to come. Perhaps the same God might change his life too. Henceforth he stopped chewing tobacco, refrained from spitting on the streets and stopped visiting the bad quarters in the evenings. All his friends were surprised to find him turned over a new leaf.

"He has no more interest in the consumption of intoxicating drinks." His best friend commented.

"He has been praying fervently to God of his belief to find him a good wife and to settle down to a righteous life." The second friend said to the others.

"I'm sure he had seen a vision" The third friend chipped in.

The school teacher heard the news from a colleague of her in the staff common room. All eight senior teachers gathered together in the room during recess on that day, which was unusual. Normally they all had the staggering timings so they come and go, eat their food in isolation, exchange a few words of the problem each one of them was facing in their home fronts. The topic of the servants, their idiosyncratic behaviors, and the extent of the stealing done by them and chronic absence from work were the topics for discussion. But today it was different.

"Have you read the news" asked the senior physics teacher to the Math's teacher. "What is it all about?" the Math's teacher asked very casually.

"The Miracle!" the physics teacher said emphatically hoping to hit the point directly. "The Miracle. Is it possible? Are we not living in the twenty first century?" The Chemistry teacher butted in to ridicule the issue.

"Why Miracles can take place any time in any century at any place." N.K., the teacher of moral science traveling that way every day said with alacrity.

"It's a hoax. There is no such thing as miracle." He replied curtly.

"You must come and see the old beggar afflicted by the dreaded disease known universally as leprosy is recovering slowly. It is believed that a man in white clothes offered him food for some days. He's not there any more. After his disappearance the beggar started recovering from the disease." The moral science teacher said to nullify all views on the subject.

"We don't believe you." They all said in one accord to prove how stupid he might be. One of them went even a step further and said,

"These dim-witted believers are trying to propagate their religion through the insignificant incident which has no base or scientific proof behind it. The fundamentalists in the country should oppose it."

N. K. Sir witnessed the scene and had really first hand knowledge of the incident felt hurt. But he resigned to his fate and said, "My own faith will remain steadfast forever. I shall not budge an inch and compromise with them. Let them think what they all wish to but I believe the incident is an act of God."

"Who is he standing close to the beggar?" N.K. Sir said in surprise. "He is the one made fun of me in the common room last week. Now what is he doing there. I wonder!" He said to himself. Since he was not able to see his profile from the back he never uttered a word next day in the common room. But he stared at him all through the day which unnerved the man.

On the next morning N.K. Sir found the man again at the spot stooping down and asking the leper questions,

"Who are you?"

"I'm a poor beggar." The beggar replied.

"Are you a miracle man?" The teacher asked him again.

"I do not know what you are asking about." He gave a quizzical reply.

In the meantime the red light was cleared and we all moved on.

"Please have it." The skeptical teacher held his Tiffin box in front of N.K. Sir. It was full of choicest savory - sweets, candies and pieces of cakes.

It surprised all of them present there in the common room, since they were aware how taut he was in his outlook. He never shared anything, neither in words nor in kind with them so long as he was working in the institution.

The Tiffin box was passed all around them. They too shared their bits and pieces with him for the first time.

After the school he met N.K.Sir outside the school gate and asked him a barrage of questions regarding God, heaven and redemption.

"We all are greatly influenced by the devil while living on earth. It induces us to commit various sins. Only after the confession of sins we are forgiven. In the case of the beggar, perhaps it was God who appeared in disguise of a young man who opened the eyes of all of us." N.K. Sir said in his simple, sure and virtuous way.

Today if one does cast a longing look at the place where the beggar met an unknown person a couple of months ago one can not find the duo exchanging the pleasantries, but instead one can encounter a family of eight, parents and six children are selling small bouquets of red roses. They are beggars, but not begging. They are laboring hard to make their ends meet in traditional way. The preservers of law act harshly and time and again have arrested them for unlawful activities. Still they persist. Someone has said these are the divine people, His own children. God works in mysterious ways.

7

Malai Mandir Bus Stop

She was there daily at the bus stop at 8:10 A.M. She would catch the bus number 620 exactly at 8:12 A.M. for a ride to her destination. A working girl, she could be a computer operator in an MNC, or a school teacher or a trainee. Whatever might be her profession she had to go there every day?

She did not appear to be a busy-body, looked very casual in her movements. She wore a pink coloured suit everyday. A small vanity bag dangled from her right arm, a shiny wrist watch with a golden colour band adorned her left arm and two silver coloured ear rings fitted her ears well. Her shoes matched her-dresses admirably.

Her thin yet smart well-maintained physic would speak volume of the self disciplined characteristic of the person. Since no part of her body was exposed to the view of the onlookers, it kept the chronic rapists at bay. Normally exposed naval, protruding and swollen breasts covered with transparent nylon tops of women create flutter in the hearts of men and stirred his passion to a boiling point. Fortunately she had none of those traits to invite the hunger of the passionate guys. Her profile was something to admire. Thin face with aquiline nose, cheeks caving in, long chin, two small pearl-like eyes embedded on it, quarter moon shaped eye-lashes placed on the forehead and perpetual Madonna like smile would draw the attention of the passers by.

No affluent, sophisticated and potential young man would pursue her as she did not carry any well-known family title after her name so no parents of the eligible bachelors would chase her. She walked on the streets of Delhi and rode the ordinary buses alone. She did not live in a posh colony, a status symbol she lacked. Her dress code was simple befitting to a modest, simple average girl. She lacked the vision of walking on the ramps half naked. Her face was not shown on the screens of cinemas halls or T. V. She even did not belong to any city of this vast land so lacked all the characteristics of an urban life.

She was a simple hilly girl. She might have been hailed from the hills of Garwal, Himachal or Uttaranchal Pradesh. Her Mongoloid feature would identify her filial connections. Due to lack of proper infrastructure in the hills of this country for human development the parents sent their children to the urban developed areas of this vast country. So the girl was here.

The old man noticed her on the first day of his arrival at the bus stop of Malai Mandir near Vasant Vihar and took a fancy to her presence there. He thought at least a company of descent sort would be there everyday. Her physical feature was nothing to attract the other men and women at the bus stop.

The waiting passengers were mostly ordinary people. There were uniformed school students waiting there with heavy bags and water bottles dangling from their shoulders. They were having endless chats among themselves, exchanging Pokemon cards and various other tit-bits. Their dresses were shabby, thin features and stooping bodies, all these were the hallmarks of the children of middle class people. A couple of rickety college students, a few bundles of papers in a side bags, squalid clothes of faded colours, would soon be haggling with the conductors for discount in the fares comprised the second category of people.

There were a few men in faded clothes with round Tiffin boxes around their shoulders, chewing forever destructive marinated beetle nuts and crushed tobacco leaves, spitting indiscriminately all over the place, starring at everyone, and sarcastic smiles on their faces also wait there every day for that particular bus to arrive.

A tall African girl, a sort of black beauty in skin-tight jeans and breast-hugging top also stands there. Some people look at her in contempt, without any reason, a few of them laugh at her, finding her odd in the midst of even people, in stature, colour and resources. Some quite appreciate her being brave and punctual with undaunted defying and 'couldn't careless' attitude. She stands there, nose in the air, clenched fists and aloof.

There are a few passengers pass their time talking to their peers. Stare at people, right and left, pass remarks at anyone they fancy without any reason, sniff the air to justify the putrid smell of the diesel and dusts, sneeze loudly without a cover and utter 'excuse me' in the end, clear the throat loudly and throw on the place where they are standing.

The old man with a philosophical mind watches the idiosyncrasies of the people. They all are strangers. He finds the scene around him quite amusing, at times stereotyped too.

Of all the passengers he finds her the most regular to board the bus there. She walks down calmly but with dignity. She comes from the eastern direction and stands under the tree jutting out into the street from the pavement. She is a well poised young lady, well-prepared for the day's work.

The old man first tried to guess her destination — Munirka, J.N.U. or I.I.T. then speculates her profession - service, trainee, teacher or student. Next he anticipated someone else to join her - her colleagues, friends, partner, peers or lover. This was his observation for over a week.

One day a girl of darker skin, short height, nothing great to look at arrived. The girl first winked at her, next smiled and in the end began to talk. The old man could not make the head or tail of the subject of the talk, but he realized they knew each other well. The conversation could not go on for long. A bus no. 604 arrived, the other girl boarded it, leaving her once more alone on the stand. Fortunately she did not have to stand for long, the bus no. 620 also arrived. She boarded it, occupied a ladies seat and was lost in the crowd. The old man also got into the same bus and alighted at Munirka, a distance of 2 K.M.

After this a couple of days passed by, the old man cast a casual glance in the direction of the girls' route but nothing unusual happened. She came, stood and boarded the bus at scheduled time. He did not care to take any notice of her after this day.

Then one day he noticed her again there. In pink suit, bag dangling from her shoulders, with a smiling face she was standing under the tree. The reason for her happiness was not far long to discover. The old man followed the direction of her eyes to ascertain the reason of her joyous feeling. The subject was a thin boy shabbily dressed, a bag in hand, was in conversation with another boy. He was standing about ten meters away from her, casting occasional glances at her and alternately was talking to a boy of his age. The old man observed next the change of places. The boy moved towards her in quick successive paces and stood before her. A conversation ensued between them. The old man tried his best to make out the gist of the verbal discourse but was clueless.

He thought perhaps they were known to each other, hailing from the same mountainous region of Garwal. What could be the topic, home in the rural district of Bhimtal where their families bringing up the siblings, rearing animals, tending the farms of fruits, paddy and vegetables. It may be they were sharing familiar anecdotes of dual interest, the sad demise of a well known character that did influence the minds of both of them in the past. It could be about a common friend who had gone abroad or perhaps, a precocious child in the village turned out to be a master-mind in a recent burglary in Delhi, or their present situation in Delhi in the midst of multiple problems, the solution of which rested in the hands of the city fathers and the avaricious politicians.

Although the language barrier debarred the old man from understanding the conversation, yet the glow emanated from their cheeks and the red hot ears spoke volumes of their good relationship. She was looking into his eyes directly, right hand occasionally placing under the chin. The boy was a bit shy so alternated his looks, sometimes casting a glance into her eyes and sometimes at the onlookers and by standards. The middle-aged office-goers stood behind them were devouring the intimacy with stares of contempt. Intermittently their tongues were lolling to savour lip services, their bodies stiffened to taste the intimacy. But it was a far cry. The boy got the upper hand; she smiled at him a provocative smile. The boy got the signal.

On the next day the boy stood under the tree half an hour before the scheduled time of her arrival, hoping the recurrence of great intimacy like the previous day. He bought a bouquet of assorted seasonal flowers, a Hindi book full of romantic anecdotes and picture depicting passionate figures of both male and female characters in intimate postures mostly cut out pictures of the film heroes and heroines and a plastic bag containing a light pink suit. They were the gifts for her. She came at the usual time, stood at a distance from the tree. She cast her eyes in his direction; a meaningful glance could be interpreted as the invitation to a close encounter. The boy was chatting with another boy, a short, under-nourished, unassuming character. His back was towards her but in a second he realized her presence there, so turned around to face her. A magnetic pull drew him towards her. He pushed the elderly office-goers, shoved the old man to make his way to reach his desired goal.

The first office-goers remarked at the impertinency, "What an uncouth fellow."

The second office-goers replied in the same tone being flustered, "Shameless Chap"

The first office-goers, "The fellow lacks manners." The second office goers, "He's an obstinate fool." The old man did not say anything. He just chuckled.

The boy stood before her with bended knees and offered the bouquets. "This is for you, happy birthday. Many happy returns of the day. May God bless you! You may live a hundred years." He rattled off all the good wishes he could master at the moment.

"Why, it's not my birthday! Who gave you the idea today is my birthday" The girl in pink suit remonstrated.

"I told you, today it's not her birthday, you won't listen." The short fellow butted in.

Next the boy forced her to take the other gifts as well.

Pretending to pick up a lady's handkerchief and offering her, reminding her presence in a party where they met which was never held, praising her blue eyes and comparing them with the lotus flower, relating her to the unknown families or calling her in fictitious names are the ploys by which the young men try to get acquainted with her heart throbs. The young man in sight adopted this method of offering the gifts to establish a bond between him and the girl in pink suit, irrespective of their age difference. She was almost six to eight years older than him. 'Love is blind' the adage could hardly be proved wrong.

On the next day the boy came first. He was casting his passionate eyes all around the place searching for his prized possession, but was disillusioned for a while. He spotted a group of children in shabby, discoloured, school uniforms, crushed and dirty. The girls among them were staring at each other and were having argument on obscure subjects — How Mummy scolded them for not getting ready in time - the fathers were unconcerned or had been giving too much indulgence, or the local boys stare hard at them and said things not to be uttered in public.

The kids hanging around their sisters were equally shabby, wearing ill-fitting trousers, soiled blazers, oft-used neckties; even ties were used to tie the pet dogs as well, hanging loose from their necks. They were fighting over the possession of the marbles, pokeman cards and comic books. Next his eyes fell on the African girl, a snooty damsel, impeccably dressed in white and black shades, the body odour, a mixture of human flesh and artificial body spray wafting from her person and would keep the waiting passengers at bay.

The two office-goers, as usual, were chatting in the local dialect and staring at all the passers by. The calm and passive, the elderly gentleman looked aloof and unconcerned.

"Who's this?" A gentle tap on his right shoulder brought the boy back from the reverie.

"It's me, man your friend."

The boy stared at his friend for at least five seconds before he greeted him. The reason could be attributed to the fact that he was expecting the presence of someone else and the tap of a tender hand could have been better.

In the meantime the bus arrived. The boy cast a longing glance at the bus stop and its surrounding areas for a glimpse of her but was frustrated. She was not there. Before boarding he hesitated, put one step on the bus and retained one on the pavement but could not decide whether he should wait or board it. He did not have to wait long, a mighty push from behind forced him to enter. At once the conductor produced his hand in front of his face for money. The uncouth behavior of the conductor aggravated the situation more. In another occasion he would have retaliated but now his mind was overcast with depression.

"What now?" He shouted. The bus came to a screechy halt with a jerk. The boy was about to fall on the girl seated in the front row, but checked himself with an enormous effort. He almost ran from the rear of the bus to the front in rage to confront the driver for his maverick behavior but halfway halted. At one glance on her face he forgot his anguish and refrained from proceeding any further. The reason for the abrupt halt was crystal clear to him. The ever watchful driver spotted the most sought after damsel of that particular trip of the day, waving at him from the other side of the road. He too did not like to miss his daily pleasure of seeing her boarding the bus. In fact he stopped the bus at the bus stop a little longer that day, waiting for her.

The boy was overwhelmed. To him no pain was greater than missing her in that particular trip. He looked at her; she beckoned him to her side. The eye contact did the job. He stood beside her since there was no empty seat. They smiled, talked and made faces with the widening eyebrows. To the surprise of all, the meeting took place for a brief period. The boy got down at the next bus stop, after waving at her profusely.

The old man observed the entire scene from the entry of the boy, the encounter and departure, with keen interest. Since he was not involved in any way to the meeting of the two souls and specially the feeling of the boy towards the girl, he studied the faces of the passengers and their immediate reactions.

The middle-aged driver had been seeing her boarding the bus for the last one year. She never missed it. Punctually every day she was there at the bus stop. In the grueling summer months bringing a bus to a stand still was hazardous. It annoyed the passengers, they perspired profusely, the heat in the bus caused uncomfortable to stay in, resulted in fray temper, and abuses hurled at the driver. A fight ensued among the passengers. The driver withstood all kinds of abuses and threats, only to carry her in time to her destination.

The conductor turned frisky. Most reluctantly he accepted the money from her in lieu of the ticket. The girl was aware of the motive of the conductor so she kept the money ready to hand over. In fact with a force she pressed the money into his hand and grabbed the ticket. She never paid the money on entry to the conductor, seated behind the gate, but forced him to come to her seat to hand over the ticket, a rare privilege, a definite breech of the general rule. The fellow also, looked for a friction; a body to body contact, a whip of body's odour and a smile. Paradoxically, he always got the stare in return.

On a particular day in the early summer month the bus reached the stand before time. Prior to reaching the stand ten meters away, the bus came to sudden halt. This facilitated the old man to board the bus, along with a lady, who was literally running in front of him. The next part of the journey was something that surprised everybody. The bus came to a halt and won't move at all at the stand. The engine was cut, a deliberate cut. There was no fault in the engine, no punctured tyre, no accident, no road block, no police interference, it was simple concern, and a concern for the most sought after passenger, the girl in pink suit. She was late so ambled away slowly towards the bus majestically, knowing fully well the temperaments of all. The driver got the lease of life and was rejuvenated, so synchronized between the clutch and gear and released the brake. He held the steering wheel firmly and smiled. The conductor heaved a sigh of relieve, got up from his seat and went to her to deliver the ticket. He inhaled the body odour of the angelic figure mixed with female body spray. He cast a longing look for the acknowledgement of the services rendered to her but was disheartened.

The office goers grimaced, winched and snorted.

"Nonsense, what is this?" The first one said to the second one":

"It's a perfect case of favoritism" The second replied.

"He's a man of dubious character." The first retorted.

"Romantic hearts." The second added.

"He possesses perfect human souls, full of love, compassion and concern." The old man quipped, realizing the disturbed minds of the two office goers.

The other passengers, traveling for the first time had mixed reactions. Some of them frowned, the disgruntled one among them. A few of them smiled, of the kindred souls and the rest of them expressed no concern. A few somnambulant ones remained ignorant forever to this glorious scene.

The old man was aware of the situation. He saw her ambling at ease towards the bus. No worry, no hurry, no chase, no fretting nor fuming, or no screaming to stop the bus. It stopped by itself. The huge material structure also felt the need of the presence of the girl. The inanimate object also became a part and parcel of a human life like its animate objects, the human beings. At no cost it would like to miss the delicate living object moving on its floor with fleeting feet, the pressure of which managed its surface to cause the greatest pleasure and rejoice in ecstasy. Perhaps this was the only time the bus had the most soothing effects on its person. During her ride the bus was pollution free, faced no traffic snarl, met with no accident, no one pick pocketed, no boisterous young lad would argue with the conductor for concession in the fare, no terrorist would dare to plant the destructive RDX bomb to take the revenge against human race, no keeper of the law would venture into it to accost for any kind of traffic violation.

She perched majestically in the middle seat, sharing with the other female daily passengers. Triumphant look on her face indicated how she had won the hearts of so many people around her. She looked straight ahead, eyes cast over the heads of all the onlookers, no fluttering eyelids, but a wry smile on her face. The old man sat in front of her and was trying to fathom the mood of her, with head turned askance and a stare. She looked aloof.

On the next morning the old man was keen to meet her again so ran to the bus stop, but was restrained by so many obstacles. At 8:30 A.M. he met the man from the publishing house at the entrance gate of West End colony from the institution from where he retired a couple of months ago. The obdurate bahaviour of the head, boor by nature, and the man turned cynical, a serious thrashing was the ultimate goal was the topic for discussion. That took five minutes. He ran after this to avail of the bus, but the vehicle had already left with its prized passenger. He missed her. A feeling of frustration overcame him.

The sworn enemies of the girl, the two office goers had the similar experiences the other day. They reached the bus stop just in the nick of time when the bus was leaving the stop at eight seven A.M., three minutes earlier than the scheduled time. In spite of adopting hostile attitude from the very inception of their meeting, they missed the rendezvous. They felt something amiss, a great loss culminated in depression. Speechless they stood there, not even staring at anyone, the usual practice. After a long while the African girl appeared on that day. They were not keen to the hostility, in fact, they seemed to tolerate her. Suddenly a host of senior girl students appeared on the scene but the duo never cast their hateful eyes on them and refrained from critical remarks. After a lapse of good ten minutes a D.T.C. bus arrived and they boarded it silently. They found a vacuum, emptiness in their hearts. In the office the day was spent in silence. The colleagues were surprised to see the change in their moods. The duo never stopped talking about others critically, but today a listless, forlorn look appeared on their faces, which surprised the others a great deal.

They too were human beings with golden hearts, full of compassion, love and care. It was perhaps the heartless, painful and boring world choked their feelings, the tedious work-load turned them inhuman and the narrow-minded colleagues induced them to be critical. May God bless their souls!

The old man was also astonished to find the African Girl at the scene after a long time. Of course today she was not her usual self. Normally her fixed eyes looked only the direction of the approaching bus from the western horizon, but today they were rotating in all directions, as if, looking for something, or someone. No one had ever seen her intimacy with anyone at the bus stop, but today it was different. She was definitely longing to meet someone, an instance of the universal bond of brotherhood, a positive human trait.

The two under nourished and shabbily dressed college students greeted each other in subdued manner. That boisterous, vociferous and ear-splitting sound of the word 'Hello' could be heard from ten meters apart before they faced each other and reverberated the entire concrete structure of the bus stop which awoke the passive onlookers from their reverie and shook the children into their marrows, was missing. They too searched for someone with their roving eyes, but missed to locate her. Personally she had nothing to do with them. She was a senior girl, eight to ten years older than them, engaged in different professional fields, one was the bread winner and the others were dependants, with diverse family backgrounds, languages spoken, caste, creed or perhaps religious convictions could not possibly have anything in common, but today, what did bind them together was the human love, care and affinity designed by the divine decree to feel the existence of each other on the earth, the creator's glorious gift to mankind.

Scheduled 8:20 A.M. D.T.C. bus crawled at a moderate speed of 40 K.M. per hour. It was carrying passengers to their destinations in that particular morning. Comfortable journey, yet there was an eerie feeling all over. The sullen faces of the passengers of the public bus had a great impact on the other travelers as well. The conductor threw a few casual questions to the passengers of 8:05 bus but the morbid replies he received, puzzled him to a great extent. Normally they exchanged greetings and referred to a few stereotyped anecdotes of familiar subjects, but today they were missing. It was a break away from the tradition; the conductor had to swallow the humble pie.

The passengers overheard the conversation between the conductor and the two office goers, sounded an extraordinary affair, such a camaraderie between them was beyond the imagination of an ordinary mortal being.

"We feel frustrated to miss the bus." One of them told the conductor

"What is so great about it? If you miss one another is here." The conductor said like a counselor.

"You won't understand, you need great heart to realize the fact." The second office-goers spoke like a philosopher.

"I really do not understand your problem." The conductor resigned.

A precocious young passenger overheard the conversation and butted in, "Hey man is there anything amiss? Has anyone fainted or dead. Perhaps someone has been a victim of a pickpocket and lost a lot of money?" "May be some one is using his fingers freely and was nabbed in the process." The other friend commented to make the affair look cheap.

"These youngsters do not have enough experiences of the intricacies and complexities of life." The first office-goers whispered into the ears of the other, lest he would be heard by them and ridiculed, the natural characteristics of the youngsters to be critical, a tendency also persisted in their hearts to ridicule others without a reason.

"They have not gone through the period of romance in their lives. Once fallen in line, see the change in them." The other added.

The ubiquitous girl in pink suit did not come to the bus stop for over a week. The old man was curious to know the reactions of the regulars. The office goers looked right, left and center in search of the golden girl. Curiously enough, they had never spoken to the girl, only stared at in contempt. But today they appeared to be lost in the wilderness. The two lanky college students feasted their eyes with the sheer look at the girl, today looked lost and frustrated.

Today, surprisingly all the well-wishers and adversaries spotted 'the boy' of her acquaintance with his crony. They were seated at the far end of the bus stand. He was dressed in a maroon shirt and grey trousers. He sat there in deep conversation with his friend. The passengers had their ears open to snatch a few words of the conversation in the hope of obtaining the news of her absence. But they were deluded for a while. Before they could board the bus a word echoed all over the bus stand, 'accident' the word came from the direction of the boys seated at the far end of a bench.

A week later she appeared again. She was there five minutes early. The regular drifted in staggering spaces, listless, aimless of the characteristics of struggling mass without destiny. Reason.....she won't be there as usual. One last look to the direction of the bus stand and they speeded up their walking strides. She had come.

The old man reached the stand first in a huff, but was rejuvenated at the sight of the girl, God's most favourite creature. One look on her forehead he was confirmed to the words uttered by the boy from the bench. The scar was marked from the corner of the right eye to the middle of the right cheek. The colour was red and dark, surrounded by a streak of white colour bordering the scar. His heart sank imagining the nature of the accident. What a pity he was not there by her side in the hour of need. He stood at a distance and guessed the type of accident, car, fall, collision or human.

The impact of the car accident would be fatal. Accidental happenings were pardonable, intentional was punishable, what was what, he could not comprehend. A fall from a high place to the ground could have been disastrous, but it could be ruled out since it was only a cut. A slip on a slippery ground could affect the bones so any kind of fracture would have been possible, but it was only a scar, so all the parts of the body remained intact. Assault by human being caused by jealousy, covetousness or lust would have wiped out the glamour, reputation and compatibility. Ostensibly it was none of those afflictions. It was something deeper than one could think of.

On that auspicious day the two office-goers left respective homes reluctantly. They had no moods to venture out of the house, in spite of having nagging wives and precocious children. The over suspicious wives intensified their tortures, both verbally and in actions. The quality of food served to them deteriorated, the calories dropped, sans vitamins and tasted insipid. The quantity of it was reduced, resulted in under weight and occasional concussions. Even the Tiffin boxes they carried to the office were half filled with unsavory dishes. 'Karela' and boiled 'brinjal', the burnt up 'chapatis', half cooked rice and the unpalatable vegetables curry served were the proof of dissension. The spouses placated them as dissolute, drunken and disreputable rogues who had no ethics and morality. Off late they had shown no interest in their wives. These men lost their appetites for food and flesh, did not show any interest in domestic chores, even avoided cuddling their off-springs. So the wives' adverse reactions were undisputable.

At a distance of ten meters away they spotted the pink suit and at once presumed the presence of the most sought after passenger. They sprinted, hopped and ran lest they missed her. At the first look at her, they were elated, but on closer look they felt they were dejected. They too spotted the mark on her cheek. Immediately they came to the conclusion she had been hit. Either it happened at home, the result of one of those unnecessary domestic brawls or she had been assaulted by rogues. The later characters were found in abundance in the city where discipline was lacking. They felt guilty for not being there on her side at the hour of need to protect her from the onslaught. In the meantime the scheduled bus no. 620 arrived. They boarded it.

The bus driver did not notice the scar, but the conductor did. On impulse and for the first time, he spoke to her.

"Sister, what happened? Did you meet with an accident?"

As usual she did not reply, but smiled a melancholic smile.

The conductor hesitated to accept the money initially. Since she showed no interest to converse or exchange goodwill, he handed over the ticket in exchange of money. The ticket cost a paltry sum of money but the goodwill that went with it was beyond anyone's conjecture. The young, conductor beat a hasty retreat and sat glued to his seat till the remainder of the journey. He was dejected, forlorn and glum.

The driver noticed the scar through the mirror in front of the steering wheel and was dumb-founded. He lost interest in driving and at one point of the drive almost collided with a truck. It came to a sudden halt at a cross-section, and avoided the impending danger by a sheer stroke of luck. The passengers were jolted, fell on each other and caused small cuts and bruises. The universal curse and diabolic abuses hurled at him. Even the girl in pink suit scowled at him.

The old man watched the reactions of all the protagonists. He observed the most astounding factor that all these people did not have any kind of relationship with her, yet their feelings, concern and deep resentment to the scar inflicted by some unscrupulous elements, anti-social brats required looking into. He prayed for the speedy recovery of the cut so that she was there at the bus stop daily to give company to all her well-wishers.

But man's proposal could never match His disposal. The girl was missing again for a fortnight. The speculation was rife among the regular passengers either she had met once more with a serious accident or got married to a handsome beau from an affluent home. Therefore, she need not come to the bus stop for the stereotyped ordeal, nine to five confinement in an office for a boring job daily. The regulars wished her all the beast in the event she got married otherwise speedy recovery.

She surfaced again a ain on a Monday at the same time. To the surprise of all she was in deep conversation with the boy. Unfortunately the old familiar smile was missing. As she was talking her eyes fell alternately on his face and the foot. It indicated nervousness on her part. The boy was quite serious. The onlookers did not like to butt in, thinking it was their private affair. But everybody was shocked to see the second scar on her left cheek, a black cover, a tinge of red showing in between the cracks of the cover and a white border. The first scar now broadened with red colour being prominent. Her face was getting distorted due to certain natural phenomenon. If it was the handiwork of a ruffian from the family, nothing one could do to cure it. She had to face the consequences. If the same person was an outsider, then there was the law of society to undertake the responsibility. If it was natural then pray to God for the recovery, since it was a curse in His sinless domain.

One afternoon in the month of March, the official spring when the assortment of flowers bloom a aplenty all around the place. The old man stood at the corner of West End colony, where a half-moon shaped garden was bursting with flowers of the season - Azaleas, Petunias, Hollyhocks, Dahlias, Dragon flies, different colours of Roses - a riot of colour presented to the view. A perfect backdrop for a photo session, meant for romance. An appropriate atmosphere existed for the couple to run around the trees, serenading and wooing each other to achieve their heart's desires. On closer look into the center of the garden he found faces with bright and sparkling eyes peeping out of the bushes. He realized they were the couples taken shelter behind the bushes enjoying their privacy in the company of each other.

"God bless these children of yours; let them enjoy the company of each other. The youth is the fleeting passage of time in the lives of each one of us. It disappears quickly as it comes. Now they are hiding behind the bushes, covered with beautiful flowers of the spring season. The flowers die sooner than they bloom so is the youth. Soon the burden of the family will fall on them. The romantic dreams will turn into nightmares. But this moment is important to them. It is colourful, romantic and full of hopes so let them be there."

"I had my youth. It had changed into this state what I'm now. But there is no regret. God's decree is evenly poised on all. The affluent, the poor, the fair and the dark, the most powerful and the under dogs, the high caste and the low cast, the R, C, and the protestant all meet their destinies alike." The old man was cogitating over so many issues while stood on the pavement near the garden.

An active brain in isolation could think and imagine so many wayward things, some were realistic and a few were weird, yet some were romantic and beautiful. A professional and specialized brain could think of only one subject of their occupation at one point of time. A professional killer has only one subject to think of. He is obsessed by one issue. No other subject could get into his brain. A patient suffering from an incurable disease could think of only of that inevitable hour.

The old man saw her riding the pillion of a two-wheeler. His eyes could not be deceived. It was the same girl in pink suit, now changed into a blue one, but the same marks on both her cheeks were permanently shown due to reflection of the sun-rays falling onto her face in horizontal shapes. The faint rays of the dying sun in the western horizon showed brightly through the foliages of the tall trees. The brightest shafts among them fell on her face and brightened the scar. The prominent reddish spot revealed the identity of the girl.

"I'm happy to see her with a boy. It means she is going to settle down. That man surely is her fiance. The couple must have had heart to heart talks about the world around them, have settled a couple of disputes arisen due to inter-action between the two families, — dowry, an obnoxious, mean and harmful system existing in our colourful and checkered society. Legal complication over the cast marriage involved both the families, has to be solved out of court amicably, or the affair with the ex-boy friend who is still interested in her, —how to tackle the same problem, — otherwise after the marriage a complicated situation may arise, the finance, the ritual and the guests. All these are the most crucial aspects of a wedding ceremony."

He saw her while she was whizzing past him in a fleeting moment. He had imagined so many things during that time. But the entire concept of her well-being as visualized by him on the previous evening changed drastically when he saw her again at the bus stop that morning. She was walking onto the bus stand with a lumpish, idiotic and boorish looking chap. All the well-wishers standing on the pavement were disappointed. The conversation regarding their relationship ensued of diverse nature, hostile, adverse and fraternal.

The two office goers cursed the young man accompanying her,

"A lumpish, good for nothing, a scavenger, a rag-picker, a demonic figure, devil's incarnate" words were used to describe the poor fellow.

The hungry-looking college students discussed between them her tainted character. They marveled at her choice of personality. The fellow of her choice was a reckless wretch, a scoundrel of the first degree and a condemned soul. She is an innocent pretty thing, should not get involved to such a low born character.

The African girl raised her head to scan through, fluttered her eye lids to express her disgust and snorted to denounce the audacity of the other character to be friend with the pink suited girl. A strange phenomena but the human heart had no limit, its affection, concern, love extended beyond social, religious and family boundaries, it touched all human souls with equal fervor. It is the rightful place for God in the entire biological structure of man.

The old man observed the whole scene enacted by innocent people around him and scrutinized the heart of each one of them. He felt good. He found every heart was filled with compassion, care and grace for each other, each one of them flourished within it. On reflexes he found out that every individual is good at heart, but it is their circumstances, family bond, social structure, political environment, economic containment and blind religious conviction change them to what they are today, all are outside agents and do not come within the purview of their hearts, the permanent, undeniable and imperishable seat of God. Ample examples are thrown all around him at this moment. He thanked God for His lovely creation; an immortal soul within the mortal body is the marvel of his greatest handiwork. He is the only one who could have conceived such an idea.

Actually the boy walked down with her was her own brother. He looked shabby in appearance, his disheveled and unkempt hairs, soiled clothes, sunken eyes, caved in cheeks and hungry look, all attributed to his outward image. But on closer look one could discover his inward self, a sober, sauve and scholarly type. Her young brother, loved to accompany her, at least once a day, to the bus stop. From the scene before him the old man could draw the logical inferences that her family was living from hand to mouth in the concrete jungle of urban settlement. Her family was just a fragment of the vast community of people living here at per with the line of poverty. She was making a great effort on behalf of her family to curve a niche in the competitive world of the struggling mass of people in a developing country like ours. He quietly saluted her effort to stand on her own feet. A great soul, the old man felt in his inner heart that he too was slowly becoming very fond of her. Hence forth, he felt dejected and the entire day was spent on useless pursuit of happiness when he missed her at the bus stop.

He was longing to talk to her, but was aware of his age. Whether he would be accepted by her as a friend, philosopher and guide, was a million dollar question. No one of those who stood at the bus stop was eligible to enter into her domain. The personal life of her was reserved for an individual male member of her community. These were only the sympathizers got involved into her affair, because they were there, a temporary sojourn for all.

The scars on her cheeks began to grow. All her well-wishers watched her intently for days. The general feeling was that the scars were not caused by the accidents, but afflicted by the mal-functioning of the flow and growth of blood in her biological system.

"Is it cancer or Leukodorma?" The first office goers asked his counterpart in rather sympathetic tone.

"I don't think any one of those ailments. I presume, it is caused due to mal-nutrition in her body. Don't you see how thin she is grown." The second office goers answered wisely, for a change in their otherwise cryptic and diabolical one sided conversation related to her existence on the earth.

"I hope so. Any kind of major disease and if it is a malign one, will entail a major medical expenditure. Will she have all that money to pay for her treatment"? He asked.

"I doubt it." The second office-goers replied. "She does not look like belonging to an affluent family." He added.

"Yes, I agree with you. All these hilly people have very little to spend. They come down to the plains in search of jobs. A microscopic minority of them does well and the rest of them struggle ceaselessly to earn descent livings till the end of their days." His philosophical discourse surprised his counterpart to a great extent.

The African girl stared at her, without fluttering eye-lids once. She tried to analyze the cause of the gradual expansion of the scars on her cheeks. The same scars seemed to have no cure. They were turning red from the original colour of black. A part of it got a tinge of maroon. Her face would soon turn into a multi-coloured complexity. I wonder what could be the reason! She spoke to herself.

"A beauty spot." The first college student remarked initially when they spotted the scar on the first day.

"She does not look all that great in that, moreover, she should put the mark in the middle of her forehead just above the nose" The second boy replied and further continued, "May be the style has changed or a superstitious gimmick."

"Whatever may be the cause she doesn't look all that great with that spot, a silly damsel she is, indeed." The second boy concluded.

That was sometime back, but today the conversation took a different turn, rather alarming.

"I hope not, she has been assaulted." The first office goers said.

"Rather not, we'll take the revenge." It is a loose remark, but spontaneous and sincerely spoken.

"How would you do it?" It may be a family feud; she is just a victim of it. It does not come within the preview of our jurisdiction. We can intervene if she is assaulted by a goon" the first office goers retorted in a convincing manner.

"It seems she's been suffering from a skin disease." The second office goers interposed.

"Then there is the doctor to consult and get cure."

"It's the obvious solution." The second office goers made the concluding remark.

The other regular passengers did not care much for her escalating condition. The old man took to heart the contrasting behaviors and feelings of human beings. Perhaps it was the way of the world. The less we ponder over it, the more relaxed we feel. Only a few among us, a microscopic number, though feel the same way. He was aware of the good souls around the place, initially resentful but now supportive. The main character of the scene was no relation of anyone of them; they had never conversed, exchanged greetings, and not even had eye contact. But what really brought them together was the human bond, natural feeling for each other.

Now almost six months passed. The small scars on her face grew into huge proportion. Her face got completely covered by a white sheet; patches of brown spots grew on them. It was a sure case of Leukodorma. The other prominent exposed parts, the hands, the heels and a part of torso also got covered with the incurable skin disease.

The old man forever watchful of the supple movements of the unfortunate and wretched girl, the pink suited female species, the figure of all the cynosure of eyes, oft-cursed, oft-praised, yet watchful eyes kept on her transition from healthy person to a diseased borne figure, which itself spoke volume of human hearts.

The two office goers stood in silence couple of days at the bus stand. They had no words to express regret in the present plight of the most sought after girl. They noticed in quiet submission the transition of the girl from a healthy one to a diseased person.

"I feel sorry for the girl. See, in what physical state she is in now. "The first office goers said on the third day, after they broke the silence.

"Yes, I do see. I really feel sorry. Is there any chance of her getting married and settling down?" The second office goers expressed his feeling rather remorsefully.

"I am afraid not, unless someone with an angelic heart descends from heaven. Look at her face, so pathetic, suffering of all kinds is written on it." The first office goers said.

"She seldom smiles. Either she is afraid to smile or a great deal of sufferings, mostly mental has suppressed it". The second office goers added to the conversation.

"Should we not be grateful to God that none of our children is afflicted by any such exposed disease?" The first office goers lowered his voice in humility while saying this.

"We should also pray to God that this girl, who was under virtual cryptic scrutiny, disgust and condemnation previously, has become a part of our family member in cognition." The second office goers concluded.

"Yes we love her as much as we love our own daughters." This last explicit remark overheard by the old man, before he boarded the bus no. 620. He could never guess who commented, but surely it was spoken from the heart of a genial person. The same weekend the two office goers retired from the government services as per the rule.

The two college students were dumb-founded. They had no word to speak in favour or against her. Being young they were not afflicted by any kind of disease, but their hearts went out to her in condemnation of nature.

"What a mysterious world we are living in?" the first boy asked the other boy.

"I blame God squarely for it. I also condemn His power of discretion. To one person he gives so much of beauty and the other ugliness. The world worships the beauty and abhors the later. What chance has she got in society to live an upright life". The second remonstrated in an angry and hateful mood.

"Yes I agree with you she has no future in our society. No parent will agree to the proposal that their son marry an ugly looking girl. What prospect has she in the marital scenario?" The first boy left the question for further discussion and boarded the bus.

"She is condemned to die as a broken-hearted person." The last remark was heard by the old man. It came from behind him as he put one foot on the first step of the bus. The two college students waited behind him to board the bus.

The African girl did not board the bus, but she stood there for a lift in the Embassy car to go to the office.

"I am ugly to look at because of my colour. The blind world of mine is colour prejudiced. Everybody worships the handsome, pretty and good-looking male, female figures. The film industry, modeling business, beauty contests and wedding markets everywhere preference is given to the fair-looking men and women. The ugly and dark-complexioned people are looked down upon. It is according to these people standing all around me. I am very ugly to look at because of my colour, physical figure and the look. But I am afraid she is uglier than me. I have the possibility to get married to a man of my type in my country, but what possibility has she got in her own country?" She said to herself, casting a remorseful eye on her direction.

"Thank God for not creating me as ugly as the girl in pink suit." This was a clear allusion to the present predicament of the girl. The old man heard the remark. It was the third in a row before boarding the bus.

"I am no judge of it." The old man said.

A month passed by after this. The girl in pink suit, once hated by all, now became a symbol of concern. The vicissitudes of life affected all and sundry people. It had changed the entire life-style of the girl. The enforced pink colour of her complexion matched with her dress, a rare combination of the skin and the cloth, which covered the former to preserve the modesty. In the wedding market, where the racket of flinching money with unscrupulous jest existed and the dowry system was rampant, she had no chance of entering into a nuptial bond with anyone of her countrymen, native or regional in the near future. Her personal life of excitement full of dreams could be completely destroyed. She was doomed forever; it seemed the entire episode of her life was providential. The old man believed in God's judgment." God had a purpose behind all His creation," he consoled himself with these words.

It was the last day for the two office goers before their retirement. The two college students also would complete their last day in the college. The African girl stood at the bus stop for the last time before her departure for her own country. The old man also was about to catch the bus from the bus stop for the last time before he went to live with his son in Dwarka, a long distance away from that place in the remote North Western part of the city. The shade of sorrows and depressions were written on their faces. All eyes were focused on the eastern side of the bus stand. A glimpse of the prized girl was most desirable on the last day of their depature for ever from that spot. From tomorrow a chapter in their lives would end and once more they would enter the world of uncertainty. But there was no sign of her.

She was absent for a week before that day, so they all pinned down their hopes that she might appear on the spot for the last time so that they could have a glimpse of her but was deluded. The bus no. 620 was late, an unusual occurrence, for a couple of minutes. All eager eyes looked toward the west side of the bus stand. They eagerly awaited the appearance of the man made mobile machine. But, instead they saw a three wheeler, well-decorated with festoon and streamers. Balloons fluttering in the air and the mellow sound of music from the stereo system filled the atmosphere. The auto was approaching the bus stand.

Since it was a new vehicle, and on its inaugural run the owner would like to display his precious possession. The people looked at it in casual manners, as if; it was an every day occurrence. Therefore, the protagonists of this episode cast casual glances at it. The three wheeler auto came to the bus stop and stopped there with a jolt. In the meantime the bus no. 620 also arrived and stood beside the three wheelers.

All passengers, regular and casual, the bus driver, the conductor and their noisy friends looked inside the three wheelers. Lo and behold, they spotted a couple seated on the back seats, attired in wedding dresses. On closer look they found the girl was none other than the girl in pink suit, dressed in her sparkling wedding attire, seated beside her was the same boy whom they spotted on the first day at the Malai Mandir bus stop. He was also attired in wedding dresses.

"God works in mysterious ways." Was the only comment made by the old man and got into the bus no. 620 with the others.

8

The Destiny

The ritual is followed strictly with clockwork precision. The old driver mopping the sprinkled water out of the car's front glass to begin with, moved onto the side-glasses and then the entire body. The middle-aged man must be doing it for over twenty years, since he is in service with them for the equal period of time. The sincerity with which he works will give the scores of the local people passing by an impression of the man, a perfect domestic help.

Every morning a girl of twelve years old will come out of the gate of the building situated at 8, Vasant Vihar, where the driver is at work, with two milk cans of unequal sizes, deposit a bunch of keys to his custody and proceeds to the nearby milk booth of 'Mother Dairy' to buy milk. The cans of two liters and one liter respectively dangling from both her hands are empty while going to the booth. The return journey is different. She stops with the burden of weight. Everyday at seven in the morning she will set out of the building, walk majestically in small strides, head down, looking to the ground, no side glances at all.

Scores of morning walkers pass that way everyday, look at her, some have curious looks in their eyes, some eye at her with sympathy and compassion, yet a few young ones, hardly handful of them, look at her with ubiquitous lustful eyes. But she is steadfast in her walk, not an eyelid flutters and no smile on her lips is discernible. The two very dangerous propositions attract the attention of the onlookers. She appears to be non-committal, disinterested and carefree to the view of the passer-by. No one knows her name, never met her or has any conversation with her ever.

Any over-enthusiastic person, keen to know her identity will be disillusioned. On the first sight one can guess her to be domestic help. A sophisticated mind will write her as the youngest inmate of the house. Whatever her status in the family, residing in the house, she performs her duty diligently, dutifully and sincerely. All the year round, she goes to the milk booth with two milk cans and fetches the ingredients for the house.

No one has ever seen any other inmates of the house, since everybody passes the house only a couple of times in the course of the morning walks. Occasionally they see the girl in conversation with the driver. They see either she is handing over the key or collecting it. A couple of times she has been entering the car and shuffling with the bunch of keys hanging from the steering. It seems she is in no hurry for the assigned work.

She walks alone with a little bend of her head, not stooping to the ground, but avoiding eye contacts with the walkers. She dresses simply in black loose slashes and white tops, wearing a simple pair of 'chappals'. Her walk seems to be casual but firm. She is the only young girl in the midst of people, fifty plus, Indian and foreigner, the former being in the majority. The calm and placid morning, the silence prevails everywhere. Occasionally interrupted by the sounds of chirping birds and the quick-feet of the health conscious people. The driver is the silent observer of every thing that goes on during that moment.

"Beti, why don't you tell Ramu to go and fetch the milk?" the driver suggested her one day.

"No, I can't allow him to go for two reasons: he doesn't put his heart and mind into the work, since he doesn't drink the ingredients and secondly it has become a part of my life. I walk in the morning's fresh air, breathe the sweetened fragrance of the plants and the trees planted on both the sides of my path", the girl replied with a sincere heart.

"I accept your explanation beti, but I really think it's a domestic helper's job", the driver submits in a humble tone.

The home belongs to Mr. De'Cunha, an ace businessman and captain of many industries. About twenty-five years ago as a young man, he had come to Delhi from Goa. Recruit of the Vasco's of Goa, Mr. D' Cunha started his career as the local representative of the company. A solo contender for the job, he established his office in Gurgaon, since his company deals with iron and steel.

Young D'Cunha worked very hard with honesty, humility and sincerity. Young bachelor had plenty of time in hand to offer for the company and his relentless services to the cause, development and growth of the company from an insignificant concern to a multi-faced company paid the dividend. The industrialist group of the Tatas offered him an incredible package. He left his original employer and became their residence manager at an early age. Complacency and affluence induce a person to look for a life partner; the man D'Cunha was no exception to it. One bright afternoon in March, he was married to Ritu Braganza at St. Mary's Cathedral in Panjim, Goa.

Within a year he got a son. He named him Cyrus, a common name among the Catholic Christian in Goa. The D'Cunha's brought up their child to the true affluent class. His schooling was done in St.Colombus, master's degree in St.Stephen's College and for doctorate in Business Studies, he went to London School of Economics. The beloved son of

D'Cunha's never showed any laxity so far academic brilliance was concerned. He went at it in full speed. While in U.K. he fell in love with several occidental dames of his age, students of self-same class. The infatuation did not last long. He adored them profusely for their exquisite beauty, ready-wit and tremendous sex-appeal, but in the core of his heart he had a doubt of their impeccable character and integrity of natural endowment. He found them all nice but cannot be trusted with everlasting relationship in a bond of marriage.

"Cyrus is long due to come home. What is he doing there in a foreign land for so long?" Mr. D'Cunha asked his wife in real earnest.

"He's been looking for a job, I presume," his wife gave him a brief reply.

"Why doesn't he look for one over here? This country has great opening for a man of his caliber. It is rising and shining," he said.

"I received a phone call a couple of days ago and had a brief chat with him too. During the course of conversation he told me not to worry about him and assured me he will be coming home shortly," she replied.

"Well if this is the case, let it be the way he likes," he just concluded the conversation.

Cyrus was in no mood to return home in Delhi. Perhaps, he had found a good pasture land in U.K. and was determined to graze there to the extent his youthful energy permitted him to do so. He found it was extremely difficult to find a suitable job to suit his temperament, desire, expectation and caliber. An only job freely available was of a dishwasher in a restaurant, or a porter in the railway junctions or bus terminals. White collar jobs were hard to come by since he was from the Asian-subcontinent where generally the people were snubbed as indolent, shirker, derelict of duties and inefficient. A few sophisticated jobs were meant for highly qualified and well recommended by the people in high places.

Cyrus did not fit into the category. He had a few male friends, oriental; all from the same college having the same status he had. His parents could not pull any string to enable him to be inducted into any commercial farms. Having an official job in the government department was unthinkable, exclusively meant for the citizen of U.K. no colored person with foreign lineage was considered for the job. He should neither dare to go near it nor even in his dreams. Although debarred from all the avenues of the job seekers, he had one option to fall back on. He could marry a local dame and settle down in a country thronged by his own peers and countrymen. It being the obvious mode of fulfilling his need at that moment, he opted for it.

Cyrus was conscious of his handicapped situation. He neither could get a decent job in the U.K. nor ask his parents for money to sustain his living in a foreign land. Finding no solution he proposed to Belinda. She was working at that moment of time as a waitress in the same restaurant in Bedford's downtown establishment where Cyrus was recently recruited in the post of junior waiter. The owner of the restaurant was an Italian migrant, set foot on the golden soil of the country twenty five years ago with a small bag contained one change of clothes and a small amount of money in his pocket but a plenty of hope to be a successful trader in the land of 'hope and glory'. He took up a job of a waiter to start an illustrious career as a successful restaurateur.

Belinda was from Italy too, so obviously she featured in the list of his worker prominently, related not in blood but as a countrywoman, a patriotic proposition indeed. She was the trusted lieutenant of the owner. Her position in the restaurant entailed her to have a close relationship with the owner who was at least ten years older than her when she was hardly thirty. Their smooth relationship outside marital partnership lasted for ten years.

"You're fantastic in everyway" the owner of the restaurant used to say initially when Belinda started living with him. But the enthusiasm of the first few years of romance waned towards the end of the decade of their relationship. Belinda lost the favour of the owner but acquired the taste of an intimate relationship. She craved for male companionship.

After leaving the house of her mentor, Belinda got entangled in wedlock with a Pakistani young man who wished to secure citizenship status of U.K. in the event he could manage to marry a citizen of the same country. Belinda was a naturalized citizen of the U.K. She was offered a substantial amount of money to perform the act of pretentious wife to an alien Asian. After a couple of years of co-habitation the husband relinquished the services of his wife when obtained the green signal to stay on in the country of his dream.

Now Belinda got the taste of money and human intimacy. Soon the amateurish nature of her extra-marital experience turned into a professional practice. Before Cyrus could get entangled in wed-lock, Belinda had married four adventure seeking Asian youths whose dreams of becoming a citizen of U.K. were fulfilled at premiums. Belinda was obsessed by her success and her appetite grew more for amassing pounds from the innocent victims in lieu of sinful act of debauchery.

One evening after the day's work, Cyrus proposed to her.

"I'd like to have a few words with you" he said with hesitation.

Belinda smiled a meek smile, she was aware of the nature of the talk. For a couple of weeks she was observing the uneasy movements of her next client. Cyrus stared at her at times during work. He fumbled and lost words when he came near her for official work. He even sweated and talked to himself as if murmuring something untoward happenings. Some days he followed her outside the restaurant at a great distance after the scheduled working hours, went out of his way to carry her baggage and wished her in every corner of the place whenever he bumped into her.

"Yes, I'd listen to you" she replied in a soft tone.

"Where can we go?" Cyrus asked shyly.

"You say. I'm prepared to go anywhere after working hours" she said.

They talked in subdued tone lest someone else would listen to the conversation and tattled to the manager since everybody in the restaurant felt she only belonged to the big man.

Next evening they met at the local park in a cozy nook of the wide expanse of the grassy area. The bench they selected was placed next to the thick bush of azaleas. The riot of colour and the sweet fragrance of the seasonal flowers created a perfect atmosphere for a romantic conversation between two buddies about to tie the knot; the conjugal affair. After a brief chat on greetings and welfare, Cyrus harped on the right note.

"I'm intending to settle down in Britain and stay here for long," he told her in a soft voice.

"Yes, so what's the hassle?" she asked him as if playing on him so as to force him to bring upon the proposal of marriage without delay.

"You know it is next to impossible to get the green card if I apply directly to the home office" he continued.

"It is indeed. So what are you going to do?" she threw the ball in his court.

"I intend to marry a local girl who has a permanent residence here" he said and waited for her reply.

"Then marry. But it will cost you an enormous amount of money-wedding fee, the party, a fat fee for the girl. You have to live with her for a couple of years and spend for her upkeepment. Then, if divorce is on card, on your own account an additional sum of money you have to pay" she elaborated in detail the financial involvement of such a weird enterprise. "Have you got any girl in mind for such an adventurous course in life" she asked as a matter of fact.

"I do not know anyone so intimately of the British nationality. I know a lot of girls from my country but they are no use in this project" Cyrus said.

"Do you want me to find a girl for you who fits well into this plan of yours?" she suggested finally.

"No. I want you to impersonate" Cyrus said in desperation.

"Well, I could do it at a premium. It will cost you a substantial amount of money," she said.

"How much do you want? I'm prepared to pay your fee." The offering of her services relieved him to a great extent.

"5000 pounds" she said.

"That's a lot of money. I do not think I have the money with me now. But if I get time, in due course I will pay up."

"Ok. You can pay me 500 pounds now and proceed with the arrangement of the wedding ceremony. I've got a few friends to invite at the civil marriage. Religious ceremony is out of question, since we both belong to different religious denominations."

"It's Ok with me" Cyrus concluded the proposal with an assertive note.

Cyrus wrote to his father for money:

"Dear Dad,

I'm in dire need of cash, an extra amount of Rs.15000/- in addition to my regular allowance. This is in connection with a project I'm going to undertake with a friend of mine to further our future prospect in Britain. You all are fully aware of my intending desire of settling down in this land of prosperity and the highest point of civilization. I'm sure you will endorse my plan and send me the requisite amount of money at your earliest convenient time.

With regards and love.

Yours sincerely Cyrus"

"Send the requisite amount of money at a convenient time" Mr. D'Cunha read the letter to his wife and emphasized the last point in rather curt manner.

"He does not think of coming back home here and pay a visit to us" he continued.

"He's going to be our alien son in the event he settles down there. I always thought of spending my old age with my grandchildren, but it looks like I'm going to be deprived of such privileges" he said in a subdued tone.

"This is the principle drawback of the globalization of life, the family life is shattered;" he quipped in a distressed mood.

Mr.D'Cunha was planning at that moment to take the advantage of the pre-matured retirement scheme and start his own consultancy business from the house, sacrificing in his own checkered career in business. This kind of request for a monetary help from a qualified young man was un-called for, however he was willing to part with it provided it helped his son to settle down in life, wherever his heart went.

Cyrus got money in due course and fixed the date of the marriage in the local civil court. He dreamt of some glorious dreams. The romance of marriage, one holy sacrament got the priority, subsequent conjugal relationships, and the mixed-blooded off springs, the fat job entailed as a consequent of possessing academic degree. He vowed to work-hard and be a successful businessman in the land flowing with milk and honey. The native land of India where his root was and his parents, their sacrifices, love and care for him was all forgotten in hope of a new venture.

Sunday, the 5th of June was fixed for the marriage; Belinda took the advance money and went ahead with the arrangement of the wedding ceremony. A lawyer's office was contacted on Mount Road where the gullible brief-less advocates swarmed in great numbers to fleece the clients out of whatever they could on an occasion such as this. This being a case of settlement in Britain and obtaining a green card, the advocate Mr. Cullis raised the issue to an extraordinary high pitch, almost triple. The chauffer driven limousine, the red carpet rolled outside the office room, several bouquets of flowers, the caterers, all were contacted. All services were desired by Belinda.

Just an hour before the ceremony, all the creditors arrived at the venue with their respective bills to be paid in advance, at least half the amount now and the rest after the actual ceremony. Cyrus was asked to reach the venue exactly half an hour before so as to see the arrangement and to complete the formalities.

The first person Cyrus met at the entrance of the hall was Belinda. His heart leapt with joy.

"Now my dream will be fulfilled!" he said to himself.

"Hello, darling how are you." Belinda greeted him with a hug and a long kiss.

"I'm fine." Cyrus too reciprocated her greeting in equal manner.

Holding his hand Belinda led him to the office door, to be greeted by gullible advocate. Inside the room a few more gentlemen whom Cyrus had never seen before were seated around the lawyers table. The lawyer took the trouble of introducing the gentlemen to the prospective customer.

"This is Mr. Martin, your caterer." A stocky, pot bellied middle aged man sprinted out of his seat to greet him. He held his hand tightly and said, "Congratulations in advance for the great occasion."

During the greeting, the robust hand of Martin gripped his hand so strongly that Cyrus was about to scream in pain. But he controlled himself, lest he became the cause of laughter.

"This is Mr.Rossini, the florist. He has undertaken the responsibility of supplying the choicest of flowers for the ceremony."

"How do you do Mr. Cyrus? I have taken the pain of bringing flowers from the European market in London. Some are flown this morning from Holland, Italy and France." He said in one breath. Mr.Rossini's baldy head sparkled as the tube light over his head were shining brightly, exposing his bald head more prominently.

"Thank you very much." Cyrus replied.

"This is Mr. Titan, our supplier of decorative materials. Red carpet has been rolled on the steps outside the office is his responsibility. In fact you'll be happy to note he has just unpacked it for the ceremony."

Mr.Titan, a diminutive figure, frail and sunken eyes greeted him with a 'high'.

Cyrus just nodded his head at the sign of courteous gesture.

Pedro was introduced to him as a chauffeur. He was supposed to supply him a limousine, appropriate to the occasion, for traveling a few distance to Belinda's house where the reception was arranged. Cyrus never saw the car but pressumed it might have been parked in a reserved parking lot in the corner of the block where the real ceremony was about to be held.

There were also two other men and a middle aged woman in the room who greeted him with genuine smiles. The men were the office clerks. They were their as witnesses to the solemn occasion required by the law. The woman was the domestic help responsible for the cleaniness of the office.

As all eyes fixed on him, Cyrus felt a little embarrassed in his stylish wedding suit. A great expectation was discernible in every person. Their intention was not to enjoy the ceremony but to fleece Cyrus out as much as possible.

Innocent as he was in this matter of intrigue and lust for money, Cyrus was rather stunned to discover the gravity of the situation. According to the contract between him and Belinda, he was asked to pay a sum of 500 to Belinda and be content with it, but these extra expenditure perhaps included in the fee, but he was wrong in his perception.

The advocate proffered him a bunch of papers and said, "these are the bills to be paid before the ceremony to these honored guests, who have taken so much pain to make your wedding ceremony, a memorable one."

"What bills?" Cyrus looked at Belinda for her approval. But she turned her face on the other side and was smiling notorious smile as if to mock the situation.

"These are the bills for the expenditure to be incurred with regard to the wedding ceremony. You know, these are very small items, the big ones will entail tall bills. Please pay up and we will proceed with the wedding ceremony" the advocate almost recited all the figures as if they were at his finger tips. The total figure was astronomical.

"Plus you have to pay my fee, which is $ 4,500/-." Belinda immediately stepped forward and demanded the rest of her fee.

Cyrus got the shock of his life. He was not prepared for all these extra expenditures. He asked his father to send him only the fee, demanded by Belinda and that was $ 5000/-. He was never prepared for such eventuality.

Everything began to swirl around him. He was in no position to produce the amount immediately, in fact never. The only way out for him was to protest. "I was not told to pay for all these expenses."

"Yes, I do agree with you. But you are required to go through the norms of the code of the civil marriage formalities. The advocate's fee is a must." The lawyer chipped in.

"Yes, I have brought it. Here is $ 50/- for your fee." Cyrus was frank about his declaration.

"How dare you insult me? Am I a beggar to accept such a paltry sum of money for the services to be rendered to you?" The Lawyer was curt in his reply.

"No, Sir, I'm not in a position to pay." Cyrus expressed his inability to oblige.

"Then you have to face the consequences." The Lawyer continued.

"And what is that?" Cyrus asked him finally.

"All these ladies and gentlemen will in one accord will sue you for cheating them." The Lawyer replied.

"I have not cheated anyone. I have come here in good faith, hoping to marry Belinda and settling down in this country."

"You can't do that. It is against the law." The Lawyer said.

"But a few moments ago it was possible." Cyrus protested.

"But not now" a unison of voice of all the people present there made Cyrus go tizzy. He had collected his last breath to protest. But in the mean time the Lawyer produced a typed paper in which Cyrus put in his signature to a single line previously to Belinda.

The paper read thus,

"I, Cyrus D'Cunha wish to marry Belinda, a widow and agree to bear the cost of the Advocate's fee of $ 500/- . (The last 0 was added afterwards)

The agreement was written up to this point with the clear knowledge and consent of Cyrus, but the rest, the most damaging part was affixed later on without his knowledge.

"It is also agreed upon that the cost of other related services to the ceremony will be borne by the client, which may amount to $ 10,000/-."

Date Signed

By now Cyrus was physically exhausted and mentally wrecked. He looked to Belinda for help. The Lady in need was accustomed to this kind of situation, turned her face the other side to avoid the eye contact.

Cyrus felt, 'This was the unkindest cut of all'. He fainted.

After twelve hours of concussion, Cyrus was woken up in a police station. On opening his eyes, he was surprised to find him in a narrow cell, lying on a cold, solid and hard bed, surrounded by no one, except a police woman standing outside the door of the cell.

Next day, he was produced before the additional judge in court No. 2. Of Old Bailey charged with cheating and illegally trying to settle down in Britain. A punishment of six month's imprisonment was imposed on him. Cyrus concealed his agony within himself. He never informed his parents about his plight for a couple of months. But Mr. D'Cunha got the wind of his son's predicament and came to see him forthright in the prison cell. The only parting comment he made was that, "Please come back home as soon the sentence is over. I will not tell your mother anything about it; lest the news breaks her heart. You also try to keep it as a secret when you land in India."

In the prison Cyrus shared a small narrow cell with other three criminals of Asian origin. They were trying to enter the country by illegal means. At the Dover Sea Port, their dingy boat was intercepted by the coast guard. After the completion of their period of imprisonment they would be deported to their countries. While in retrospection, Cyrus realized and thanked God that he had a destination but his comrades in sorrow had no place to go to.

"I shall go back home in India. My parents will be eagerly waiting for my arrival. The tainted record of my stay in Britain will be buried here." He reiterated his two vows in several occasions to his fellow prisoners, which firstly, he will never, in his living memory set foot on the soil of this wretched country, infested by the con men, lecherous characters and scoundrels. Secondly, never to have any encounter with the female species on earth. "I consider them the most disgraceful element of all creations of God, a great cheat, heartless creatures, seeking pleasure at the cost of others, lustful, avaricious etc. etc....

The rigorous imprisonment for six months was over in no time. Cyrus was getting ready to go home in India. But his sixth sense directed him to meet Belinda for the last time and ask her what prompted her to do it. He was honest to her, paid her the money she demanded to solemnize the wedding and remained faithful to her till the final day.

Today he had come to the hotel as a guest and not as a waiter. He bore a defying attitude and there was a mark of revenge in his gesture and posture. The manager did not like the spark emanating from his eyes as if to devour the entire wicked world in one shot. Looking at the man and realizing his evil intentions, he immediately rang up the owner. He was at an orientation conference for the staff of his chain of hotels. Sensing trouble from the nature and intensity of the call, he rushed to the restaurant only to find one of his ex-employees was seating at a table in an inebriated condition.

"What the hell, why have you called me here?" He accosted the manager. "I thought there is an emergency." He turned to Cyrus and said, "Hey, you what do you want here? Do you want your job back?"

"No, I have not come to see you. I have come to meet Belinda." Cyrus said in a curt voice.

"Belinda!" he burst into a hysterical laughter. "Oh, that swindler! You won't find her here. Go and look for her in Old Bailey." So saying, he walked out of the restaurant in long strides with thumping footsteps.

At the Heathrow airport before boarding a B.A. flight to India, Cyrus picked up a copy of the Times and read in the second page the following news clipping,

"The Caption;------Wedding rackets busted."

The London police busted a gang of imposters posing as marriage agents, duping tourists and job seekers from the sub-continent of Asia. The group comprises migrants from different parts of Europe, mostly from Italy. The leader of the group calls herself Belinda along with a brief-less advocate, run the racket under the nose of the local police outpost. She has been luring young Asian aspirants to the wed-locks at an enormous cost. The modus operandi of the gang is almost identical wherever it functions. They try to fleece out $ 8000/- on the average at each encounter from the innocent, unsuspected, yet willful young men whose dream is to settle down in Britain and obtain green cards. A thorough investigation to the nefarious activity has been entrusted with the Intelligent Department of the Scotland Yard." Cyrus read the clipping several times while waiting at the transit lounge of the airport before he was called for the security check. His reaction was nothing but blank stare at the ceiling of the room. Only utterance he had made was that, 'Why me?"

From the day one of his arrival in Britain, Cyrus was convinced that his destiny had led him to this illustrious country, firstly, for higher studies and secondly, to settle down permanently in the land of hope and glory. He could never think of going back to his country where his root was and his parents eagerly anticipated his arrival.

Cyrus pondered over the entire episode of his life while seated in the comfortable window seat in the middle of the plane. A sumptuous meal was served but Cyrus ate very little of it; soup and desert went untouched. He never looked at the airhostess while the drink was served. A kind of hatred towards the entire world especially the women folks were brewing in his mind.

"I shall never ever have any kind of relationship with anyone of them. Excepting mother, I shall not look into the eyes of the female species hovering around me in future. (He did not look at the hostess into their eyes, not even touched the over-head switch once to draw their attention for anything). In dire need I will shun them. I curse them from the bottom of my heart. They are an imbecile lot." He was fretting and fuming and would have pierced through the heart of Belinda, if he had a knife in his hand at that moment

"Are you feeling alright? Shall I get you something cold to drink? What do you want, wine or beverage?" A barrage of questions hurled at him by a pretty airhostess.

"Whoom.." he only grunted as a reciprocal gesture and turned his eyes away from her. She felt it was rather unusual and rude on his part, but she was used to such barbaric behaviours of men.

He was received at the airport by his father. Mr. D'Cunha welcomed his son with open arms and whispered, "I've not said a word to your mother about the incident so you behave accordingly."

Cyrus was really perturbed mentally, particularly while abroad in B.A. flight as how to face his mother who was so proud of the integrity of her son's character and he did not want to hurt the most vulnerable part of her, that was the heart.

According to Cyrus, this was the end of a chapter in his life. Henceforth, he vowed not to tread on a shaky part as to have intimate relationship with the female species.

Part II

The first evening at home went off uneventfully. Cyrus stayed inside the house most of the day and had no encounter with anyone except his parents. His food was brought in by the old Nepali maid, twice during the day. That too when he was in the wash room. Perhaps, the maid was instructed by the mother in no way he should be disturbed, or co-incidental.

Cyrus brooded over the entire episode of his life happened in pristine disastrous situation. The more he thought, the more he was agitated. His mind got filled up with hatred and the revenge became the order of the day. But who was he going to slaughter? Belinda by now was serving her jail sentence far away in a British cell. To him she was the representative of the entire women folks all over the world. The name is a slur in his simple career, a slut, to be condemned for not possessing non-idealistic life, a curse, to be isolated from the entire human race. The romance he was contemplating turned now into a tainted obsession.

It took him almost a fortnight to come back to his senses. The mind we possess is a treacherous object. It can make or mar an individual unless one can put a rein to ones wild thoughts. It is a most astounding phenomenon that such a small element, the head can give rise to so many contrasting ideologies... criminal, benevolent, social, constructive, destructive, romance, artistic etc.

Mr. D'Cunha was aware of his son's predicament and kept quiet, hoping he would overcome it by natural process of cleansing a contaminated mind. Mrs. D'Cunha remained a non-

- interfering person, but observant of her son's present condition. She felt it but was unaware of her son's sordid past. "In no time he would get acclimatized and then, he would lead a normal life." She said to him. The D'Cunha's thought of two goals for their son — a coveted job in an MNC and the marriage to a girl from a wealthy family.

"Son, have you thought of applying to any company for a job of your caliber and choice? You're well qualified now." Mr. D'Cunha harped on the usual topic every parent would have done so.

"Yes Dad. I've been looking out for a suitable job. I have applied to several companies through internet, both domestic and multi-national companies. I do browse through different sites whenever I can. Hope to get an answer any day."

"I'm glad to hear it. Will you be interested in my company? It has a good reputation in the international market." His father suggested.

"I don't know. I can't decide. I don't think I can continue living in this city. Its atmosphere gives me nauseating feeling. Its people and its primitive culture, tradition and weird religious conviction throttle me to the core. The living standard here is low, too much restriction imposed on the relationship between sexes, poverty lies at the lowest rung of the economic strata and there exists an unnerving chasm between the microscopic opulent class and a vast majority of the poverty-stricken people" he said in disgust.

"Are you being affected by such discrimination? Have you not been provided with everything?" his father quipped angrily.

"My life is subject to God's discretionary power. I have been born in an affluent family so I have everything. The opulent parents can provide everything to their children, which are beyond the reach of the poor. I'm lucky in a sense I belong to you." He made the statement like a philosopher

"I'm sure you will agree with me, it is your ardent duty to maintain the same standard and to grow in it. Eventually enhance the property, wealth and reputation of the family by applying yourself fully." Mr. D'Cunha said.

"Dad, I've just come from a traditionally rich country. The people there have been enjoying their lives in all respects over two hundred years. The spirit of adventure imbibed in them from time immemorial induced them to plunge into conquering the world. The efficient administrative system enabled them to hold the countries together. The bracing climate coupled with immeasurable wealth amassed from all over the world, specially from our country have enriched their soil, in turn they have decorated the urban settlement with super structure and developed the educational system resulting in rich culture, tradition and heritage. I have lived there during the period of my maturity. It has opened my eyes. A kind of taste has developed in me for good things." Cyrus spoke like a mature individual.

"Do you find anything amiss here" His father asked.

"Why there is so much poverty all around us?" Cyrus.

"Ignorance, illiteracy and lack of administrative control, perhaps are the reasons." Mr. D'Cunha said.

Cyrus now got an executive job in an MNC, dealing with the imported car accessories. He was appointed the manager of the local office based in New Delhi. Since Delhi was developing fast in all fields of business activities, employments multiplied. There was a great demand for young executives holding foreign degrees, salaries offered were handsome; perks available were adequate and supplementary aids were aplenty. He was allocated a luxurious flat in a multi-storied building in Gurgaon, but he preferred to stay with his parents at Vasant Vihar. The decision made had a filial characteristic and it was a mark of affectionate, kind and considerate heart of a young man.

"You could have stayed at the companies flat. It is closer to your place of work. The locality offered excessive facilities and comforts one is required to live a healthy, comfortable and satisfactory life," his father commented on the day of his appointment.

"I know it Papa, but I would like to stay with you and look after you." Cyrus said with an affectionate tone which moved his parents greatly.

"You have to marry soon. Then surely you need a spacious accommodation for an expanding family. Your spouse may not be willing to live with us." His mother butted in and exposed the reality of life.

"I won't marry. The presence of a girl in my life will be a curse. I stay at a distance from them," Cyrus fretted and fumed after this statement.

"But it is natural that every man should have a woman in his life for company, household activities and expansion of human race." His mother vented the parental feeling in a lucid manner. She continued, "Why are you so averse to female companionship? It is indeed natural for every man to get attached to the opposite sex. Have you any bitter experience?"

The last question shook Cyrus to the marrow. In a flash the forgotten chapter of the pristine insalubrious bitter experience struck him like lightening. He could not find any word to reply his mother's query. His father pursed his lips tightly and looked the other way. Butting into the conversation would have had a disastrous effect. He was also a part of the secret episode of his son's sordid past.

Cyrus discharged his duty honestly and efficiently. He managed the entire departmental works skillfully. Maintained a strict discipline in the department and infused enthusiasm in the hearts of his subordinates to work hard in their respective job. He used to say 'a good work will have good return. Only a dedicated worker can reap rich harvest'.

Cyrus left home everyday at 7.00 am and returned at 7.30 pm. Some days were longer when the foreign directors or auditors visited the office. He returned home sober. Never touched the drink and uttered a single foul word. No servant came anywhere within the vicinity of his room. Once in a while he had the indistinct view of the old maid, who came in tip-toed into his room, dusted the furniture, arranged the bed and went away noiselessly with fleeting feet standing on the toes. Cyrus did not appreciate his things in the house being touched by anyone.

Soon the pressure of work multiplied. Cyrus had to visit different branches of the company in India, occasionally went abroad as far as Hong Kong and Singapore. Hardly had he paid any attention to the household matters. He was quite ignorant of the existence of the other inmates besides his parents in the house. Of course he knew the old driver well. He drove him to school and other places as well in his younger days. Over three decades the old driver had rendered relentless services to the family, honestly, and efficiently; rare display of gratitude and loyalty.

Cyrus got into the mainstream of the business world. Now the time had come to display his ingenuity. He had decided to throw a social party. At dinner he broached on the subject.

"Dad, I wish to invite all my friends and business associates to a social gathering at our house on a Saturday a fortnight hence."

"It's a good idea. I will help you to organize the party." His father consented to the idea without hesitation.

A list of name was prepared. It figured a couple of his friends with their spouses and the rest, the majority of them were his business associates, four of them were females, holding the same executive posts in some other companies. The food menu was prepared by his mother; a connoisseur of exotic food buff. She was well known in her circle of elite friends for her skill in producing culinary flare of exquisite tastes.

Mouth-watering snacks were served with choicest drinks. Main dishes comprised Chinese, Indian and Continental cuisine. The deserts of three kinds, ice-creams, fruit salads and Indian sweets went untouched. The most attractive item in the menu was the 'momos', shaped, boiled and served with worster sauce and hot soup, by the Nepali maid of long-standing and her fourteen year old daughter.

"Who is she? Cyrus asked his mother at one point of the peak moment of the party when everybody was soaring high under the influence of heavy intake of the alcohol, pointing at a pretty young lass.

Before he could figure out who could that be, the girl disappeared through the kitchen door.

"She must be our old maid". The mother just said and disappeared too. Being a mother of the only son for over thirty years and a couple of years more, a good wife too, she knew exactly the feeling of her son towards the female companions. A strange phenomenon though, but giving time, she knew, over the years he would change and yearn for a female companionship. It's a law of nature.

The party went off well. A couple of men were high but the rest of them, not many, who were there behaved normally. The ladies found it was a sober party so they went on talking on different subjects. The most familiar ones comprised fashion, food and films. A few infernal episodes were related ranging from rape to elopement but eventually they fell flat on the listeners. The person was avoided by all till the end of the party that went well over midnight.

Mr. D'Cunha mixed with the guests freely and encouraged the male guest to drink as much as they could but to the limit of sobriety. He coaxed the ladies to help themselves with the food and testify the culinary skill his wife acquired recently.

Mrs. D'Cunha floated between kitchen and the sitting room supervising the preparation of the food and also keeping the guests busy with their drinks as social commitment befitting to the hostess.

Cyrus did not have a moment's rest. This was the first party he had organized to entertain his peers in the working place. He was determined to make it a success.

"Let's sing" Cyrus suggested suddenly when he realized the revelers seemed to be quiet. A chorus of falsetto voices sang in dissonant chords and different melodies. 'Hotel California' sounded as if the place was on fire. 'My heart is burning' gave the impression the ship was still tossing and turning, it simply refused to sink. 'Country Road' would have driven the original singer mad or stirred him up in his grave. 'Old Lang Syne' sounded as if the Tuba had developed a crack. A couple of songs sung from the film titled 'The Sound of Music' woke up the children in the neighborhood. The Austrian patriotic music 'Adel Weiss' sung at the finale of the movie. The highest note attacked by half a dozen revelers in unison gave the heart attack to the septuagenarian old lady next door. The pariah dogs left the place in disgust.

"It's a fab party' remarked Robert Juneja, swayed to and fro at the end of the party.

"G-o-o-d d-r-i-n-ks", drawled Bhaskar Bose. Cyrus had to escort him out to the car.

"Surely your mother has the taste. The food was good. But when do we expect your better half adding more flavour to the curry?" asked the pretty Sunita of the Escorts Group of Companies.

"It's out of question', Cyrus gave a curt reply and turned back to enter the house'. A big clash was averted at that moment. He was about to collide with a young girl. She was dashing out of the room to avoid confronting him. A split second delay would have done the needful, but she sprinted out and disappeared from the view at once.

"She is a nuisance." He hurled a remark at the vanishing figure.

By now, Cyrus' dislike of women, an unnatural phenomenon though, became known to all his friends and business associates. They discussed the topic among themselves, had quiet laughter and declared the issue is funny and temporary.

"He has not met yet a killer Jane, who could bowl him out." A friend of Cyrus said to another.

"Yes indeed. He has not come across the right person." The second said in reply.

"Is there anything wrong with his hormone? He most probably has a very little of male hormone in him." The third friend said.

"Let us organize a freak party and see his reaction there." The first friend suggested.

The party was organized in a farm house. A strict rule was imposed with consensus votes that all male members should bare their torsos and the girls in their scanty skirts and short tops would participate in the party. Drinks and food were the responsibility of the individuals. Cyrus refused to comply. He went to the party fully dressed in casual clothes with a couple of bottles of whisky. Since, the purpose of the party was lost; no one showed any interest to strip as they intended to do. Cyrus came back home in a huff.

Next they took a drastic step as to brief the girls in the office to be more free and dashing with him. The girls pushed him, poked him, giggled, taunted and sighed deep breath in his presence, but to no avail. Cyrus stood on his ground firmly like the northern star. The friends, companions and business associates declared his behavior 'weird'.

"It's a natural instinct to be friendly with the opposite sex, but Cyrus is an exception." The friends said to each other.

He was a workaholic, devoted his entire self to the cause, enlistment and prosperity of the company. He never raised his head from the screen of his computer. He always discussed the matter of his file in brief with his subordinates and co-workers and dismissed them in no time. He avoided his colleagues in the dining room for lunch and arranged a separate place to have his lunch in staggering timings. He defeated all the plans his friends devised to get him acquainted with the female species on earth.

The management group of the company was highly pleased with his result oriented performance. It was unanimously decided in the board meeting that he should be promoted to a full-fledged manager of the company in the next financial year for his hard, sincere and devoted work. The news upset some but the majority of his contemporaries felt he deserved it. The news leaked out to Cyrus by the over-jealous personal manager of the CEO. She wanted to curry favour with him.

Mrs. D'Cunha attributed it to his gene. She had seen how her husband in the past almost gave his entire life to the cause of the company, its growth, profit and expansion. Mr. D'Cunha took it to his stride.

"Who are you? What are you doing in my room? Who sent you here?" Cyrus asked a barrage of questions to a girl. She was dusting the furniture of his room. The girl did not show any kind of feeling nor she replied, but walked out quietly with her head down, eyes on the floor in a restrained manner. This infuriated Cyrus to a breaking point, he dashed out of the room on the trail of the girl and was about to assault her, but was interrupted by Mrs. D'Cunha. She heard the commotion from her son's room and came out in time to intervene.

"Who's she, Mama? And what is she doing in my room? Cyrus said in agitated mood. He was fuming and fretting. It seemed he was about to throttle the girl.

"Son, listen to me. She is our domestic help. She is a part of our family." The matter was forthright with her explanation.

Mr. D'Cunha took stock of the situation so stepped forward to pacify the son. He knew very well the agonizing moment his son was passing through, he could never forget his tragic episode in the past. He felt his son needed an explanation.

Part 3

Kanchi left Kathmandu in the wee hour of a winter morning. She was pregnant with three month old baby, puffed up belly, conceived by her husband, Kancha. The drunken habit of her husband, subsequent brawl and inhuman treatment meted out to her all through her stay at her husband's house made her take a drastic decision. It was self-willed and firm decision to depart from the house where women found shelter, protection and love. Her dream of living a meaningful life for her self and for her would be born child shattered. Kanchi knew it very well her own parents were not in a position to keep another person in the house.

Kanchi boarded a bus at the bus stand, the destination of which was not known to her. After an arduous and painstaking journey the bus reached Biratnagar in the evening. During the journey, she sat beside a genial Nun who was rushing to the Convent of Jesus. Mother Superior summoned her suddenly to discuss a matter of high magnitude. When she heard the sordid affair of the helpless woman travelling beside her, she took pity on her and took her to the Nunnery. The Mother Superior was not pleased to allow her in the Nunnery as she was carrying a baby in her womb, but she felt it was an act of God, therefore, it was her ardent duty to come to the rescue of a helpless creature of His creation.

The baby was born after six months. It was not in the tradition of this particular convent to rear the baby along with the mother. So, she asked her if she would like to stay in a family anywhere in India.

"I will send you to India. There is a benevolent and God fearing couple in New Delhi who want a domestic help. You have to live with them as a member of the family. They have a twelve year old son. The accommodation will be provided."

"Yes mother, I'll go." She gave a short reply.

Mr. D'Cunha made an arrangement with the travel agent to fetch her from the Biratnagar Nunnery. Mrs. D'Cunha welcomed Kanchi in their midst with open arms. Cyrus was not aware much of the existence of a new entrant to the family. He used to see Kanchi for a while during the day. Much of his personal need was looked after by his mother. Sporadically he met her at the dining table serving food. A thirteen year old boy spent most of his time outside the family boundaries. He had little time for his own, but plenty for others. His boarding school days kept him busy with studies, extra-curricular activities and camaraderie. Holidays spent in the hills or sea resorts. College life made him a stranger at home. Being the only child, Cyrus was pampered by both parents. U.K. days made him an alien. 'Home sweet home' was an isolated conception. The net result, Cyrus did not know who was who, at home and now after twenty five years he did not wish to know who were living all around him.

During Cyrus' absence from home, Minu, the daughter of Kanchi grew up. Frail but sturdy, short but beautiful, Minu was sent to the local central school. She was a bright student. The D'Cunha's never involved her in domestic chores but gave all kinds of financial help to further her studies.

"We have no daughter. Minu is our daughter. We are going to educate her and keep her in our house and treat her as a family member." Mr. D'Cunha said to his wife one night. His frequent visits to the other parts of the country on official duties, left Mrs. D'Cunha alone and lonely. Small Minu fulfilled her heart with the emotional needs.

"She is shaping up well. I do not mind keeping her at home with me. We have to consider Kanchi. She can not live alone."

"Kanchi won't mind staying in the servant's quarters alone. Every mother would like to see her child prosper and live happily."

Kanchi could guess the intention of her benefactor. In a way she felt happy that her daughter's life was well secured. Recently she had been receiving letters from her husband begging her to come back home. He promised her that he had turned over a new leaf, had given up all bad habits and had a steady job.

"I do not know the authenticity of the statement." Mr. D'Cunha remarked when Kanchi came to bid farewell. Kanchi dropped a few drops of tears. It was difficult to discern whether the drops meant sadness or happiness. It was a mixture of both.

Cyrus could not reconcile with the idea of entertaining a girl in the house. "They all are sluts, cruel, heartless, selfish demon, etc, etc. I vow in the name of all jilted men like me to take the revenge."

"She must go, she must go." Three words remained uppermost in his mind. In sleep he uttered them as well. At the dining table he inserted in between sentences. In the office, in conversation with his colleagues he said those words. While dictating he quoted that magic words. The typist had a good laugh. The old driver could not figure out what he was saying, 'Chick dust God, chick dust God', only sound entered his ears.

It took Cyrus a week to devise a viable plan for her ouster. The easiest way to placate a person was to call her a thief. In the morning, he hid his purse behind the cupboard containing ten thousand rupees and half a dozen credit cards. He raised a hue and cry as soon as he entered the house in the evening.

"Dad, Mom, I have been robbed" He screamed at the top of his voice.

"What do you mean by robbed? Who has robbed you?" Mr. D'Cunha enquired.

"I do not know, but I can't find my purse. I distinctly remember I left it under the pillow before I went to bed last night. This morning I forgot to take it with me. Now I cannot find it." Cyrus blurt out.

"No outsiders come here." He said innocently.

"It is the work of an insider. I strongly suspect the girl. Throw her out of the house." Cyrus insisted.

"You have no reason to implicate her in this affair." Mrs. D'Cunha butted in. "She has not taken the purse. You dropped it behind the cupboard. She found it. Here, take it and count your money."

Cyrus was crestfallen. He was defeated in his evil design. But he was not ready to give up. The next step will be to torture her physically and mentally. How? He could never go near her because she had been well protected by his mother. She had been allotted a special room, the guest room adjacent to her mother's room. "What a privilege, I wonder!" He said in disgust.

"I can push her out of the room. But mother will be heart broken. I can frighten her in the guise of an evil spirit. But if she ever dies as a consequence of the attack, I will be blamed. I can assault her. Engage a few muscle men to attack her on the way to the milk booth. It would be too obvious to be dealt with. The police will find out and those criminals will give away the name of the instigator. The plan will be termed as an act of terrorist. The name of my family will be sullied. I can poison her to death. But after the autopsy has taken, the doctors will find out the reason for her death. I will be implicated. I can starve her to death, but she is too close to my mother. So I have no control over her food or eating habits. I can kill her with a sharp knife. The subsequent result will be a long legal battle in the criminal court of law. I will rot in jail and my career will be ruined."

"But why should I destroy my career for the sake of a silly girl? Moreover, she has not done anything to me. It is I, Cyrus D'Cunha, the heir apparent to the said family, without a solid reason is trying to harm an innocent girl to take revenge on the female species, one of them has harmed me in the past."

"I better change my strategy" Cyrus said to himself.

A week after the incident Cyrus was sent to Mumbai for a week on company errand. There he kept himself busy with office works all the days long. In the evenings when there was no party to attend, he used to go for walks. The Marine Drive in front of hotel Oberoi - he loved to walk. He hated the much talked about Juhu Beach, a place infested by stalkers, musclemen, vendors, un-skilled masseurs, gays and anti-social elements. The Bombay Central, a place completely swallowed by prostitutes, touts and drug addicts. He could not enter any hotel or restaurant there, as to his embarrassment; he found the clients were entertained by sluts and belly dancers with their erotic dances. The lobbies of the five star hotels were occupied by call girls and young men bent on making first bucks. A couple of them winked at him on his first visit to the elegant place.

"Shameless characters', he remarked at them. "God rescue these fallen souls. These are your children created in your image. Please forgive them of their sins." He walked out of the most sought after places, where things were happenings, celebrities wasting their easy earned money and the romantic lovers meeting their partners.

Cyrus returned home on a Sunday evening. To his immense pleasure, he found his room was sparklingly clean, furniture were dusted, curtains cleaned, books arranged, flower vases installed with assorted seasonal flowers and a tag was fixed, declaring 'Welcome Home'. A kind of an aroma, pleasing to the smell was wafting in the air. His wardrobe was arranged, clothes were neatly and carefully hung from the hangers matching tie and shirts tucked into the suit. He felt a touch of class, taste and feeling. It was obviously the handiwork of feminine touch.

"Wow, Mummy! I am so thankful." So saying he laid down on the bed.

At that moment Mrs. D'Cunha was recuperating from the viral flu. Cyrus entered her room and noticed the girl was sitting next to his mother. Her right hand was on her forehead

"Mum, what happened. Are you sick?" Cyrus asked her quite sympathetically.

"Yes, my son. I was suffering from flu. Now, O.K." She said in a rather subdued tone.

"Is there anything I can do for you?"

"No my son I have been well looked after by Minu. Where is she?"

Poor Minu went out of the room tip toed. So no one could hear her departure.

Within a week Cyrus was also infected by flu viral. His mother tried her best to nurse him while awake. Minu did the rest in his sleep. She cleaned the room, arranged his medicine on the side table to be taken at staggering timings. She was careful not to awaken him during her presence there. The hatred he harboured against her and the entire human female species had amused her greatly.

"How can a man live outside the social ambience. Gregariousness is human nature." Minu told her friend in school one day.

"Goodness gracious. How do you know all these?" The friend asked her in surprise.

"The English teacher told us while explaining one of Shakespeare's Plays." She replied.

The friend did not realize the inner meaning of it. It was Minu's inner outburst.

"How can Cyrus be so cruel, heartless and obsessive?" She questioned herself, but there was no answer for it.

Cyrus was aware of Minu's presence in his room during his sickness. Initially he resented and was about to scream, but restrained his emotions, realizing the fact, if Minu did not work, his mother had to do it. Her age would compel her to go slow. She might get sick. Minu was capable of doing her job, nursing him.

"I will allow her to do the daily chores but with a limit." He consoled himself

After recuperating in the house for another week, Cyrus began to go to office to clear the piled up works that kept him busy for a fortnight. During that period he would leave the house early in the morning and come back very late in the evening. Every morning, he would find his breakfast was ready and kept warm on the table and at night, food was served hot and fresh by an invisible hand.

"I find an invisible hand behind this work. I feel someone lurking behind the door observing every activity of mine. Surely it's a female who is catering for my taste and trying to bring solace to my, otherwise, troublesome, obsessive and vindictive mind. Who is the person?"

Each time he sat at the table for food he could hear a mute shuffle in the kitchen. Initially he thought it was mother or she might have employed some one as a cook. If mother, she was omnipresent. If another character he could wait to meet the person.

But soon he heard a different tune, smelt an exquisite smell. A kind of pleasant aroma mingled with human flesh, of female kind and light cosmetic smell wafting in the atmosphere. He felt good.

The light commotion in the kitchen caused him to stir to a magnetic pull. One morning he could not control his patient and barged into it and what he saw made him recoil and storm out of it immediately.

Minu was stooping down on the sink. The water was pouring out from it ceaselessly. She was washing the pile of used up utensils. She was stunned at his appearance. Cyrus looked into her direction, saw the two beady eyes; squint, a sign of Mongolian origin, embossed on a beautiful face. He was emotionally stirred, but lost word to speak. So beat a hasty retreat.

The same evening he saw her again, standing outside the gate, chatting away with another girl of her age. The rendezvous could have ignited a destructive fire in his heart a few days ago but now it was different. He felt relaxed; a kind of joy overcame his anguished heart. He heard a stray remark while passing by.

Minu - "I liked Madhuri Dixit in 'Khal Nayak'.

Friend - "I like Sanjay Dutt. He is so handsome and a macho man he is."

A peel of laughter followed. Cyrus was overwhelmed. "Are they making fun of me, or enjoying themselves?" he thought. "But never mind. This is no business of mine." He said to himself and walked ahead.

The driver just arrived after dropping his parents to the club. He noticed a mark difference in the nature of his boss's son. He had been the small boy growing into manhood. Every twist and turn in his life was noted carefully by him. Today, it surprised him to see the boy feeling ecstatic for the first time after his return from abroad.

Cyrus pretended to be sick and requested his supper to be brought into his room. It was obvious Minu would do the needful. The expectation was great, but disillusionment was even greater. His mother walked in with the tray, laden with a bowl of vegetable soup and a couple butter less toasts.

"What do I care! It is the duty of my mother to look after me when sick." He consoled himself.

"Who else will come? I have no place in my heart for anyone," He continued thinking.

On Monday morning Cyrus was late in leaving home. The office car waited outside for him for over ten minutes. It was seven 'o clock sharp. Minu went out every day at this time to fetch milk from the local milk booth. She had just left the gate before Cyrus deposited the bunch of keys to the driver. Cyrus noticed her walking stealthily with measured space, head bent, two unequal milk cans in hand. He came and stood outside the gate.

"Uncle what's the date today?" He asked the driver.

"Well I'm not sure. It may be 8th or 9th of March" the driver said after a minutes' hesitation. Interestingly he noticed Cyrus's face was aimed at his but his eyes cast over his head towards the direction of the girl. It was amusing but interesting to observe.

Cyrus stood there for a couple of minutes and cast a longing glance towards the direction of the girl, pretending as if looking for something or forgotten.

The week end he stayed back home and tried to catch up with the sleep lost due to heavy pressure of work, outing with the directors of the company and attending endless parties. At about eleven am he woke up, went unto the window to stretch and saw Minu was standing under a tall tree in the farthest corner of the garden with a water can. She was bending down and began to water the small bushes of Azaleas, Petunias and 9 'o clocks. One quarter of her bosom was exposed. It stirred his soul to an immeasurable extent and filled his heart with pleasure for which there was no word to explain. He remained glued to the scene.

The sudden appearance of the old driver on the spot distracted his attention from the girl. The old man offered her the 'Prasad'. He stayed put for a while doling out directions to the effective watering of the plants. While doing so, Minu smiled a million dollar smile. Her diminutive and frail body swayed delicately with the sprayed water from the nozzle of the water can. The flowers gave out a pleasant smell. The revitalized dry soil mixed with the fragrance of the fresh blossoms of the seasonal flowers and mingled with the body odour of the human flesh, hit his nostrils. Cyrus was transformed. The fatigued body of his turned into, like newly cut fresh flowers or recently plucked red Kulu apples.

Mrs. D'Cunha observed the entire proceeding from her window, hiding behind the curtain and felt satisfied. She made the only comment of the incident to her husband. "At last our son has come of age."

Mr. D'Cunha said nothing but smiled. He felt satisfied and replied, "'I'm glad of it."

On Sunday, the D'Cunha's were rather surprised to see Cyrus was standing outside the door waiting for them to board the family car. They were about to leave home for the morning Mass in the parish church on Poorvi Marg. It was a Sunday ritual in which all the family members traditionally participated. Cyrus never joined them after his return from abroad.

"Good morning son." The parents wished him almost simultaneously. Their observation ran riot at that point of time. Cyrus was a prodigal son as far as the religion was concerned. He did not attend the church services after his return from U.K. but now what forced him to stand before them and prompted him to accompany them to the morning Mass. They wonder!

Mrs. D'Cunha was dumb-founded but Mr. D'Cunha took things in his strides, being aware of the short episode of his son's sordid past life.

The local parish church was full to the capacity worshippers. Being the elders of the church, D'Cunha's had two permanent pews reserved for them in the first row.

Cyrus had to occupy a seat in the second row just behind his parents.

The church altar where the great supper would be enacted following the traditional rituals was constructed in the far end of the church facing the pews. A cross was hung just behind the altar on the north of the church. The celebrating priest stood between the cross and the alter while performing the ritual, invocation, nunc diminic, creed - all these were time immemorial services repeated during each service.

During the sermon the Priest stood before the lectern. The celebrating clergy was the retired Bishop of the Delhi Diocese. He was hailed from Italy. Fifty years ago he touched the soil of this country as a young priest, fresh from Milan's Novitiate. A handsome, tall and vibrant young priest drew the attention of the parishioners of Mapusa Cathedral in Goa. Wherever he celebrated the mass, the church was overflowing with the worshippers. His meteoric rise to the exalted position as the Arch Bishop of Mumbai and later on the post of general controlling the entire country was due to his dedicated services accepting poverty and leading a life of celibacy. Now after retirement he had been put in this church as an assistant to the vicar. He was a voracious reader and had written a few dozens of commentaries, discourses and biblical interpretations. A genuine servant of God, he had worked among poverty-stricken people of this country during his tenure of fifty years. His flocks knew him well and he knew the folks among whom he worked. Today's sermon was based on love. "Gods love is so wonderful" he began.

"God had created this world to nurture human beings and all other creatures. He had made man in his own image. He wanted man to look after himself, the creatures and all other elements on the earth, water and air. He also wished man to stay away from the devil and lead a righteous life. But man always fall prey to sinful acts. They lie, murder, con, steal, rape and indulge in many other sinful acts. Only a few among them like the pillars hold life together and follow it as prescribed in the Holy Book. But God is just. He considers all, both the holy men and the sinful ones as his children, He wants them to live together in Godly fear and wisdom. The rich have isolated them from the main stream of life and live in the land of Utopia. The poor are forced to live apart from the rich and cluster themselves into hovels, shanties and huts. The murderers, rapist, con men, swindlers, smugglers commit their respective crimes and fill up the prison cells.

The Bible says, all of us have to stand before the creator one day and give accounts of our good works and misdeeds while living on the earth. A few good ones will pass the tests and enter paradise but the rest, the majority of them will hang around the hell for a long time. Extreme cases will enter the precinct of the condemned area and suffer.

But God is kind. He does not discriminate between any two classes of people. In fact he loves the fallen ones more. He wants to show them the right path of righteousness. All his emotions, sense faculties and talents are the gifts of God, to be used for his inward and outward developments.

On closer look God found the human beings have drifted apart from the path he had chosen for them. Over the centuries the man amassed a lot of wealth and forgot God. He began to worship mammon. His carnal desires intensified and he had begun to commit various sins. A place in hell is reserved for each individual.

But God is merciful. He wants each one of us to be living with Him in paradise forever after the judgment day. He wants to give us a chance. Man is too weak to mend his way. He needs a support, which will lift them up. So God sent His only Son on the earth to die for them on the cross and be redeemed. For the atonement of all sinners he made the supreme sacrifice. Unless the creator loves all his creations, he won't do such a thing. How many of us are ready to sacrifice our only son..... None, I presume. Our worldly love is artificial expression of our emotions. God's love is genuine."

This moved Cyrus greatly. He came back home as a different person. He wanted to love everybody. The same night he prayed to God and asked His forgiveness

"God, forgive me. I've sinned against you. I lost my senses due to certain reasons, which are known to you. I will endeavor to do my best to love all your creatures."

A fortnight later, Cyrus was sent to the U.S. office as the finance director of the MNC.

A month later he e-mailed to his father,

"I need someone to look after my household affairs. Kindly send Minu to look after my house and give me company."

9

The Providential Decree

A controversial row regarding the supremacy of God over the Universe was raging in the firmament and was causing an unpleasant mental disturbance among the celestial beings. The Arch Angel and the Angels dwelling in the realm of the paradise. the heavenly abode of all of them were at the receiving end.

The Angel Gabriel could never reconcile with the idea of the devil being the superior authority of the universe. He heard several times from the mouth of the devil itself saying.

"I'm the supreme being and rule over the world. There are more wicked people on the earth than the sages." The devil used to boast of his power.

" What makes you to say that?" the Angel Gabriel enquired of him one day to ascertain the truth of the statement.

" See there are more evil-doers than the benevolent ones on the earth. The former are my creation. the later are of God's. You can describe my followers in many words - Cheats, thieves, liars, swindlers, con men, avaricious persons, rapists, murderers, terrorists, etc. but only one mono-syllabic word 'holy' can be attributed to God's people" the devil went on elaborating on the evil points of his view.

" But one word can be used to describe your followers. It is 'bad' just the opposite of good. God's word carries more weight than yours.

Four letters word makes the word 'Good' but only three letters constitute the word 'Bad'. Good people bring joy and happiness, but the bad people usher in misery, suffering, loss and dejection. What is more weighty and meaningful?" The Arch Angel summarized the view of God and his followers with conviction.

Such a burning issue of God's undisputed power and authority over all His creation challenged by a fallen angel could not be tolerated by the celestial beings. Even the earthly mortal beings were perturbed when the news infiltrated into the earthly domain of man. Both the heavenly bodies and earthly beings craved for a solution in favor of their creator.

The ill-propaganda of the devil infatuated his supporters to such an extent that they coaxed, cajoled and in the end forced him to confront God and challenge His authority. In an opportune moment the devil sneaked in to heaven and dodging several guards on the way reached the judgmental throne to face God.

"I know your evil intention of dethroning me from the coveted post of being the supreme head of the Universe. But I fear you'd not be able to do so. I am the creator of this universe. Both the living and dead, animate and inanimate objects are my responsibility. Their welfare on the earth is looked after by me. I decide their fates on the earth and here after".

"You're wrong. It is I, being an evil spirit, steer them into the evil doings. I feel nice when they suffer, elated when they cry for help and rejoice at the death due to the long sufferings, incurable diseases and fatal accidents. I cause the children fall and break their bones to make the mothers cry, create palpitation in the hearts of the young lovers, inflict pains at the break of it, force them to go to wars with the consequent results of arson, looting, loss of lives and property. I inflict incurable diseases on them, they struggle all their lives to find a permanent cure. I get a gratifying and heartening kick when they suffer, bleed and cry heart-breaking cries." The devil would have giving a list of sufferings the people could have but God stopped him from going further in his evil design.

" I initiate their birth on the earth, sustain their lives, see that they can be united with me afterwards. Everything that is good is my creation" God humbly mentioned a few things, in fact the most vital ones pertaining to human lives.

" I turn your people into thieves, dacoits, swindlers, con men, killers, murderers, rapists, terrorists. I feel their hearts with greed, lust, revenge and ill-will. They torture, cheat, hit, bite and loot at my command. I get immense pleasure of watching them bleed". The devil's outburst shook the entire world. All the prisons, police lock-ups and hide-outs of the criminals got busy with devilish activities.

" Please leave me now. I have got works to do" God said to the devil.

"You can't dismiss me so abruptly. You have to prove your all pervading power and authority. As you know I score much higher than you. Those great wars fought all over the world from the very inception of the civilization, specially in Greece, Rome, India, America are my doings.

I am the architect of the two great wars fought in the last century" the devil expounded its evil deeds in the most devilish manner.

.. He has evolved treaties, truces, amnesty groups, U.N., U.N.O., N.A.T.O., O.N., G 14 groups to bring succor to the belligerent nations" The Arch Angel gave him the short reply on behalf of God.

"Its no use of arguing. Lets prove each other's point of view. Nonetheless I will prove you wrong. I'm mightier than Him, in strength, vigor and shrewd manipulation of things." The devil delivered the most pungent, evil and derogatory thought as an ultimatum. God smiled a serene, pure and holy smile.

At that moment a local passenger train hauled by a steam engine attached to it was leaving New Delhi Railway Station. Its destination was Katgodam in the Uttaranchal Pradesh, situated at the foot hills of the Great Himalayan Mountain Chain. The passengers comprised mostly the people of U.P., and its adjoining states. They were simple, poor and god fearing people.

Some were holiday makers, would be touring Nainital, a hill station of Uttaranchal Pradesh. The lofty mountain ranges of the great Himalayas nestled a few health resorts worth visiting for its bracing climate, pollution free air, scenic beauty and romantic atmosphere. One could relax in a tension free environment, flex muscles and enjoy exotic food in a resort, several of which cater for all types of clientele.

Some were labourers. They would take up jobs in hotels, resorts or guest houses as waiters, dish-washers or domestic help. They belonged to the lower rung of discriminatory social system existing in the country, had been placated as the scheduled caste or the sudras. They were literally poor, ignorant and illiterate. They were of migratory nature, would be moving out of Nainital at the end of the season.

Some were farmers, would be taking up works in the fruit orchards of Nainital, Bhimtal, Sattal and Ranikhet in dual capacities as contractors or labourers.

There was a group of mendicants making a trip to Nainital to hear the final verdict of the chief justice of the Uttaranchal high court. The disputed land from where they had been uprooted by the land owner in Ramgarh. During his absence they forcibly acquired the land in the name of the Goddess 'Kali', a decade ago. The Sanyasin's contention was that the land they had obtained then was of no use. It was lying fallow, no harm using it for the services of god. The head of the group was convinced the verdict would go in favour of them.

A group of fifty people, male and female from the village of 'Kiru' near Bhopal were going to attend a religious meeting under the aegis of a healing mission, at Sattal. The meeting had been fixed for a couple of days. Almost half of the delegates were ailing people suffering from different diseases, another half was escorting them. It was their blind faith in the healer and his God had drawn them together and inspired them to forge ahead. The healer would talk a lot to these people and then touch them in the name of God. Their faith would surely see them through, not the healer. But the man would take the credit.

A gang of robbers comprised twelve notorious characters of a renowned underground group of U.P. were traveling incognito. They boarded the train in the guise of the members of a marriage party. Their avowed intention was to loot the train at gun point then move into Nainital, rob the tourists of their belongings, spread panic in the hearts of the innocent tourists who would come here from all corners of the country, also from the globe in drove to while away their spare time for sometimes, spend their hard-earned money and relax in the company of their dear ones. The miscreants bent on depriving them of this pleasure.

Before they could plunge into their intended activity, they involved themselves in nefarious activities. They winked at a few unsuspected dames, pinched a couple of unconscious young men and pushed some elderly gentlemen to provoke them to loose their temper before the onslaught.

A honeymoon couple occupied two seats in an isolated cabin of the three tier compartment. Their was the love marriage. Since the day of their intimacy they had been weaving plans of comfortable settlement in the serene atmosphere surrounded by beautiful and congenial environment of the mountain.

"Where only you and me will live in the protected arms of nature, away from the humdrum of the city life" the man quite often whispered the same thought in her ears.

" We'll have a bony boy and a pretty daughter as the symbol of our true love" she made the reciprocal statement.

"I'll name the girl, Neha" he added.

"I'll name our son Anand." She said.

"The house will be built on the bank of a swift flowing river, the sound of which will forever sooth our tired bodies and lull us to sleep" He expressed his emotional thought more explicitly.

"Our small house will stand on the periphery of a mountain, surrounded by lofty verdant forest trees. The wind blowing through them will forever remind us of love of god, expressed through the creation of His" She added fuel to the emotional fire to their passionate concern for each other.

"The snow clad mountain, the enormous gorges, tricky and misleading creeks, the running rivulets filled with gliding touts, sardines and mackerels, the lush green meadows and lustrous valleys spread by assortment of flowers giving a panoramic view of the creators love and care for mankind. The entire picturesque scenario will be a part of our house." The man concluded his graphic narration and looked into the eyes of his wedded wife for consent. She replied in the customary feminine manners of turning the protruding half of the tongue, rotating eyes and the chin thrust forward.

The devil confronted God and said,

"See I am going to destroy that train with all its occupants. You take a lot of pride in yourself in boasting of creating those mortal beings on the earth, try now to save them."

God looked at him with sympathetic eyes and turned His head on the other direction as if not to hear a word of what the devil had said.

The train moved out of the main station slowly. After blowing whistles one after the other at several level crossings it entered the corn fields, dotted with the huts of the farmers, presumably the owners of the fields or bonded labourers, the later were living at the mercy of the former.

The driver looked a contented man. Smoked a few 'biris' to kill the monotony, sang a few verses from different film songs, was hoping to eat his evening meal which his sweet and loving daughter of twelve years old handed him over in a tifin carrier box before leaving home. He had pinned down a lot of hope in his daughter for a bright future and prosperous life.

Miriam was born to Mr. and Mrs. Lalwani after fifteen years of the marriage. They traveled to several holy places for God's blessings, irrespective of their religious convictions. They paid obeisance to all the Gods and Goddess found in the length and breath of the country -Hardwar, Hrishikesh and Varanasi in the north and Tirupathi, Mahamallapuram and Kanchipuram in the south of the country, to name a few. They visited the tombs of all the holy men. In Ajmir Shariff they donated sheets to cover the tomb of St. Salim Chisti, in Meerut they visited the church built by lady Fatima and took the vow of leading an austere life till their first child was born.

For a few years - colleagues, relatives, friends, neighbors avoided them. He was accused of being not potential and she barren. They could not go to the local temples or churches, the priests would not accept the offerings, the worshipers would stare at them in disgust, the young upstarts would jeer at them, the boys of school going ages pelted stones at them. But good God gave them patience to bear the assaults inflicted upon them. One bright evening she threw,within six months she had the bulge in the stomach. The first week of the ninth month she gave birth to a baby girl. All speculations of their detractors were proved wrong.

During the last twelve years, each day of his life was bright and beautiful. He left home everyday for duty holding hands of his beloved daughter and came back home when greeted by her again. That sparkling smile on her face and the feminine touch eased the tension of the day. His tired body found the rest in her company, the mind the solace.

" Will you add fuel to the fireplace, don't you see the coals have burnt out and turned to ashes?" He commanded the assistant. He did not quite like the company of this particular man for his insolent, rude behavior and negative view of life. But the railway rules forced him to work with him on rotation.

"I know my job.You need not boss over me". The fireman replied curtly.

" I'm not asking you, but ordering you to add more coals to the fire, otherwise it will extinguish and steam will be lost, resulting in the loss of speed of the train" the engine driver did not quite loose his temper but said harshly.

The fireman lost his temper so replied in the most atrocious manner, "Why don't you do it yourself instead of ordering me".

"This is not my part of the work. The railways have employed you to do the work". Why don't you do it yourself? I'm bound to report the matter to the authorities of the dereliction of duty". The engine driver cautioned him.

The young fireman was rather ambitious. He wished to rise high on the ladder of success immediately. In the beginning he wanted to occupy the place of the engine driver, but lacked the knowledge and skill of the job. He was ambitious for two reasons - one to earn more money, two the post entailed respect and a stupendous prospect of demanding high price in the dowry market. He required more money to build a house before plunging into the life-long imprisonment of the marital life.

" Son, do not squander your hard earned money. Now you got a permanent job in the Railways and this small quarters to live in, but a time will come after your marriage when you'll be requiring more space for the expanding family." His father used to say to him periodically.

"Yes father, I know my duty," he replied in this manner whenever the topic of such nature came for discussion.

Fifty percent of the salary he would give to his mother for the household expenses, not quite enough though, and the rest of it he would keep for himself, squandering on the alcoholic drinks and visiting the freaky women living in the red light area of the locality. He was always in need.

"This man has drawn his salary today. It's quite a handsome amount. If I can get the money I can pay Jane, she will be mine forever." The fireman thought.

"Hey you, why aren't you working? Don't you see the coal is burnt in the fire-place. Throw some more coal into it." The driver ordered him once more. It appeared unnatural to the driver since the process of replenishing the furnace after every ten minutes was a routine affair.

Up in heaven the devil was ecstatic. His evil design would be fulfilled now.

"See your creatures," he told God. "They are at dagger's drawn. I will cause a friction between them thereby the entire movement of the engine will be immobile, resulting in the full-scale destruction of the train and all the passengers. Consequent result will be the death of all the passengers" the devil turned to God, with a wry smile on his face. He further asked." Can you save the situation, it has reached the boiling point?"

" I have created the world to sustain human lives so that they worship me and live righteous lives. It is not for destruction." God made a brief statement to confirm His authority.

The fireman filled the furnace to the full, stuffed more coal than required and moved towards the engine driver.

"Hey, what do you want?" the engine driver asked the fireman sensing his evil motive.

"Hand over the money you've received today." He told him firmly.

"What audacity. Why should I do for heaven's sake? This is my money. I've earned it by the sweat of my brow. Get back to your place at once, I order you". The engine driver ordered his subordinate firmly.

"I won't go back. Who the hell are you to order me?" The fireman asked him with a defying tone.

"I'm your boss. I shall surely report the matter to the higher authority," he passed his final verdict.

The fireman went back to his place near the furnace, stood there for a while, fuming and fretting due to excessive anger, ruminating over the thought of taking the revenge, later on. But the thought of grabbing the money turned him insane. He lost control over emotion and ran out of patience, picked up the shovel and moved towards the engine driver. Before the driver could make out of his motive and react, the fireman hit him with the shovel on his head. The engine driver dropped down on the floor instantaneously from his seat and became unconscious. The fireman pulled out notes of twelve thousand rupees from the pocket of his over all. Next he stood motionless for two reasons - estacy being rich, by twelve thousand rupees - agony - unexpected murder of an innocent person and observing the mess created on the floor of the engine near the furnace. Half burnt coals of immeasurable quantity and of burnt out coals strewn all over the engine. The incandescent coals were staring at him for his life. The sight of the engine and vitiated atmosphere inside it choked him to the core. Next he found breathing was impossible. So he came out of the engine and stood on the steps by its side to breath unpolluted air. It did not bring any relief to him he fainted on the steps. His hands could not hold the side railing for long, the body weight pulled him down and he fell headlong on the stony ground beside the railway track. The train puffed away merrily towards its destination.

The devil chuckled and looked at God sarcastically, as if to say, "see my power, I'll cause a great accident to occur, the train will bump into a formidable barrier ahead of it, overturn and kill all the passengers. The impending result is the great disaster. If you have the power try to stop the train".

"If you do not create something you do not have the right to destroy anything created by others" God said briefly.

The Arch Angel heard the comment and said to the people on the earth, " I am speaking to you on behalf of God, you murderers, war mongers, warriors, autocratic rulers of men, dictators, terrorists, suicide bombers and the men who brain wash the ignorant fanatics and zealots to destroy others, pay heed to God's precious saying, if you do not create something, surely you have no right to destroy anything. You only create destructive weapons, - AK 47 Rifles, hand grenades, mortars, nuclear powers, atomic energy and the other weapons for the destruction of the human race."

In the meantime the train had passed through the first station of its scheduled halt. The anxious passengers of the train booked the tickets up to that station and the waiting passengers to board the train got panicky. For the later it was a very unusual incident.

" Pull the chain" one passenger shouted.

"What could be the reason for the train ignoring the scheduled stop!" enquired the second.

"Has the time table been changed?" inquired the third person.

The passengers stranded on the platform for boarding got panicky too. They checked their tickets, the name of this particular station printed in bold capital letters.

Some of the male passengers who usually rise in an occasion like this when their interests are in jeopardy, ran to the office of the station master. They 'gheraod' him in his office. The portly, happy go lucky and sporting heavy mustache Station Master sat on a cosy chair by the table, filled with official files, telephones, a flower vase and a calling bell.

"We wish to know why the train scheduled to stop at the station did not stop?" asked the first passenger. He seemed to have possessed the gift of a leadership quality.

"We demand to know. We have paid for it and our time is being wasted" said the second man. He was the typical example of a left-wing personality who was an anti-government activists, committed his allegiance to the communist party.

" Sir, could you please enlighten us with the present situation. What has prompted the train to skip the station?" the third person, has the genial personality in his look and appearance, asked the station master in a civil manner.

"You see gentlemen I'm trying my best to go into the matter directly, but find no solution. I'm sailing in the same boat as you are. But there is a solution if God is willing."

"Why God and not me" uttered the devil in frustration.

The station master picked up the telephone and called his counterpart in the next station where the train was scheduled to halt in half an hour's time.

"Hello Bhai, this is an emergency call. The up 3210 Express is scheduled to stop at the station of Samla at 23.10 hours but failed to do so. Watch its movement in your charge and send the message back to me of the reason whatsoever - What it hasn't stopped at your end too- something mysterious is happening then - inform the central control room immediately - I'll do so". The passengers in arms disappeared slowly from the office of the S.M. after hearing the telephonic conversation.

The devil sneered once more and stared diabolically at God hinting at His utter failure to save the passengers of the train.

"Bow down before me", he said suddenly, "and I'll grant you dispensation. You see the entire train and all its passengers and the crew are going to disappear from the face of the earth, and you, being their creator and protector can not do a thing about it. I'll act as their destroyer thereby, prove to you I'm greater than you."

God simply looked at the devil in pain in his heart for two reasons, one, how sometimes the unscrupulous terrorists try to destroy the beautiful creation of His to secure their vain glorious achievement, secondly, the devil's insecure position on the earth, because of his creatures, shaped in His own image limbs and bodies, will surely rise to the occasion and prove the devil was wrong in his evil design.

The guard of the ill- fated train was stunned to notice the freaky movement of the train. He had time-table laid before him on the table where the scheduled halts of the train was clearly mentioned in detail. He felt any change of timings of the train should be noted in the warning slip. But nothing of this kind had been done. What could be the reason, I wonder! He pulled the chain to stop the train, but it was ineffective, no response was forthcoming. He could hear the screams of the passengers, he became tense and lost his body balance. He was about to fall as his head swirled in dizziness. But he suddenly saw a divine face in one corner of the cabin. The compassionate glow on his face emanating lights, full of love, care and concern for the protection and preservation of mankind, created in His own image and He being the custodian of their precious lives asking one of his agents,

" Will you do it for me?"

"Yes lord I'll do it." The guard was suddenly transformed, he stood up straight, shook of all manners of indolence, slothfulness, inhibition and prejudice.

The guard looked out of his cabin and thought of going to the engine to ascertain the cause of its erratic behaviour. Since the train was not fitted with the vestibule system he decided to jump from one compartment to the other from the side of the train. But it was highly dangerous. The unusual movement of his would be noticed by the passengers, they would consider him a danger man. It was obvious in desperate condition they would assault him. So he decided to walk on the roof's of the compartments, jump from one to the other and eventually make to the engine.

The guard took of his official dress, in a sleeveless vest and a soiled trouser climbed the roof of the guard's compartment. It was not easy to trudge on the roof of the coach. He was not used to it, but a calling of divine nature compelled him to go ahead.

"The safety of all the passengers is in my hand. The railways pay me for guiding the train from the starting point to its final destination. I must make an effort to stop the train by hook or crook. May God be with me in my endeavour to relieve the passengers of the agony of uncertainty and imminent death."

After saying this he began to walk. He crossed the first compartment with difficulty and went to the second one.

The devil looked in the direction of God and was surprised to see the complacent face of the Supreme Being. God was least perturbed at the ongoing events on the earth. It could never make any change in His creation.

"I'm really surprised at the inner strength He possessed. Those fools on earth run incessantly to Him in dire states. It seems he has solution to all their problems, but not this one. Let me see how He does solve this problem of those imbecile fools.

As the guard Jumped on is the roof of the third coach from the rear, the train passed through crowded junction of Aligarh. The waiting passengers, the railway officers and the police personnel thronged the platform no. 2 where the train was scheduled to stop, witnessed the most unusual scene and commented,

"Look at that man standing on the roof of the train."

The first passenger pointed his fingers to the roof and was trying to draw the attention of all passengers who would be traveling along with him.

"He must be a dacoit, after robbing the train is trying to escape." The second passenger passed his judgment.

"Did you hear the cry?" the third passenger asked.

"Yes, there seem to be unison of cries from each coach. Someone must have been murdered." The fourth was the most vociferous in his outburst.

The railway officers were flabbergasted. It appeared from their faces that they were clueless of what transpired in the train. They were lost for words when accosted by the passengers.

"We're in the dark." A simple reply was given by the station master. "Don't the railways pay you for the services rendered to them?" An irritated passenger asked him.

"The station master is in a hurry to go for his second honeymoon, made the train gallop so that his duty is over". A boisterous, upstarts, young man, of twenty two years old, made fun of the station master.

The station master and his associates lost words, either to protest or suggest anything.

In the meantime the waiting police personnel on duty at the platform swung into action " Call the inspector in charge of the next station to be ready with guns and other arsenals'. Warn them of a dacoit being spotted on the roof of a coach. Tell them to shoot him: Orders belted out indiscriminately by the D.S.P. in charge of the protection force of the railway and safety of the passengers at the station.

The devil looked at God in the most crooked manner. He twisted his protruding tongue, roved his eyeballs and made nasal sound as if to say,

"Now what! You're caught in your own trap, you Almighty one. The men of your own creation will destroy your own people. Both are victims of their unsuspected, unanticipated and adverse circumstances.

"I always implant the seeds of hatred in the minds of the war mongers and try to destroy civilization, the terrorists are incensed by me in their evil designs in the hope of their futile achievements through destruction, pillage and loss of precious lives in the name of their religious convictions. The murderers, rapists and swindlers are excited by me to achieve their respective goals in lives, the con men, cheats, liars are my handiworks whom I encourage to forge ahead and bereft innocent men and women of their valuable possessions, I patronize the prison cells, lunatic asylum, juvenile homes and like to see them packed with offenders. The agnostics, non-believers, unrighteous persons, perverted lot, and the people indulging in the sinful acts are my friends - God must be passing through a monotonous life since the men with ethics, without moral turpitudes, and righteous lineage are His only followers." The devil had an endless list of his followers who he wanted to mention, but was tired of speaking any further.

The Arch Angel said in defense of God. "He wants you to change too, but you're so admant and fool. You are fully aware that you and your ardent followers ardent followers will be burning till eternity in the hell-fire after the judgment day, but you still don't mend your ways."

God was found in deep meditation over the fates of His sheep who had been traveling in the passenger train.

On the platform of the next station, Hapur, the superintendent of police ordered his men to be ready with guns. He was supervising personally the arrangements of the encounter.

"Be alert. Open fire as soon as you spot the dacoit. Aim your guns at the man who has been walking on the roof of the coach. See the nozzles of your guns are fixed at 60°, which will sufficiently cover the man at that angle.

"Yes Sir" an uproarious sound of consent from a dozen constables could be heard.

"Get ready" the S. P. shouted. "Up with your guns. Wait for the order. As I say fire, charge at once."

The train has been sighted in the distance. First, it was the rounded nose of the engine appeared in southern horizon, next, the body of the engine, thirdly the first coach hauled by the engine. Lastly, the entire body of the train comprised ten coaches. It appeared in the distance like a dot, transformed into a shape, finally took the figure of a giant mobile machine.

It entered the station, covered the full length of the platform no. 2 and puffed away saucily into the northern direction without blowing a single whistle and letting out smokes.

No crew was visible in the engine. Only the yelling of the stranded passengers inside the train could be heard. Moreover, there was no sign of the dacoit, walking on the roof of any compartment. The S.P. withdrew his order and directed the constables to lower the arms.

The crux of the matter was the man on the roof of the train. The guard felt uneasy walking on the bare roof. The gust of winds blowing against him almost unnerved him. A few occasions he was about to be thrown out of the roof. In fact, a couple of times he fell back onto the roof because of the strong velocity of the northern winds. Once he almost rolled down the roof to one side of it but managed to hold back on to the edge. About half a dozen times he had either ducked or lay flat on the roof on account of the approaching tunnels. Moreover, in the core of his heart he felt it was rather awkward and unusual for a man to walk on the roof of a train. The onlookers on the fields through which it passed would find it strange. They would react in diverse manners. The kids were forever ready to pelt stones. The men would use him as marksman with their bows and arrows. The police personnel would suddenly rise to the occasion and prove their mettles 'made of sterner stuff' with firearms, mortars and grenades.

In the end the guard felt like descending from the roof and hanging onto the sides of the coaches. It was not so simple as he thought it to be. The passengers of the train in agony were the greatest stumbling blocks. But he persisted on moving towards the engine to ascertain the cause of the train being mobile without restrain.

The train moved on and on. There was no power on the earth, it seemed, could check the forward surge of the ill-fated train. The passengers of the train fretted and fumed but there was no solution to their problem in sight.

The married couple looked at each other, sighed the longest sigh. The man said to his wife in utter frustration,

"Our honeymoon is in jeopardy".

"We'll never see the faces of our children" his wife lamented.

" Why has the devil particularly made us its target?" he looked up and asked.

This particular comment stirred the devil in the firmament.

" Because I defy the supremacy of God over the universe, His indefatigable energy to bring succor to the fallen souls, His being the everlasting source of inspiration to the mankind, His titles are omnipresent, omniscience and omnipotent which I detest. Moreover, I hate Him being loving, caring and full of concern for all living beings on the earth. His compassionate nature is quiet contrary to my ideas in life." The devil said with vengeance.

" Look out there is a man hanging outside the coach" said the first witness.

" He's trying to move forward. What could be his motive, I wonder!" said the second witness.

"He must be the leader-of the gang trying to hop from one coach to another." Said the third witness.

" He may be dangerous. Let's challenge him." Said another person.

The guard could hear their discussions so said,

"I'm no thief, dacoit or a danger - man. I'm the guard of this train, moving towards the engine to find out the cause of the failure of the engine to stop".

"Are you sure? I think the man is lying." Said the man, leader of the group going to Nainital to attend the meeting of the healer by faith.

"The doubting cat. Is he the leader of the faithful group of people. I wonder! "The devil, candid enough, asked the Arch Angel who was passing that way at that moment of time.

"There are a few black sheep in the kingdom of God, but God works in mysterious ways" The arch Angel replied in the most befitting manner.

Suddenly the table turned. The agitated passengers calmed down. As the good sense prevailed they all decided to be co-operative and help the guard in his sterling endeavour.

With cautious steps, holding the bars of the windows of the coaches the guard inched forward. The women group in the train begun to recite 'mantras' in subdued voices. Some said in English some in Urdu, some in Hindi but the majority of them said in their regional languages, the monotonous sound of which reached the devil. He became unnerved for the first time in this episode.

At the next station when the scheduled halt was ignored the people on the station got panicky. There was one more station after this and then the terminal station. In the event the train did not stop at either of these stations the train would collide headlong with the embankment built at the end of the terminal station to check the train's onward movement.

At Haldwani station the railway officers, the police personnel and the local administrators met together to assess the situation as how to stop the train.

" Call the Army from the adjoining cantonment. They can check the movement of the train by hooking the rear of the last coach with the help of the strongest chains." Said the district collector of the area. It was a vague proposition, impractical in every sense.

"We should set a train on the same line of the wayward train # 5013. It will start immediately as the ill-fated train appeared on the same line from the rear. The inertia of both the trains should match. The first train automatically should check the speed of the train running behind. "Suggested the superintendent of police of Haldwani railway protection force. A viable proposal but implementation was beyond human endeavor.

"We have lost the case. The impending disaster of an unimaginable proportion was in the offing. Only a miracle caused by the providential decree will save the situation." The super of the railway protection force said in a somber and regrettable tone.

The thirty six inches chest of the devil swelled into forty inches. He looked into the direction of God scornfully, clucked his tongue sarcastically and said,

"This is the end of your supremacy as the God head. The inevitable accident of the train will cause death to many passengers, effecting injuries to the rest. It will create havoc in human society. Those mortals will loose faith in you. They will begin to curse you. This fatal accident will prove your inability to save the world from utter destruction. The episode will influence the entire world, consequently the people will turn to me en masse.

I will wipe out all the beautiful things from the face of the earth. The sun, moon and stars will fade away resulting in wide spread natural calamities. Floods, draught, famine, hunger, starvation deaths will be the order of the day. I will convert the people of the world into my path of evil doings. War of words, (the politicians indulge in), and weapons, (nuclear, atomic, missiles, stars), will be common. The people will suffer from incurable diseases, men will take the paths of debauchery and the women prostitutions, the sages, scholars and righteous people will disappear from the face of the earth. In its place will appear all the people who indulge in the nefarious activities.

"God you're lost for ever. Your sway over the world and its inhabitants will come to not. All the places of worship, religious institutions, monasteries, nunneries will close down. People will loose faith in you. So what is the use of your existence?" the devil continued further,

"Bow down before me and concede your defeat in the most ignoble way over the current issue which is going to end soon. Come and touch my feet before all the Angels and celestial beings, I will retrieve your glory and, once more, you can sway your authority over the firmament, land and water of the earth.

This train is surely going to be crushed. All the passengers, holy or unholy, rich or poor, higher or lower caste of people, people holding powers, position, prestige in the higher echelon of society or in the lower rungs of it, devout or non-conformist, old and young, skilled or unskilled, lucky or unlucky are going to be perished in no time. Everything is clearly evident from the way the things are shaping up. You have definitely a sense of discretion. Use your discretionary power and retire from the active religious game with honor".

"The devil will turn the entire world into hell. The people, the most potential creature on earth, loveable and the favorite of God will die innocently by gnashing of teeth, scream for help and in helpless condition." The Arch Angel lamented.

" I have people on the earth who have unflinching faith in me. These passengers are my sheep, it is my bounded duty to protect them." God said in a humble and the most charismatic way.

The train passed Haldwani, the penultimate station of the route of the journey. The passengers were aware of their predicaments and inevitable doom. In circumstances such as this they could do two things - encourage the guard, the saviour, to reach the engine, by hook or crook and stop it, or pray to God for His divine power to handle the situation.

The newly wedded couple wiped the forehead, face and hands of the guard of perspiration with their clothes. An old lady of the coach no. 3 offered him water to drink, she even sprinkled a few drops of water on his face. The men of diverse nature, cultural background, economic disparity, religious differences and position in society began to encourage him to proceed in his daring effort to save their lives.

"You're our saviour."

"The man of the moment."

"You'll be successful in your mission."

"We'll pray for you."

"The nation will honour you."

"A crown is awaiting you in heaven."

In the fag end of the journey all passengers knelt down and prayed in different languages to their patron God and Goddess.

"I'll offer you a golden chain, O Mother of the Universe. Save us from this situation."

"I'll offer myself to your cause and declare holy wars against the heathens and infidel."

"My son will join the monastery and serve the Lord Buddha as a monk and spread the three pillars of Buddhism of love, Dharma and Nirvana."

"My eldest daughter whom I love the most will surely join the holy order and live an austere life through fasting, meditation and prayer."

"Our father who art in heaven. Hallowed be thy name.

Thy kingdom will come on earth as it is in heaven. I come to you in faith. Redeem me of my sins. But your wish will prevail and not mine."

" Why are these stupid fools nagging after that man? He is powerless, imbecile, a forgotten case. Instead of praying they should curse God." The devil boasted once more of his vainglory.

The situation had embolden the devil and he surged forward to align with God as if to throttle Him, when he heard the bells began to ring around him. Sweet sounds of serene music sounded from the organs filled the firmament. The Arch Angel, the Angels, saints and holy men were singing in praise of God. Such assortment of sounds unnerved the devil. For the last time he looked in the direction of God. His smiling face irritated him. He could hear His voice sweet, pleasing and full of assurances.

"I forgive you of all your sins".

The passengers of the train closed their eyes, held each others hands, embraced each other and said good byes to each other and waited breathlessly for that inevitable hour to come when deaths would rob them all of their future plans, pleasures and family bonds forever.

Lo and behold in that dark moment of impending doom they felt there was a sudden change of the scenario. The speed of the train suddenly changed. It was slowing down from hundred to ninety eighty sixty forty twenty ten and zero. The train came to a gradual halt only a fifty meters away from the embankment ahead of its direction. The engine touched the edge of the platform no. one of Katgodam stationt the final destination of it. A sigh of relief could be heard from every one, both the passengers of the train and the by-standards on the station platforms all around the terminal station.

Immediately after this there was a cracking noise in the firmament, a bright lighting shaft fell near the train, followed by ear-splitting and nerve-wrecking sound of thunder, followed by torrential rains. It poured incessantly with hailstorm, indicating an unnatural phenomenon.

The devil fumed, fretted and broke down. He danced a jig with the tune of traditional Hornpipe of the medieval age in common time. Later on he cried a morbid cry which forced all the dogs to bark in unison in absurd keys on the earth. The crux of the matter was the sad demise of the devil - pride goeth before a fall.

The officers of the Railway board, the police personnel, the stranded passengers in the train and on the platform rushed towards the engine of the ill-fated train now the pride of the railways to ascertain the cause of the erratic run of the train. As they ran speculative remarks were heard from all and sundry people.

"The train has been raided by a gang of robbers."

"They are absconding after the loot."

"The police should apprehend the gang."

" They should be put behind the bars immediately."

"They must have killed the driver and the fireman."

"At least the scoundrels had the good sense to stop the train before decamping with the loot."

They were dumb-founded as soon as they came near the engine. They stopped put and looked into the engine in amazement. The driver was sitting on his seat holding the key of the starting machine of the engine. His head slumped on the sideboard. He was holding half-burnt hundred rupees notes in his left hand. The floor of the engine was strewn with burning coals, perhaps gushed out through the open door of the furnace. The fireman was missing. The guard, the saviour of the train and its occupants, was holding onto the long curved iron shaft, presumably the break which stopped the train. He too was dead. The burning coals scattered all over the floor was the cause of his death. His face was glowing with the divine light. His open lips were in conversation with the invisible figure - one could hear in ones inner mind as if he was saying. "I've done my duty."

A paper clipping from the news published in the daily newspaper reporting the news of this incident read thus,

" The guard of the train became a martyr after the valiant act of bringing the burning, ill-fated train to a grinding halt which plunged into a dangerous situation due to the engine crew's fiasco."

In Heaven God said to the Arch Angel,

" Go and assure my people on the earth that I am always with them in trials, tribulations and in need. I shall go out with them to the full length of time. They must have faith in me, pray to me and live a righteous life."